THE SOCIAL CONSTRUCTION OF EDUCATIONAL LEADERSHIP

Studies in the Postmodern Theory of Education

Joe L. Kincheloe and Shirley R. Steinberg
General Editors

Vol. 255

PETER LANG
New York • Washington, D.C./Baltimore • Bern
Frankfurt am Main • Berlin • Brussels • Vienna • Oxford

Anna Hicks McFadden
Penny Smith

THE SOCIAL CONSTRUCTION OF EDUCATIONAL LEADERSHIP

Southern Appalachian Ceilings

PETER LANG
New York • Washington, D.C./Baltimore • Bern
Frankfurt am Main • Berlin • Brussels • Vienna • Oxford

Library of Congress Cataloging-in-Publication Data

McFadden, Anna Hicks.
The social construction of educational leadership :
southern Appalachian ceilings / Anna Hicks McFadden, Penny Smith.
p. cm. — (Counterpoints; v. 255)
Includes bibliographical references and index.
1. Women school administrators—Appalachian Region, Southern—Social conditions.
2. Women—Employment—Appalachian Region, Southern—History.
3. Educational leadership—Appalachian Region, Southern.
4. Appalachian Region, Southern—Social conditions.
I. Smith, Penny. II. Title. III. Series: Counterpoints (New York, N.Y.); v. 255.
LB2831.824.A66M34 371.2'00974—dc22 2003025250
ISBN 0-8204-6812-6
ISSN 1058-1634

Bibliographic information published by **Die Deutsche Bibliothek**.
Die Deutsche Bibliothek lists this publication in the "Deutsche Nationalbibliografie"; detailed bibliographic data is available on the Internet at http://dnb.ddb.de/.

Cover design by Dutton & Sherman Design
Cover photo of Qualla School reprinted by permission
of Hunter Library, Western Carolina University

The paper in this book meets the guidelines for permanence and durability of the Committee on Production Guidelines for Book Longevity of the Council of Library Resources.

Printed in the United States of America

To the male and female senior educational leaders in Western North Carolina who so ably lead the school systems in service to the children of the region.

CONTENTS

LIST OF TABLES

ACKNOWLEDGMENTS

We are grateful to Hunter Library, Western Carolina University, and the Jackson County School District for the use of the cover photograph. Some of the findings of this study were previously published in *Women as School Executives: Research and Reflections on Educational Leadership*, edited by Stephanie Korcheck and Marianne Reese, a 2002 publication of the Texas Council of Women School Executives. Findings were also the subject of papers presented at conferences of the American Educational Research Association, the National Council of Professors of Education Administration, and the Southern Regional Council of Education Administration. This study would not have been possible without the assistance of Mary Buchanan and Carol Oxendine, administrative assistants in the Department of Educational Leadership and Foundations at Western Carolina University. We are also indebted to Western Carolina University, who awarded Anna scholarly leave to complete this project and Penny a Hunter Scholar award to research aspects of school history in the region. Finally, we are especially indebted to Margaret and Jack who know and understand the sometimes crazy ways we work.

PART I

The Context

"Sometimes when I want to talk about an issue or maybe somebody in the local government, that is a point of frustration to me. I really have to be careful because they have extended family working for me . . . Probably the best piece of advice that was given to me before I took this job was that, whether they're your enemy or working with you, they are both camping in the same store. But if you tell one something different from the other, it's going to come back and bite you in the rear end. And they aren't going to trust you anymore. And trust is a big issue up here."

Male Participant

·1·

SOUTHERN APPALACHIAN CEILINGS

The nested regions of Southern Appalachia and the southern mountains of North Carolina provide a good base for examining specific cultural change: the growing access of minorities to educational administration positions in the South. This book highlights the role of geography in shaping social expectations and the responding accommodation behaviors and then turns to what people in the region have to tell us. Their stories are about the importance of public schooling to local, primarily rural communities; the dedication of educators to both their jobs and those communities; and the ways in which administrative diversity is challenging traditional concepts of who should lead school systems. The book also discusses a way to (re)consider access to positions of power and how power is exercised.

The people whose experiences are related here include senior-level school leaders, coworkers in subordinate positions, and school board members. Most of them began their professional careers in the late 1960s and the 1970s and are baby boomers who came of age at a time of social unrest that disturbed, admittedly with mixed results, gender and racial stereotypes. Because these people work within specific temporal and geographic contexts, their cultural frame of place proved central to our understanding of regional change. We wondered if being born and raised in Appalachia made them more viable candidates for leadership roles than someone who was from somewhere else. Was being a Southerner important in securing a job? Were the same dynamics at work for men as for women?

Are women now more attractive as administrative candidates than they once were? Are racial minorities, male or female, more attractive candidates? If so, why? Were there attributes or behaviors Southern Highlanders expected to find in a district-level administrator that were unique to the region? If so, what? How were those expectations shaped? Were they the same for everyone? Was there anything in their stories that might contribute to an understanding beyond a particular place?

The book is in three parts. The first paints the backdrop, examining the cultural frames of Southerners and Appalachians through historical and sociological texts leavened with remarks from regional writers. The second section describes the performers, school leaders who tell us about their professional lives. It compares them to their peers elsewhere in the country and to each other, introducing the concept of geographically situated leadership. The third part moves beyond Carolina's mountains to a consideration of general constructs that might be applicable elsewhere.[1] It concludes with relating some unpleasant consequences of current access trends and performance expectations.

Why We Became Interested

When each of us came to Western Carolina University (WCU), part of the exotic dance of faculty selection for a tenure-track slot included an answer to the unspoken question, "Can you live *here*?" *Here* meant in Jackson County or one of its near neighbors. *Here* also meant in a place "likely more remote and isolated, more parochial, than the places to which you have been accustomed." Jackson County has only three main roads, two of which run east–west and intersect the third, which runs north–south. Only one of those routes has four lanes for its entire length and then only when the department of transportation is not repairing or improving the surface. The other two roads wind and twist, ascend and fall sufficiently to discourage timid drivers. Smaller roads end in a cove or on the way up a mountain, following a creek until the hills narrow too much to support a home. The largest town, Sylva, has slightly more than 2,000 residents. The other two incorporated towns, Webster and Dillsboro, have 454 and 137 inhabitants, respectively.

An exit from the county necessitates climbing mountains—the Cowees to the west, the Plott Balsams to the north, and the Tanasee Ridge to the south. The highest and most remote section of the Blue Ridge Parkway follows the county line to the east. The Great Balsams separate the populous north from the golf and gated communities to the south. There are no enclosed malls and no major department stores. People, including job candidates, either love the place or hate it. Asheville, the region's only claim to urban amenities, is an hour away.

Our educational leadership graduate students, both locals and more recent arrivals, felt a need to let us know that people here are *different*. They are cautious around newcomers. One could live among them twenty years and still be considered an outsider. Religion is important, likely to be fundamental, very conservative, and deeply personal. Local politics are sometimes governed by disputes that reach back to the Civil War. Patronage and nepotism might have diminished, but they have not disappeared. It is a traditional values kind of place, where men make a living and women, whenever possible, stay at home. Who your people are means something.

We should not, they told us, anticipate lively discussions about postmodernism. Modernity is still suspect in some quarters. Granted, we would not find the misbegotten characterization of Southern Appalachia depicted in *Deliverance*, but we might want to remember that they filmed part of the movie in this section of the state.

At the same time we were apprised of mountaineer states of mind that might conflict with what our students assumed were our ways of making sense of this world, we were also told about the virtues of the Southern Highlands. Young people do well in the region's public schools. They collectively perform the best on North Carolina's new high-stakes accountability tests in spite of having fewer resources than most high-performing systems downstate. The region produces nationally recognized writers, crafters, and musicians. There is good community and professional theater here, and the region is home to a number of summer camps; Olympians train on a local river. Many of the largest Protestant denominations have state or regional retreat centers here. Visitors to the Blue Ridge Parkway trace the final miles of their journey on the ridgelines of the region, ending at the Carolina entrance to the Smoky Mountain National Park. The poet of Chicago, Carl Sandburg, made the Southern Appalachians his last home. Asheville's Biltmore, built by George Vanderbilt, is the largest private home in the United States open to the paying public. Thomas Edison and Henry Ford rusticated here. Modern forestry began in what is now one of several national forests in the region, and part of the Eastern Band of the Cherokee's reservation sits in Jackson County.

We came to WCU with few set expectations about our work in the area. We both had at one time been high school English teachers. We were both former secondary school and system-level administrators. We began our careers in administration when there were few women occupying senior-level leadership positions, took our initial coursework at a time when women were in the minority in those classes, were taught mostly by men, and usually worked with and under the supervision of male superintendents. Understandably, when we moved into higher education, we both set research agendas that included a scholarly consideration of the roles played by gender in educational leadership preparation and practice. We did those things independently and in different states, joining the faculty at WCU in the same year (1996). We began working collaboratively on this research project about four years ago (2000).

Almost immediately upon our arrival, and independently, both of us noticed educational leadership changes in the senior-most positions in the region. The cautionary stories about conservative local mind-sets that we had received from our students and colleagues magnified these stories. There appeared to be a tentative gender shift in the making. By the time we were hired, there was a female superintendent in one of the local school systems. By the time we arrived on the job, there was a second female superintendent in the region. Additionally, there was also a growing acceptance of outsider school leaders, men who had not been born and raised in the region. Although there had been few outsider school leaders in the past, superintendent searches increasingly included candidates "from off."

Even the school leadership program was changing. No female had occupied a tenure-track position in school administration before we came. By the time we began this study, WCU's K–12 educational leadership faculty had a majority of female members, and a woman chaired the department in which they worked. Ideological shifts were palpable. We wanted to understand the interplay between the cautionary tales we were told and the changes we saw taking place.

We turned to school administration literature, knowing that gender, once an ignored variable, had become a staple in educational research. We found that little of that research had been undertaken in the South in general, and in the Southern Appalachians in particular.[2] Were trends noted elsewhere applicable here? Did women in the Southern Highlands negotiate different paths to power positions in public schools than their downstate Southern sisters? Than women elsewhere? Once in positions of power, did they lead differently than their male counterparts? Differently than their female colleagues in other parts of the United States? We started our research with a standard comparative approach in mind. We would look at school leadership through the experiences and perceptions of local female school leaders, comparing what we found here with what was known about comparable educators elsewhere.

The Place

Western Carolinians, be they native, transplant, or visitors, are place conscious. Where they are matters. Their part of the state is geographically challenging but sublimely beautiful. True, the signifiers of the modern homogenization of America have breached the mountains. They have not, however, succeeded in domesticating them. Yes, there are golden arches in small towns and Wal-Marts in a few of our more rural counties. Yet, here, too, a few wild places remain. It is still possible to get virtually or figuratively lost in wilderness.

Transplants who choose to live permanently in the state's southern mountains come for a variety of reasons. A look at Asheville suggests the breadth of that diversity. It has been lauded in national magazines as a best small city in America, one of the best places to retire, the best place "to live and work," the "most alive" small town, one of the country's top ten whitewater areas, the destination of one of our nation's fifty best road trips, a top five mountain-biking town, one of the ten healthiest places to live, and one of the top twenty-five destinations for art lovers.[3]

Adventurers are attracted by geographic challenges. Prospects for biking, hiking, climbing, backpacking, camping, kayaking, canoeing, and fishing lure them. Natural beauty, the possibility of solitude, and tradition entice musicians, artists, and writers in disproportionate numbers. Here one can find aging river rats and retired Appalachian Trail through-hikers sharing space with potters, bluegrass musicians, and cloggers. They live beside organic farmers, sustainable agriculture advocates, and people living "off the grid." Here, too, are herbalists, acupuncturists, and most varieties of massage therapists. A nationally ranked writing program is down the road from the regional Outward Bound school.

Snowbird retirees migrate south in winter. They reappear in spring, running northward from the return of heat and humidity to their summer homes in the Carolina mountains. We calculate the seasons by the number of Florida and Georgia license plates on the roads. By midsummer, part-timers are a majority in some parts of the upcountry. They and seasonal tourists swell the numbers in towns like Brevard, Cashiers, and Highlands. Their decision to spend time here is based on a congenial combination of weather, topography, cost, the promise of relative safety, and the prospect of sufficient amenities to make the transition easy.

Natives are reluctant to leave at all. Even if they depart, it is often a temporary move. Teacher education graduates will sometimes wait years for a position in their home county, working as teacher assistants or in nonprofessional jobs, rather than moving east to school systems that have immediate openings. Prospective school leaders patiently wait their turns in local districts, rather than seeking faster routes to administrative positions elsewhere. Native Appalachians appreciate the same recreational opportunities that attract newcomers and tourists to the region, but their primary reason for staying is family. This part of the state is home.

Natives speak fondly of "old homeplaces." Family lands sit by a creek or on a mountain named for its original white settlers. Hillsides hold structures that have stood on that land for decades: a barn, part of a log cabin, an old springhouse, or the remains of a stone chimney, all sentinels to a time past. There are remains of a family cemetery. To old-timers, the land is *that family's* place, even if that family no longer lives there.

Natives know their neighbors, at least the permanent ones. It is not unusual that they are kinfolks, close, a few cousins removed, or in-laws. They have shared memories, histories in common, even if intervening years sent them in different directions. Once, they attended the same churches, occupied the same classrooms, shopped at the same stores, and worked side by side. They sat on the curbstones of various main streets and watched the same parades. High school football games are still prime time on Friday nights.

Even when people leave to find jobs elsewhere—a common Appalachian experience—they return for vacations, weekends, family gatherings, and retirement. Mary Sutton Buchanan, one of our department's secretaries and a sixth-generation Jackson County native, is a typical example of boomerang migration. Her husband, Dan, left the region first to join the military and then to find a job. They had their children and raised them in Norfolk, Virginia, and Charlotte, North Carolina. When he retired, they returned to her family's homeplace, the property on which the Sutton family originally settled in the nineteenth century. Their son Danny lives there too, having built his house close to that of his parents. He and his wife recently took their newborn triplets, one of whom is named for her maternal grandfather, back to Sutton Branch. The children are the eighth generation that has lived on that land.

Mary's husband, Dan Buchanan, also owns part of his family's homeplace. His sister lives there. Keeping it "in the family" is a way to keep memories alive and family close. "We were," Mary says, "always coming back, always coming home."

Place worked its magic on us, too. The more years we are here, the more attuned we become to its importance and to its division of residents into those with homeplaces and those with homes, to those who dwelled intimately within these mountains and to those who were new to them. Did the influx of newcomers, both permanent and temporary, alter gender expectations? Did it enhance the likelihood that outsiders might be more acceptable?

The Study Expands

What originally was to be a comparative study with geography and gender as variables expanded over time. The more we looked at change patterns, the more we became convinced that increased professional opportunities for women were linked to and preceded by those tendered to nonnative males. We began to talk about a quality that we labeled "insiderness," an attribute necessary for one to be considered a viable candidate for a superintendency. We had by that time narrowed our study of administration to the superintendency or senior-level district positions traditionally considered prerequisites for the top position. If there has been and continues to be a pattern of discrimination, it would be most obvious in the roles that entail the greatest public exposure and that are perceived to have the highest status.

Changing demographics played a role in the growing acceptability of geographic outsiders for local educational administration positions. More newcomers were moving to the Southern Appalachians, and more of them were staying beyond the summer. They were coming from other than border states, bringing sensibilities that were neither strictly nor even necessarily Southern or mountain. Not all of them were Caucasian. The Latino population, for example, has significantly increased, and that growth shows no signs of abating. Today, Mexican restaurants can be found throughout the region; ten years ago they could be counted on one hand and were clustered near Asheville. Stores cater specifically to Spanish-speaking patrons. The shelf space for foods associated with south-of-the-border cuisine expands yearly and construction jobs are no longer English-only sites.

The persistence of temporary outsider experiences by native residents has also challenged regional insularity. Factories here have closed, forcing families downstate in pursuit of jobs. Simultaneously, city residents seeking another kind of lifestyle buy deserted back-road farms. Although wild places remain, globalization has come to the mountains in a variety of ways that contribute to unsettling cultural norms.

In the third year of our study, another leadership barrier was breached when a local school system hired its first African American superintendent. We, consequently, included the variable of race, but admittedly pay it less attention than it will need as racial diversity increases in the region. So, herein we examine gender, geography, and race as they distinguish between insiders and outsiders and as they are considered in decisions about access to and performance in school system leadership positions. How do people in a particular place socially construct those roles? How have those constructions changed over time? Why? And, of what consequence might the changes be?

Researcher Bias

We bring to this project certain attributes that can be considered simultaneously advantages and disadvantages. We are females who are unapologetically feminists. We are Southerners, with different southern experiences. One of us was born and raised in South Carolina; the other was born in Virginia into an Air Force family that spent most of its traveling time in the South and then retired to Texas. We have been classroom teachers, principals, and central office administrators. We are proud to have been engaged in public education and find more right with it than wrong. We remain hopeful about its future in spite of the popularity of reform initiatives that we find antithetical to our concepts of education and inimical to the well-being of children. We have, then, the advantages and disadvantages of insider information, opinions based on experience and predispositions. Our cultural baggage assists us in having an intuitive understanding of certain issues that would be less explicable to a noneducator or someone without considerable relevant school experience in the South. We acknowledge that it also colors the ways we look at our data.

Our perceptions and, to a certain degree, the quality of the data we collected from interviews and surveys are circumscribed by our status as non-Appalachians. It is impossible to gauge the level of trust we have attained in our years of working with educators in the region and, even were it high, we would still lack the understanding that comes from being born and coming of age in the place. The meanings we construct from what we learned and the implications we draw from our conclusions are necessarily place bound and tentative. We went in different directions than we initially thought we would go, encouraged to take a different road by our conversations with study participants and our reading of the region's historical record. Initially, we thought we would be telling a story about simple discrimination, intensified by cultural layers that each emphasized strict gender coding of roles. And, of course, we were wrong.

Southern Appalachian Ceilings

Ceilings are ubiquitous. Everyone encounters them: man-made ones in buildings, natural ones in forest bowers or caves, temporary ones protecting us from building sites or the weather. In a literal sense we are surrounded by them and have always been. They describe limits, like a price ceiling, or natural boundaries, like a lowering fog. Most of us have bumped into one or two of them, forgetting to duck or charging up a ladder too fast.

The phrase "glass ceiling" is part of our national discrimination vocabulary. It is not difficult to conjure up a number of images of excluded people observing a thing desired through some kind of transparent barrier. It could be youngsters looking at a glass case of candy in a country store. They might be the children described by John Steinbeck in *Grapes of Wrath*, youngsters who want a treat that costs more than their father can afford on the family's trip to California, or Charles Dickens's characters gazing through a window at a Christmas dinner they cannot afford, or third-class passengers looking up at the men and women on the first-class deck taking tea to the tune of an orchestra. The barrier can be horizontal or vertical, but a barrier it is and a tantalizing one. Those people on one side of the glass can see through its transparent panes to something they want and from which they are inexplicably or unreasonably excluded. In the context of educational leadership, the object of desire is an executive position, and the rationale for exclusion is who they are.

Not everything desirable is attainable. Sometimes it costs more money than we have. It might be age inappropriate—an automobile, say, for a twelve-year-old—because it requires an expertise not yet attained. We might want to be World Cup soccer stars, but we are not Mia Hamms. We might wish to be Nobel Laureates, but we are not Jimmy Carters. We might want to author Pulitzer Prize–winning novels, but we are not Toni Morrisons. That special person is too young or already taken or too rich or too famous or too interested in other things. At other times, reasons for exclusion are less transparent or fail to make sense. Defenders of the status quo resort to a time-honored explanation, "That's the way it is," or they resort to a common variation on that theme: "Because we said so."

Being women of a certain age, we are both familiar with those responses. Why couldn't girls play in Little League? Because, when we were growing up in the pre–Title IX era, organized sports were for boys. If the weather was too cold for a dress, girls could wear trousers under, but not in lieu of, them. There did not appear to be, at least to a prepubescent female child, anywhere one could appeal such matters. Several decades ago, many college women had mandatory dormitory curfews. After a certain hour, they had to be safely tucked inside their residence halls. College men lived free; college women slept locked up. Absurd? "That's the way things were done."

At approximately the same time, and extending backward for centuries, separation for people of color, particularly African Americans, exceeded the trivial. There were actual barriers of separate doors, separate water fountains, the balcony in the theater, and a web of invisible lines that one dared not cross for fear of physical retribution. The presence of color, not unlike the absence of a Y chromosome, meant loss of opportunity, even though the explanations for why that should be the case, both legal and cultural, seemed by mid-twentieth century (and before) to be weak. "It's the way some things are."

Ceilings are both real and intangible. We have all experienced an unexpected knock on the head from real ones. Most of us have encountered, on a scale sliding from slight to profound, the effects of cultural ceilings. That such has been the Western human condition should not surprise us, because hierarchy and its corollary, segregation, have been and continue to be part of our heritage.

The Great Chain of Being

From Plato onward many Westerners thought the world was an orderly place and that within it there were appropriate, distinct roles for its inhabitants, large and small, to play. Although the interconnections among the roles were never quite as distinct and immutable as a formal caste system, there were similarities. Within a divinely ascribed order was an explicit ranking of members, from an ultimate creator to scruffy rabble to inanimate objects. By the time of the Neoplatonists, medieval church fathers like Thomas Aquinas were energetically coupling Christianity with the natural-world descriptions of Aristotle. Eventually, order was manifested in what Alexander Pope called "the great chain of being," a concept whose evolution is explored at length by Arthur Lovejoy (1936) in a book with that title.

So accepted by the Western Christian world was the sense of proper place that it became one of those "beliefs which are so much a matter of course that they are rather tacitly presupposed than formally expressed and argued for." As such, it was rarely examined "with the eye of logical self-consciousness." Unexamined notions "often are the most decisive of the character of a doctrine . . . and still oftener of the dominant intellectual tendencies of an age" (7). *The Great Chain of Being* provided (for many people, continues to provide) guidance for what roles we were able to (can) play and how we were (are) to play them.

Transgress nature's ways, disturb the natural order of things, and court chaos and disaster. William Shakespeare (1601–03), that touchstone of occidental thought, captured the essence of the danger in his play *Troilus and Cressida*.

> The heavens themselves, the planets, and this center
> Observe degree, priority, and place,
> Insisture, course, proportion, season, form,
> Office, and custom, in all line of order;
> . . . But when the planets
> In evil mixture to disorder wander,
> What plagues and what portents, what mutiny,
> What raging of the sea, shaking of earth,
> Commotion in the winds! Frights, changes, horrors
> Divert and crack, rend and deracinate
> The unity and married calm of states
> Quite from their fixture. O, when degree is shak'd,
> Which is the ladder to all high designs,
> The enterprise is sick . . .
> Take but degree away, untune that string,
> And hark, what discord follows! (22–23)

Frights, horrors, sickness, and discord—scary stuff all that. Challenging the way things were supposed to be was not a trifling matter.

As E. M. W. Tillyard (n.d.) made clear in *The Elizabethan World Picture*, the result of disturbing the universe was a theme to which Western scholars returned throughout the medieval and early modern period. It was not only wrong that it violated natural law, it was also a sin. The connection between the sacred and a particular order served to reinforce that order. Kings ruled by divine right, in much the same way that divine decree had designated Adam below the angels, an earl below a duke, a woman below a man, a servant below a master, and the animals of the field below humankind.

Court not revolutions. Unlatch the chain at any point and the entire system comes tumbling down. According to Pope (1733–34), writing more than a century after Shakespeare, "whatever link you strike, Tenth or ten thousandth breaks the chain alike." "The whole must fall" (413–14). The power of natural order did not end with the Middle Ages; the political upheavals of the eighteenth century secularized it. Thomas Jefferson (1813), for example, could write to John Adams about "a natural aristocracy among men" and wax eloquent about how stratification based on "virtue and talents" (1305), rather than accident of birth, will advance the cause of good government in a young republic. Whatever the agent of sequence—intentional design or impersonal nature—an orderly chain remained. As kindergarten teachers continue to remind their students, there is "a place for everything and everything in its place."[4]

Chains and Change

Part of the genius of our current form of government is its ability to expand the size of the chain's links, to widen political space through legislation, executive order, or practice. Our predecessors have broadened the definition of who can occupy particular places in the body politic. For example, in 1841 Thomas Dorr's "People's Convention" challenged the restriction of the franchise to only the propertied classes. The Civil War granted citizenship to all African Americans and the suffrage to black men. In the next century, women's suffrage campaigns successfully challenged gender prohibitions to the ballot. Our national narrative is a collection of stories about various outsiders eventually becoming insiders. Over time, Americans have woven a wider social fabric, one made of multicolored, multitextured threads.

Granted, access proceeds more like the process of punctuated evolution than steady linear progress. Legally, it comes in fits and stops, in backlash and reform, as the history of Jim Crow laws attest. Behind that halting change, however, is a general trend from narrow to wider access. Where once a link was closed, it can be uncoupled and enlarged. What was once beyond the pale, unthinkable, and, consequently, unnatural, becomes first recognized, then subject to discussion, dispute, and reconsideration. In the 1960s, police armed with dogs met African American Civil Rights marchers. In 1984 and again in 1988, however, Jesse Jackson contended for the presidential nomination of a major political party. In 2003 Colin Powell is the secretary of state and Condoleezza Rice is head of the National Security Council.

Legal ceilings are named and, consequently, accessible to debate and change. We are conscious of them, and our awareness makes them amenable to inspection. Cultural ones are less distinct and lack the clear labels of legislated discrimination. They become a part of our collective unconscious, mythic illusions we do not question.

With consciousness, boundaries become visible. We can see through them, literally and sometimes figuratively. Awareness necessarily precedes asking questions about them. What are the reasons someone sits on one side of the glass and someone else sits on the other? We legislate laws. We do not legislate culture or ideas; they are more subtle. An idea, even an unjust or immoral one, once conceived, cannot be easily padlocked. Like the contents of Pandora's box, loosed on the world, a thought assumes a life of its own. However, traditions, reified by cultural norms and rarely examined, are stubborn. The world would not and did not spin out of control when an African American took a seat in the U.S. Senate, but some people were convinced that it would and did. When women began to sit on juries, the hallowed halls of justice did not tumble; some people were convinced they would and did.

The persistence of belief in proper roles for the better sort and the meaner sort, for men and women, for people of different races or classes or places, is one of the legacies of our penchant for orderliness. A vestigial organ in our body politic, this conviction has remained long after its reason for being has ended.

There are glass ceilings in any striated society. In this book we are concerned with one ceiling as it occurred and as it is changing in one place. Until recently, in the southern mountains of North Carolina, local white males, almost exclusively, served as system-level public school leaders. Those were not proper positions for women, for people of color, or for geographic outsiders. Today that chain is uncoupling.

Occupational Glass Ceilings

Many people first encountered the idea of segregation as it applied to gender and employment access in the Center for Creative Leadership's pioneer study

Breaking the Glass Ceiling (Morrison, White, Van Velsor, and the Center for Creative Leadership 1987). The study for the book began in the mid-1980s as the Executive Women Project. It included the results of interviews with women in senior leadership positions in Fortune 100-sized corporations and with both male and female informants in positions to judge their performances. In addition, it used the comprehensive database of surveys, skill assessments, and simulation performances for center workshop participants disaggregated and analyzed by gender. Although Ann Morrison and her colleagues address the absence of females in the top ranks of corporate America, in many ways their findings apply as well to the top positions in the nation's school systems.

Acknowledging that the 1970s and 1980s represented a time of increasing access to administrative positions, the *Glass Ceiling* authors point out that women continued to suffer from arrested executive advancement. Women might reach middle management but they were unlikely to reach the corner office on the top floor. There was a definite limit to aspiration, one that applied not to individuals but "to women as a group who are kept from advancing higher because they are women" (13). Once through an initial management-level barrier, they encountered "a wall of tradition and stereotype" that kept them from rising above that level (14).

Among the external constraints were some of the usual suspects. The work itself required extensive personal and temporal demands. Those demands were exacerbated by the persistence of the idea that women held primary responsibility for household and family obligations. Being the outsider, the token, a member of a very small minority carried an extra burden, both psychological and physical, which did not appear likely to go away at any time in the near future.

In examining the factors that contributed to successful leadership ladder climbing, the authors cited the need for women to "find and master a narrow band of acceptable behavior" (98). They must do the job as well as their male counterparts, including sometimes outdoing them, while remaining feminine. Although there did not appear to be many significant differences in their self-perceptions or in behaviors in situations requiring the exercise of leadership, women were "perceived quite differently by many people, including the savvy insiders who can make or break their careers" (53). In this instance, perception is reality and culture's child. It follows social norms and behavioral expectations. It also shapes them. Insiders expect certain things. Those from whom such things are expected learn to conform, if they, too, want to become inside players.

Our society expects business leaders to be men. The equation is simple: if leaders are men, then leadership must be coded male. Leaders embody masculine behaviors. As Elizabethans continue to whisper in our cultural ears, it is how things were meant to be. Being female in those roles is unnatural. Women dare not be too masculine for fear of desexing themselves and being inauthentic or, worse, sexually suspect. Simultaneously, they cannot appear too feminine, because that would be contrary to the ways that top leaders are expected to behave. They must, then, act out a contradictory set of behaviors. Success resides not in what one knows or can do but in how appropriately one displays who one is.

Punching through the initial leadership ceiling, according to Morrison, required establishing credibility, finding advocates, and "outright luck" (134). Timing and placement, although insufficient in themselves, were all too often necessary. Once within the higher echelons of the corporate world, once above the ceiling, women still found themselves outsiders. Their advancement dead-ended in staff rather than line positions. They had limited influence and were supervised rather than supervising, and they discovered that advocates dwindled to a precious few. Many of them voluntarily derailed their careers, tired of juggling multiple responsibilities and shouldering against the ceiling. Having not signed on to play Sisyphus for life, many of these women sought alternatives to traditional advancement.

The basic parameters of the arguments developed in *Breaking the Glass Ceiling* continue to appear in general leadership literature that addresses barriers to senior-level executive positions. Today, however, they exist in an altered socioeconomic context. In response to critiques like Betty Friedan's 1971 manifesto, *The Feminist Mystique*, the newly reconstituted women's movement began a conscious examination of the nature of women's work and gender segregation. Friedan's initial complaints were those of educated, white women of privilege—suburban housewives whose hours at home resulted not in a sense of fulfillment but in an existential angst that had no easy name. Entangled in a cultural web from which they could not escape, many of these homemakers sought a degree of social and economic emancipation.

Friedan spoke from a position of privilege, and her audience was far from universal. Women of color and poor women had always worked, both within and outside the home. They wanted different kinds of freedom, and, ultimately, the women's movement fractured along lines of class and race. Yet Friedan's work did initiate a scholarly focus on gender and labor that contributed to explorations of such topics as occupational segregation, wage gaps, unpaid domestic work, production of biological capital (children), and glass ceilings. Patriarchy, like racism, extended into most corners of the Western workplace. Books like *From Working Girl to Working Mother* (Weiner 1985) and *Out to Work: A History of Wage-Earning Women in the United States* (Kessler-Harris 1982) gave way in the 1990s to more focused polemics on specific employment practices (see, for example, Strom 1992), specifically feminist interpretations of labor practices (Baron 1991a and b), and comprehensive critiques of the status quo independent of class (for instance, Kemp 1994).

Work was gendered, including unpaid work in the home. Work gendered female was less important than work gendered male, thereby worthy of less remuneration, lower status, and limited autonomy. It was not simply valued less, it was degraded. It became what males did not want to do. Men were judged by what they did; women were evaluated by the fact that they were women. As Kessler-Harris (1982) points out, "male and female children were socialized to particular expectations of the family and household. All else seemed outrageous and it was treated as such." When women "strode bravely into the work force, they landed in its lowest places without coercion with their full consent and understanding and even encouragement." Echoing Lovejoy, Kessler-Harris observed that "this was part of no grand conspiracy, no human design. To most people it seemed totally natural" (viii).

Friedan's complaint challenged that naturalness. The Executive Women's Project looked at a slice of its consequences, the dearth of women at the top of the corporate ladder, and provided a ready name and description of the forces that kept them outside the last rooms of power. They were optimistic about a coming, seemingly inevitable, change in the status quo. Yes, "the problem has no easy answers or quick fixes" (Morrison et al. 1987, 165). "There is," Morrison and her colleagues confidently wrote in the 1980s, "light at the end of the tunnel for executive women" (174).

Yet after consciousness raising, bra burning, street marching, sit-ins, harassment suits, post-1960s Civil Rights legislation, Title IX, and affirmative action, there were still gender-based inequities. In 1995 the Federal Glass Ceiling Commission issued two reports, one documenting the persistence of a glass ceiling (*Good for Business*) and the other listing ways that business, the government, and society might prevent its continuation (*A Solid Investment*). The commission found, nearly a decade after the Center for Creative Leadership's work, that women and minorities continued to encounter advancement barriers. For example, even in the mid-1990s nearly 97 percent of senior leaders of Fortune 1,000 and Fortune 500 companies were white, and nearly that many were male. Commissioners urged the continuation of affirmative action, encouraged sensitivity to stereotyping, advocated diversity training, and asked the government to lead the way by monitoring its own efforts to promote minorities to senior-level positions.

The reception of the report was as tepid as its recommendations. Probably few Americans even knew that their taxes supported a Glass Ceiling Commission, much less that it issued a series of findings that today sound like a "you can do it" lecture delivered by someone's well-meaning elder aunt or uncle. Their reports seem dated, well-meaning relics of a passing or past sensibility.

Part of the reason is that our national politics are today in a different place. Denials of sexism abound, as do calls for the introduction of a color-blind society. We reduce questions of economic inequities to complaints about encouraging class warfare. Glass ceilings are old news, a little like sunbonnets and hoop skirts—quaint, but dated.

Yet the term and the condition persist. Disproportionate representation of a particular sex (male), a particular race (white), and a particular status (insider) in the upper echelons of public service, the military, and the for-profit and not-for-profit worlds continues. The reasons are as dated as Shakespeare's orderly universe. True, there now are more women in power positions. Also true, however, is that change does not occur in isolation. Increased access, as we will argue later, changes whatever women have accessed, sometimes in ways that make the attainment a hollow victory. Once one is on the other side of the glass, the candy might not be as sweet as once it looked. Glass ceilings are culturally constructed; their naturalness is an act of humankind, not of nature. Cultures are shifting things. Ceilings are moveable barriers, not static points on a fixed continuum.

Ceilings and School Leadership

In *The One Best System*, historian David Tyack (1974) traced the development of America's schools from scattered, autonomous one-room buildings to the bureaucratic urban models that characterize most public educational institutions today. One aspect of that transition was the movement from male teachers working with varying degrees of independence to male administrators supervising a corps of teachers, most of whom were female. He likened the resulting organization to a "pedagogical harem" (45). "Hierarchical organization of schools and the male chauvinism of the larger society fit as hand to glove" (60). The existence of a harem was not cast in stone. As will become evident later, it is likely to be exiting in the future, perhaps to be replaced by a sorority.

In 1987 Charol Shakeshaft addressed the question of missing female school administrators by looking first at the past and then at their contemporary status. What roles did women play as schools became organized into systems and educational administrators increased in number and type? How did roles allocated to women compare to the roles given to their male counterparts? How do they compare today? There had always been female school leaders. Indeed, at one time they existed in larger proportion and with somewhat more influence than they did in the 1960s and 1970s. By then, there were differences in the routes women took to leadership positions and the ways in which they constructed their work.

Women had never constituted a majority of educational administrators, even though by the beginning of the twentieth century they occupied a significant majority of the entry-level positions (teachers) in the profession. Most of the women who ran schools in the nineteenth century founded them. Most women in administrative positions in public schools held elementary school principalships and worked in rural areas. When they did achieve senior-level positions as superintendents at the county or state levels, as they did between 1900 and 1930, their roles lacked the status, salary, and power of high school principals or superintendents of town districts, positions filled by men. Admittedly, there were a few exceptions (Ella Flagg Young, who superintended the Chicago public schools between 1909 and 1915, for example, and Susan Dorsey, who was in charge of the Los Angeles schools from 1922 to 1929), but they were few in number. With the maturation of the school district system, access to superintendencies narrowed.

The coming of the Depression, centralization of districts, application of scientific management techniques to schools, establishment of efficiency as a prime measure of accountability, and the creation of specific forms of credentialing as a prerequisite for employment (some school leadership programs did not admit women) placed limits on access to top positions. Following World War II, there was a renewed emphasis on moving men into public education, an initiative aided by the G.I. Bill. Prosperity returned. It was accompanied by a middle-class *Leave It to Beaver* view of the proper responsibilities for educated women. They were to be wives and mothers in America's growing suburbs. America returned to Tyack's harem as the preferred (proper) organizational structure of public schooling. Gribskov (1980) notes that the declining influence of women's organizations and clubs, groups that had been instrumental in working for suffrage and progressive social reforms, also contributed to a decline in female access to public power positions. Williams 1979) argues that desegregation disproportionately hurt minority access to leadership positions, particularly for women. Certainly, by the time Shakeshaft began her review and Morrison and her colleagues were looking at females in the executive suites of the corporate world, there were fewer women in leadership roles than one might expect given their numbers in the world of education.

With the solidification of 1950s feminine mystique ideology and the reappearance of complaints about the potential feminization of America, access became more problematic for reasons that were strictly gender dependent. Marriage meant that women entered the job market, but not careers. They were place dependent, tied to their husband's economic fortunes. They also got pregnant and periodically suspended their professional work for family responsibilities. As a result, they were perceived as less predictable employees because they might move or take a temporary leave of absence. If they remained single, they were accused of being too masculine or of being subject to the eccentricities of frustrated spinsters. Either way, they were denatured as women. If they married, then their energies and time were first obliged to their husband and children. Subject to divided priorities, they were considered poor candidates for leadership roles.

There simply was not much wiggle room available. "Real" women did not aspire to be school administrators. Women who did were not real women; they were abnormal by definition (they aspired to a man's role) and that fact alone served as a disqualifier. As Shakeshaft (1987) observes, "by dividing the world into two kinds of behavior . . . and labeling behavior of competence as male, women must choose between being called competent or being identified as female" (113).

Shakeshaft looked at both building- and system-level administrators. Jackie Blount (1998) specifically addressed the topic of gender and the superintendency in *Destined to Rule the Schools*. She found, not surprisingly, that women were underrepresented in the upper ranks of school leaders and that their exclusion was the result of systemic discrimination. Women presented themselves in greater and greater numbers at the schoolhouse door, first as teachers and then as candidates for other positions, but it was the number and supervisory power of male administrators that grew. "The present configuration of school administration is inextricably woven into traditional gender definitions that are premised on males controlling females" (161). It is unlikely, Blount concludes, that power inequities will diminish without structural change. Attaining the top leadership positions might be less than sweet. The superintendency "is not a neat center of power in public schooling" (162).

In 2000 the Census Bureau designated the district superintendency as "the most male-dominated executive position of any profession in the United States" (Glass et al. 2000, 17). By that date, 13.2 percent of school superintendents were women. Although that percentage had doubled the proportion of women in those positions in 1990, the numbers failed to reflect the disproportionate number of women (72 percent) who filled professional positions in K–12 education. "Where," Glass (2000) wonders, "are all the women superintendents?" Still behind that old glass, Blount and Shakeshaft might respond.

Ceilings and the South

Two decades of enthusiastic Southern governors have encouraged us to think of Sunbelt states as areas of relative growth and prosperity. Sunbelt is an apt name, aligned with images of bright horizons and rising fortunes, of a sense of optimism. Better to be on the sunny side than where the rain falls. Today's

South is Atlanta and Dallas and Charlotte, modern, high-rise, and skyline cities with the accoutrements of success—professional sports teams, new stadiums, malls, boutique shopping sections, and restaurants with outside tables and extensive wine lists, serving cuisine rather than comfort food. In its most recent incarnation, today's New South is a place where commerce means more than cotton, and manufacturing includes products other than textiles and furniture. Rather than being the region from which people migrated, it has become the place to which they move. The old industrial corridor of the northeastern and central states might be rusting, but these are boom times in some places below the Mason-Dixon Line.

Yet, for all its recent success in a troubling and erratic economy, the sun does not shine everywhere equally. Economic and cultural ceilings persist. The states in which one finds the largest number of houses without indoor plumbing are, with the exception of New Mexico, in the South. Of the states with the highest illiteracy rates, most are in the South. There are fewer dentists per 1,000 residents in most of the southern states than in the rest of the nation. By 1992 all of the states without laws against sex discrimination were in Dixie. That was also true of the states with the lowest percentage of white women employed in occupations traditionally reserved for white males (Reed 1994, 12–20). When data on the superintendency is disaggregated by gender and place, one of the regions with the lowest percentage of women is the South (8.4 percent), eclipsed only by the Rocky Mountain states (Glass et al. 2000, 82).

Ceilings and Appalachia

When Michael Harrington penned *The Other America* (1992), one of the places he used to illustrate "otherness" was Appalachia. Since the nineteenth century, when wilderness romantics, progressive do-gooders, and economic exploiters rediscovered it, the Central and Southern Appalachians have served as a place for cultural voyeurs to wax eloquent or strident about simple virtues and plain living, ecstatic religion, Little Abners and Daisy Maes, ignorance, sanitation, and hookworms. If the South were the region left in the dust of the Civil War, condemned to be the supplier of raw materials for Northern industrialists, Appalachia was left out. It became America's place that time forgot. Its rediscovery was part nostalgia and part economic exploitation.

Like the South, Appalachia spent decades as a stepchild of a growing national economy. It, too, had a history of ceilings. As Richard Jackson, a North Carolina mountain native, puts it in *Our Appalachia: An Oral History* (Shackelford and Weinberg 1977), "Appalachians have stood to the side of mainstream

America because it's a colony. Its resources have historically been used to swell the wealth of people outside its boundaries" (379). Poor, with an extraction-based economy, Appalachia, like the South proper, had a set of role expectations that worked against upward mobility of women. At the time the individuals in our study came of age, children were raised to become their parents, sons following fathers and daughters following mothers. For women, that meant overseeing the household and tending to children. As late as 1976 one observer could write that "interests outside the domestic realm are considered to be the primary concern of men" (Hicks 1976, 42). "Segregation along sexual lines is, by urban American standards, quite marked" (46). Ten years later, another observer wrote that "a wife accepts the authority of her husband as a natural fact of life" (Beaver 1986, 98).

Layers and Caveats

The southern mountains of North Carolina sit astride ancient fault lines. They are not now a hotbed of seismic activity, but evidence of earthquakes can be read in their geography. The Blue Ridge Mountains are a result of colliding tectonic plates followed by millions of years of erosion. Those plates provide a way to think about ceilings, about transparent barriers that separate some of us from others. They rearrange themselves over time, slowly and in small stages. Rearrangements produce and gradually increase stress. Too much stress and the earth splits, altering the landscape in dramatic fashion.

When we looked at the gender divisions in our part of the United States, what we thought we saw was a ceiling made thick by multiple layers of discrimination. Whatever ceiling effects attached to gender elsewhere in the United States also existed here. If, for example, a general cultural division persisted in excluding women, as well as other minorities, from executive positions in New York, we assumed that it extended southward. When it edged toward Virginia, it bumped into and slid across a ceiling already in place, one that separated perspectives Southern from viewpoints elsewhere, reinforcing an already existent set of national expectations. Regional attitudes about the proper places of Southern ladies and racial minorities had long been and linger as shapers of access and performance. When those two ceilings moved from the coastal plains into the upcountry, they encountered Appalachian patriarchy. Three layers of discrimination kept people in their places. We erroneously thought their effect would be additive. We found that it was paradoxical.

In the process of reporting our work, we resort at times to making things simpler than they were or are. For example, there is neither one South nor one Appalachia. Even within the fifteen counties of our study,[5] there are notable differences. Regions are complex, varied, in flux, and populated by different people with different aspirations, expectations, and motivations. The world is plural. We are also aware of the crudity of looking primarily at gender, race, and geographic outsiderness. There are, admittedly, other variations of minority status alive, well, and here. It will often appear that we have homogenized regions, minimized diversity, and ignored confounding variables that might have produced another story than the one we tell. Our goals are to link certain ceilings to certain cultural assumptions, to make claims about the importance of place, to introduce ideas about changes in particular settings, and to consider a possible set of unintended consequences. This is an opening chapter in the story of Southern Appalachian occupational segregation.

Theoretical Constructs

There are some fundamental ideas that helped us shape the ways we went about looking for information and attempted to make sense of the data we collected. Two frames of reference undergird the others. One is a feminist perspective about gender that includes the belief that there are certain basic inequities that flow from the ways societies define gender roles. In the Western world, those inequities disadvantage women more than men, particularly in terms of political, economic, and cultural power. Cultural differences and the consequences of those differences are mutable. Because they can change, when they disadvantage one portion of the population, they should be addressed. That last statement is normative and purposefully so. Knowledge, we believe, can and often should serve a social function.[6]

The second is that both of us were initially English majors and that one of us later did graduate work in history. We think that human beings leave evidence of who they are and how they got to be that way in their stories as much as in things that we can enumerate and treat statistically. Although we admire the methods of social scientists and occasionally use them ourselves, we are intuitively more at home with the messier attempts of humanities practitioners and artists to describe and make sense of their world.

Evelyn Fox Keller (1983) titled her biography of Nobel Laureate Barbara McClintock *A Feeling for the Organism* because that phrase captured her personal, initially misunderstood approach to science. McClintock talks about the necessity of looking intently at individual plants, of taking the time to "hear what the material has to say to you."

> No two plants are exactly alike. They're all different, and, as a consequence, you have to know that difference. . . . I start with the seedling, and I don't want to

> leave it. I don't feel I really know the story if I don't watch the plant all the way along. So I know every plant in the field. I know them intimately, and I find it a great pleasure to know them. (Quoted in Keller 1983, 198)

Getting to know her plants? Intimacy? Not quite the perceptions that we have come to associate with the cold, hard sciences. According to Keller, one reason that McClintock's work was so long overlooked was that she conducted her studies outside the domain of normal science. For McClintock, the study of living things requires taking more than reason and an empirical eye to a laboratory. It necessitates an appreciation that is less rational, looks at wholes as well as parts, observes with feeling, and appreciates the value of natural settings.

We are neither Kellers nor McClintocks, but observers of far more modest skills and purpose. Yet we share their predilection to consider texts important, to listen well, and to trust, at least at times, a less-than-exact story rather than a chi square or an ANOVA. In addition to that foundation, the work of social constructionists, cultural historians, and standpoint theorists have helped shape our academic mental landscapes.

Sociology of Knowledge

Early in the twentieth century, Max Scheler introduced the term "sociology of knowledge." Our introduction to the idea came in the late 1960s through *The Social Construction of Reality*, by Peter Berger and Thomas Luckmann. The authors set out a number of propositions that we have found useful.

The knowledge to which we attend constitutes the reality of everyday lives. It forms the building blocks of meaning in any society. Another way of characterizing that type of knowledge is that it is commonsensical. "The reality of everyday life is taken for granted" (1967, 23). That is, it is readily accessible, nontheoretical, broadly distributed, and palpable. It is sufficiently part of an omnipresent background to be beyond doubt. Indeed, to doubt its veracity is to call reality itself into question.

Language is the mechanism that we use to understand and communicate that reality. It establishes names and generates patterns. Language actualizes the moment and makes it stable, creating a "social stock of knowledge" that can be transmitted from one generation to the next (41). We describe reality with signs and symbols, thereby imbuing it with shareable meaning.

The reality that language perpetuates is socially constructed. Communities engage in the work of shaping reality together. Who we are as individuals is intertwined with and inseparable from who we are collectively as a society. Reality becomes the agreed-upon description of how things are. Sufficiently repeated, it becomes habituated. Once habituated, it becomes institutionalized. Occasionally, it is reified, merging with the natural world (90–91). When particular realities become attached to specific power interests, they solidify into ideologies. Acting within socially defined constraints, we perform our particular, socially determined parts.

"Knowledge," as Berger and Luckmann make clear, "must always be knowledge from a particular position" (10). Ideas stand in relation to other ideas or things. They are situated, rather than existing somewhere "out there" in some absolutely knowable form. Truth claims, then, are always tentative. There exists the possibility of choice within accepted options. The road less traveled, the course followed by revolutionaries and heretics, leads outside the boundaries of normal; to follow it is also a choice.

One of the best-known scholarly applications of these ideas is Thomas Kuhn's (1973) *The Structure of Scientific Revolutions*, which was originally published several years before Berger and Luckmann's theoretical summary. Kuhn sets out to distinguish between the nature and operation of normal science and revolutionary science, pointing out that most scientists engage most of the time in the former. Normal science takes place within specific parameters, assumptions governing what is proper to study and the ways in which those studies can be properly conducted. Communities of scientists collectively determine governing assumptions. They monitor their application through access to and preparation for the profession, provision of space and funds for research, approval and distribution of findings, and rewards for performance.

Those assumptions constitute the paradigm within which legitimate, as opposed to revolutionary, research can be done. Normal science is impossible in the absence of a paradigm, yet not all paradigm candidates are equal. Those that achieve hegemonic positions tend to be more successful than alternatives, at least initially, in addressing research problems then defined as important. Within the parameters of a particular paradigm, scientific progress is often quite rapid, because scientists focus almost exclusively on problems that can be addressed by a given set of assumptions.

All paradigms degrade. Over time, investigations become ever more refined and technological innovations reveal things that cannot be explained by current theories. Anomalies, events that cannot be explained by the paradigm, appear.

The more troubling and numerous the anomalies, the greater the likelihood that questions challenge the assumptions themselves. A critical mass of anomalies can precipitate a crisis. In a period of crisis, rules are loosened. Critics propose explanations that do not correspond to accepted knowledge, and competing paradigms appear. Debate ensues. Proponents of the original paradigm attempt to suppress differences and force adherence to the traditional perspective. Because they possess power (they are a profession's gatekeepers) and because they are willing to exercise it (public ridicule or exclusion of contrarians from positions of power), paradigm shifting is not something that happens easily or often.

It is the nature of normal science to suppress novelty. To question normal science is to question how one sees the world itself, to question reality. Paradigm shifts mean we suddenly see the world differently. The example Kuhn uses in his book, the transition from a Ptolemaic to a Copernican cosmology, illustrates that point. Applying his insights to other disciplines, one can understand why altering a single concept—say, the divine right of kings—might call into question an entire way of seeing, like the traditional great chain of being. The world, like what we see in a kaleidoscope, changes with a slight turn of a wheel. If the king has no inherent right to automatic and permanent placement on a particular link of the chain, then his fall will provide the space necessary to conceive of governments without him as legitimate.

Definitions of gender are social constructions. Because they have been paired with notions of the sacred (for the Christian Western world, the explicit and implicit gender hierarchy that begins with Adam and Eve), enacted over time and thereby habituated, they have become part of our ideological background noise. They frame the assumptions that we use to negotiate relationships, personal and public, between men and women. They constitute, in the language of Kuhn, our gender paradigm. Socially constructed reality is always subject to change. As Berger and Luckmann point out, "institutionalization is not . . . an irreversible process, despite the fact that institutions once formed, have a tendency to persist" (1967, 81).[7]

Cultural History

High school history classes tend to be chronicles of kings and conflicts. For students in the United States, that tendency means ignoring the history of North America until Europeans arrived, rushing through exploration and colonization, pausing at the revolutionary period, and then moving through a litany of the presidents, their deeds, and their misdeeds. The other chronological bracket we routinely use is war and then usually the major ones—the American Revolution, the War of 1812, the Mexican-American War, the Civil War, the two world wars, and Korea. History, even in some colleges, rarely ranges outside things political, diplomatic, or martial. A nod to economic history might include fluctuating business cycles and the triumph of American ingenuity through industrialization and technological innovation. Extending the story to the everyday—to marginalized people, social inventions, and culture, both high and low—is not the stuff of a heroic past designed to enlarge patriotic sentiments. Yet that story is the one in which we live our everyday lives, both personal and professional. Consequently, we turned to social and cultural historians to understand the ideological expectations of a particular place.[8]

Modern attention to the intersection of mind-sets and geography comes from the work of several French historians, who, collectively, are known as the Annales School. The name is derived from a journal they began in the late 1920s, *Annales d'histoire économique et sociale*. Although their roots were in Marxist historiography, these scholars have more in common with the Italian Antonio Gramsci, who emphasizes the role of power in establishing and maintaining cultural hegemony over the masses (Appleby, Hunt, and Jacob 1994).

The Annales historians explored the role of geography in shaping how different cultures develop. For example, in the 1920s, Marc Bloch (1973) looked at a specific phenomenon, the king's touch as a cure for disease, comparing its different development in two countries. In the resulting book, he introduced his readers to a concept that he labels "collective illusions," an apt name for ideas a particular society naturalizes. Fernand Braudel, in his multivolume history of Phillip II's Mediterranean world (1972), spent the entire first volume discussing place. "Geography," he writes, "is no longer an end in itself but a means to an end. It helps us to rediscover the slow unfolding of structural realities, to see things in the perspective of the very long term" (23).

Bloch distinguished between exceptional and general causes. For every event, there are some precipitating and immediate causes. For example, a misstep might cause one to fall into the Grand Canyon. However, were there no larger and more general causes, the event cannot occur. First there must be the canyon. Although necessary, the chasm is insufficient reason for the fall (Gaddis 2002). For Braudel, it is where we begin to understand the event. The place to begin is with the place itself. From geography come the prerequisite conditions to a history of *mentalités*, the development of shared mind-sets or cultural structures. A recent, popular treatment of the role of place in character formation is David Fischer's *Albion's Seed* (1991), which posits that the location from which British colonists emigrated influenced both where they settled in the New World and how they structured and behaved in those settlements.

Anthropologist Clifford Geertz introduced the idea of "thick description" in 1973. "Culture is not a power, something to which social events, behaviors, institutions, or processes can be causally attributed; it is a context, something within which they can be intelligibly—that is, thickly—described" (14). To Berger and Luckmann (1967), "the process of becoming man takes place in an interrelationship with an environment" (48).[9] Insider knowledge perpetuates particular meanings to which outsiders are denied or lack the ability to access. As knowledge becomes increasingly complex, certain domains become inaccessible to outsiders. Few people understand the intricacies of fractals or string theory, so each remains an idea primarily accessible to physicists or educated amateurs. Powerful places—places that retain vibrant, relatively homogeneous cultures—are ideologically well-positioned sites from which to observe access changes, to witness the transition from outsider to insider.

Geography, the nature of a particular place as well as one's position therein, is central to our story. There are other contributions from cultural historians and anthropologists that we find attractive and that inform the work we do. For instance, we use evidence from a number of different disciplines, believing Geertz's (1983) claim that scholars have entered a period of "blurred genres" in their attempts to make sense of everyday life. We concur that "man is an animal suspended in webs of significance he himself has spun" (Geertz 1973, 5). We value the power of local stories to tell us something useful and interesting. They are the scaffolds upon which our arguments are framed.

Standpoint Theory

Karl Mannheim (1936), an early proponent of a sociology of knowledge approach to the social sciences, notes that traditional concepts of objectivity necessitate "the rejection of all those forms of knowledge which are dependent upon the subjective standpoint." "It is impossible to conceive of absolute truth existing independent of the values and position of the subject and unrelated to the social context" (79). Social scientists must take into consideration the interplay among various points of view, striving to find ways to integrate them. To understand a complete story requires acknowledging the limited nature of specific narratives. Truth resides somewhere in the midst of contending social realities. To minimize errors or limitations that necessarily arise from a particular perspective, scholars routinely collect multiple perspectives. They triangulate their data.

The historian Carl Becker detected a crucial limitation in Mannheim's argument. Sociologists and historians arrive at Mannheim's error-lite position through a lens that is itself socially situated (see Novick 1992, 160). Because the integrative lens that filters multiple perspectives tends to be white and male, collecting differing viewpoints still privileges a particular position. Early work by Gilligan (1982) and Belenky et al. (1986) pointed toward alternative reality constructions when a fundamentally dissimilar position was used to gather and analyze data. Research done from a woman's perspective produced a different voice, a different way of knowing. Some feminist academics began focusing their studies on women and using a deliberately feminist methodology for conducting their research. Not coincidentally, their critique of their colleagues' previous work centered on the fact that early generalizations were shaped by white, middle-class, male worldviews even when the authors were women or people of color.

Feminist research theorists claimed that it was membership in certain social groups (for example, gender, race, class, and sexual orientation) or the intersection of such groups (for instance, a working-class, Latina female) that shapes how we see the world and how we act therein (Smith 1987, 1992; Hartsock 1983, 1987; Harding 1987; and Rose 1983, 1986). They adopted a variation of the Marxist contention that the proletariat has a more profound understanding of how society functions than do members of the bourgeoisie. Rather than using an economic standpoint exclusively, they expanded the concept to include other populations at the margins. To achieve "strong objectivity," a concept developed by Harding (1993), a researcher must work from the standpoint of minorities. The standpoint of majorities or dominant groups was weak objectivity; inquiry was better begun with/by marginalized groups.[10]

Like standpoint theorists, we believe that knowledge is situated and that it is plural (Haraway 1991). Local knowledge is an important, indeed crucial, counterweight to a universal interpretation of how things are (Collins 1991a and b). Particularity is good. Context matters. The world of the every day is a (the) proper subject for study.

Most of us have heard the phrase "beauty is in the eye of the beholder," a line from an 1878 Margaret Hungerford novel. It echoes Hume's earlier and perhaps more apt "beauty in things exists in the mind which contemplates them" (Bartlett 1980, 676, 357). The same can be said of our social, as opposed to our natural, world. It can even be said of the parameters, frames, or standpoints that we use to view that natural world.

What's in a Name? The Dissembling Study

Dissembling was once a necessary part of life as a Southern lady. According to *Webster's New World Dictionary* (Guralnik 1970) it means "to conceal under a false appearance; disguise;" "to pretend to be in a state of; simulate; feign" or, as a verb, "to conceal the truth, or one's true feelings, motives, etc. by pretense." To some people, that set of behaviors makes one a hypocrite. To others, however, it provided and provides a wedge from a position of dependency and subjugation, literal or symbolic, to power. It is an alternative to servitude and a viable option to negotiate the shoals of social restraints. In a way, dissembling is a liberating act, even though some of its elements in particular places and at particular times might be conventional. It provides a way to disturb cultural norms from within.

One way to look at the space created thereby and the parameters within which successful dissembling can occur is Erving Goffman's *The Presentation of Self in Everyday Life* (1959). In it he reports on a study of the ways in which people present themselves in ordinary work settings to various audiences. Social establishments can be studied, Goffman maintains, by looking at impression management. Performances, the ways in which people present themselves, must conform to certain expectations to be judged authentic by their audiences. To do that, performers pay attention, with varying degrees of consciousness, to certain elements of that performance. For example, behavior differs depending on where a performance occurs. What a performer does to manage her front-stage behavior, her formal professional behavior, differs in degree and sometimes in kind from how she behaves backstage with friends or family members. It also varies depending on such factors as the audience for whom it is intended, the purpose of specific performances, the props and time available, the quality of a particular script, and the presence of other performers.

Although Goffman's delineation of the elements of impression management might sound excessively contrived (he uses a stage metaphor throughout the book), the tool he provides for looking at social interactions is useful with regard to dissembling behaviors. Both male and female candidates for a superintendency manage their performances before the school boards that have the power to hire them. They dress for the role, talk the part, and, in general, conduct themselves according to the expectations they believe that audience has for the position of district leader. The more consonant their performance with those expectations, the most authentic they appear, and the more likely it is that they will win the role. Rather than being hypocritical, certain dissembling behaviors are conscious choices designed to enhance the likelihood of an authentic social interaction.

An example of contrasting interpretations from American history provides another way to look at crafted and consciously chosen behaviors. Stanley Elkins (1963), amidst considerable and probably deserved controversy, reinvigorated the study of the South's "peculiar institution" when he argued that the constellation of docile and childlike behaviors exhibited by African Americans in the antebellum period was the effect of the unusually pernicious and closed system of slavery that one found in the United States.[11] These behaviors, to which he affixed the label "Sambo," while serving well as a survival mechanism for those forced to labor as a slave, ill prepared men and women for emancipation. Individual behaviors could digress significantly from those of the group, but Elkins argues that most slaves exhibited those general or group behaviors. They had been infantilized by an institution from which there was little chance of escape. To Elkins, most slaves became, rather than elected to perform as, Sambo.

The historian John Blassingame (1979) agrees with Elkins that a Sambo phenomenon existed, but he disagreed about what it meant. Blassingame noted that the characteristics traditionally attributed to Sambo personality types—submissiveness, docility, loyalty, childishness, an aversion to hard work, cheerfulness, ignorance, and a degree of irresponsibility—were considered, at least by white owners, to be inherent. They were part of the African's nature. It was probably more than a happy coincidence that these traits corresponded to attributes that made the justification for slavery likewise appear part of nature's plan. Yet, according to Blassingame, the appearance of such behaviors was actually a mask created by slaves to dupe their owners and to counterbalance the power they wielded. (Bloch would have called Sambo a collective illusion.) To minimize work, slaves cultivated an impression of slow-moving ignorance. To secure space and time in the slave quarters for some semblance of a stable life, they gave the appearance of faithfulness to their master and his family. Psychologically dependent Sambo existed in the master's head in much the same way that the image of the helpless Southern ladies existed in the minds of their fathers, brothers, and beaux. A closer approximation to the whole story was available in the slave quarters or on Goffman's back stage, where masks dropped and Sambo disappeared. "Puttin' on the master" was simply another way of dissembling.

Elkins's argument is that slaves internalized these externally validated identities. Placing people in dependency roles, over time, makes them psychologically dependent. Sartre (1968) addresses the danger of such internalization in *Anti-Semite and Jew*. Fanon (1971) makes some of the same points in *Black Skin, White Masks*. The Helsinki syndrome demonstrates that the kidnapped often identify with and become like the kidnapper. The physically oppressed, even the culturally colonized, sometimes identify with and long to become like their oppressors or colonizers. Accommodation behaviors designed to expand opportunities for power become something else when they are wholly assimilated.

Our experiences with female and race minority administrators, as well as dispositions born of our own professional and personal histories, incline us toward the Blassingame position. Even in the most closed of systems, there is negotiation space. There are front and back stages. In relatively open systems that already embrace a modicum of diversity, negotiated space is even wider. As Berger and Luckmann (1967) write, "pluralism encourages both skepticism and innovation and is thus inherently subversive of the taken-for-granted reality of the traditional *status quo*" (125, italics in the original). Diversity begets diversity. A crack in the glass ceiling can lead to others.

A less serious, albeit somewhat accurate, take on the topic of self-invention and successful negotiation of potentially troubling environments is the recent work of Jill Conner Browne (1999, 2001, 2003), whose audience is about as far removed from academe as it is possible to be. The creation of the Sweet Potato Queens as a vehicle for a good time; Southern humor; advice to women of a certain age, weight, and class; and gender role subversion illustrates what more somber historians, anthropologists, and sociologists have to say about finding ways to bend the system to attain particular goals. "Life is too short—and too long—to spend it being miserable. Life may indeed be short, but it is, for a fact, wide. It is high time we started settling for more" (1999, 207).

Coming Attractions

This book is divided into three parts. The first one, chapters 1 through 3, provides the study's context. It begins with a more precise and complete description of what we label "Southern Appalachian Ceilings." It includes an introduction to the theoretical constructs we found helpful in shaping the ways we addressed those issues (for example, the works of Erving Goffman, Thomas Luckmann, and Peter Berger). We then review the constraints that two interlocking cultures (the South and Appalachia) place(d) on access to positions of school leadership. We conclude the section with a summary of changing perceptions of who should lead public schools and how they should do it. In that third chapter, we look at how the profession defined educational leadership and at how it was constructed in Southern Appalachia, a place where at least our study participants believe that women remain ladies and good ol' boys are good.

The five chapters that set out the details, findings, and analysis of the professional narratives of our sample of regional school leaders make up the second part. We describe our sample, the data we collected, and how we gathered it. We indicate the ways that these leaders, local policymakers, subordinates, and the broader public currently construct the role of school leader. The eighth chapter ends with a definition of situated leadership, an exploration of its efficacy, and a model that appears to explain the access patterns we found.

In our concluding part, we set our snapshots in motion, addressing evidence of widening access (adjusted ceilings) and altered performance expectations (situated leadership with parochial twists). Among the concepts we discuss are insiderness, insider elasticity, accommodation behaviors, dissembling, assimilation, and professional socialization. Finally, in the tenth chapter, we turn to what might be considered the dark side of the changes we found, looking at some potential, perhaps unintended, professional as well as educational consequences of those changes.

·2·

CRACKER-BARREL WISDOM

The Geographic Context

For decades, soda crackers came in barrels to country stores throughout rural America. Positioned near a potbelly stove and sized to hold a soft drink, checkerboard, or deck of cards, barrels became temporary tables around which local raconteurs gathered to trade gossip, seek advice, socialize, and, in Appalachia, to pick and sing. Sites for small community casual conversations, country stores also served as cultural centers, teaching the art and craft of belonging. They were places where young men waited out rain or winter, old men found audiences for their memories, women purchased those things their farm did not provide, adolescents flirted, and children savored the twin delights of penny candy and grown-up stories. Often doubling as local post offices, country stores were where the packages from Sears or letters from family members, traveling neighbors, and distant friends arrived in the days before rural home delivery. In the absence of newspapers, they served as venues from which neighborhood members took their news of the community and the world outside.

If wisdom is the ability to judge well, to reach conclusions based on experience or knowledge, then cracker barrels can (did and still do) serve as extension schools for whole communities. They taught truths embodied in place. They affirmed the natural order of things there and then. This chapter is about the South, Appalachia, and the fifteen counties in North Carolina's southern mountains that made up the region we studied. It focuses on culture, on assumptions about gender, race, and place, as well as the attitudes that influence those assumptions. What did it (does it) mean to be a Southerner? To be an Appalachian? To be a man or woman coming of age in Southern Appalachia?

The places in this chapter are like parts of a collapsing telescope. Each one is nested within a larger cylinder, in focus only when they are connected together. The South makes sense only against the backdrop of the nation. The Appalachia that we consider is not the entire region, but those parts that fit within the South. What we include about Southern culture in general is true, with shifts of perspective to account for differences of place, for Appalachian culture, too. Both regions, for example, are religious, paternal, and individualistic to a degree different from much of the rest of the country. Here we spend more time considering the South and less looking at Appalachia, because it will reappear periodically later in the book. When we turn to a consideration of the counties that form our immediate setting, we shift from a cultural description to a look at the places and people living there today.

What emerges is a snapshot, rather than a motion picture or a panorama. We do not trace, with careful attention to nuance and complexity, change over time nor do we provide readers with a 360° view of the Southern Highlands. What follows is a slice of perceived reality, subject to all the flaws of any metanarrative. It is cracker-barrel wisdom, born of observation and anecdote, subject to alteration with a simple exchange of persons doing the telling or a different emphasis on the elements of the tale. Rarely do any of us construct our realities on more than such stories.

The South

An initial problem in writing about the South is definition. Which geographic South does one have in mind? The states located below an extended Mason-Dixon Line to, but not including, New Mexico? The states of the Confederacy? The antebellum slave states, not all of which left the union following the 1860 election of Lincoln? The climatic South, those states with a subtropical temperature range? The South defined by the Census Bureau? The Deep South?

Which historic South should we consider? The Virginia Founding Fathers or the antebellum South of John Calhoun? The Civil War or the War of Northern Aggression South? The South of Jim Crow, the Ku Klux Klan, and segregation or the South of Ida B. Wells, Booker T. Washington, and Martin Luther King Jr.? The Tom Watson Populist South or the Henry Grady New South? The sharecropping South or the Sunbelt? Strom Thurmond and Jesse Helms or Jimmy Carter and Bill Clinton?

Another difficulty is what population to consider. Do we look only at lifelong residents or do we include snowbirds, recent arrivals, or other transients? First-generation Southerners or descendents of Civil War combatants? Country folks or urban and suburbanites? Does it even make sense to consider

Southern and/or Appalachian regionalism as a distinct entity? Is being Southern or Appalachian any more unique than being a New Englander or a Midwesterner? At a time when the United States is increasingly interconnected globally, does any meaningful regional identity persist?

The states that we considered "the South" for this project are Alabama, Arkansas, Florida, Georgia, Kentucky, Louisiana, Mississippi, North Carolina, Oklahoma, South Carolina, Tennessee, Texas, and Virginia. We used the sample defined as "Southern" by the University of North Carolina's Center for the Study of the American South in its Southern Focus Poll. Rather than addressing changes over time in Southern or Appalachian images, we chose to highlight aspects of regional culture that frame boundaries of expected behavior and personal identity that linger today.

Most of the time, general descriptions of regional folkways are about majority race and dominant class perspectives. Because locally hegemonic positions structure community expectations, they are the ones to which we paid attention. An accurate and complete picture of the South is plural, not singular. What one set of people sees as positive, another might view as negative. For example, some scholars link the South's uniqueness to its battlefield losses in the 1860s. The Civil War created the tragic context within which all subsequent history occurred. Conversely, to most slaves Appomattox was not a tragedy. To black Southerners, the Lost Cause was never a loss.

White Southerners were in the majority after Reconstruction. They believed that their defeat was the result of logistical advantage rather than a fair evaluation of relative merit. To defeated members of the Confederacy, Dixie represented a higher moral order than the victorious North. They cast the conflict and themselves in heroic garb. Majorities, after all, write the history books and all histories are flawed, shortsighted by necessity or will. They relate partially accurate, but always insufficient, narratives, regularly dressed up as historical absolutes. In the South, battlefield defeats led to a sense of failure that, in turn, led to compensatory behaviors resulting in the glorification of Southern gallantry. It culminated in self-identities perpetuating flawed ideals of honor and chivalry. The history of the South has a privileged, white, and male storyline.

Other narratives coexist. There was never only one South. But our emphasis is on the norms created by people in power, the South that white men sought to protect and perpetuate. Men hold the chairs, usually in some local order of privilege. They form the rings around cracker barrels. It is their wisdom, their explanations about how things are and should be, that provides the stage upon which our educational leaders perform.

Regionalism practiced in the South is qualitatively and quantitatively different from that found elsewhere in this country.[1] There are simply more people and places describing what it means to be Southern than there are for other parts of the United States. Every region has magazines and specialty journals dedicated to pursuing things unique to that place; the South has them in excess. *Southern Cultures*, *Southern Exposure*, and *Southern Living* all address particular audiences about things regional. The first considers difference in a cerebral, albeit often humorous, way. The second serves as a venue for regional muckraking. The third celebrates the genteel gardens, food, and fine houses of the prosperous for the prosperous wannabes. One can pluck from the magazine shelves *Southern Accents* (home furnishings), *Southern Lady* (refuge of belle aspirants everywhere), *Southern Horsemen* (for the gentry), and *Southern Review* (a literary journal).

That is only the tip of a publishing iceberg. There are *The Georgia Review*, *Sewanee Review*, *Mississippi Review*, *Southern Literary Journal*, *Southern Quarterly*, *New Delta Review*, and *The Chattanooga Review*. Want to read the latest in Southern history? Try the *Southern Historical Review* (journal of the Southern Historical Association), the *Georgia Historical Review*, or the *North Carolina Historical Review*. Popular Culture? *Oxford American*, maybe, or *Living Blues*. The University of Mississippi hosts the Center for the Study of Southern Culture, the University of South Carolina houses the Institute for Southern Studies, and the Deep South Regional Center can be found on the Tulane campus. The University of West Florida is home to the Center of Southern Foods.

There is a Museum of the New South in Charlotte, and battlefields dedicated to the Old South seemingly everywhere. The University of North Carolina Press published the *Encyclopedia of Southern Culture* (Wilson and Ferris) in 1990. One can belong to the Southern Order of Storytellers, the Society for the Study of Southern Literature, and, by invitation, to the Fellowship of Southern Writers. There are individual state oral history projects as well as the Southern Oral History Program. Regionalists can select from among general interest magazines (*State*, *Texas Monthly*, *Florida Monthly*, and *Mississippi Folklife*, perhaps) or specific site alternatives (*Blue Ridge Country* or *Smokies*). There are online 'zines in various stages of development, such as *Dead Mule*, *Way South*, *Southern Scribe*, and *Southern Quarterly*), and our current favorite, on the basis of name alone, *Y'all.com*.

Regional specialists appear infected by the same intellectual bug that bites some scientists, causing them to pursue grand theories of everything. Southerners and commentators on things Southern chase after an elusive, albeit definitive, explanation to describe the region's uniqueness. For Ulrich Phillips (1928), it was the idea that the South was and should continue to be the province of white men. To the Agrarians (Twelve Southerners 1977), whose 1930 manifesto, *I'll Take My Stand*, is still in print, it was the continuation of a traditional lifestyle, a refusal to embrace modernity. The Vanderbilt Twelve defended the South's opposition to narrow specialization, crass materialism, technological progress at the expense of greater truths, and dehumanization. They stood for values that tied it to the natural world: orderliness, wholeness, a sense of place, purpose, and posterity. For C. Vann Woodward (1960), Southern identity came from the region's poverty in a land of plenty, its military failures in a country known for its success, and its "tortured conscience" slavery in a nation of "innocence and social felicity" (16–21). David Potter (1961) thought the South was the product of persistent and prevalent folk culture. For Frank Vandiver (1964), understanding the region meant understanding its pattern of offensive defense to challenges. George Tindall (1964) argued that to comprehend the South one had to examine its various and sometimes contradictory mythologies, the inconsistent stories Southerners constructed to explain themselves. Bertram Wyatt-Brown (2001) suggested that particular ideas of honor and grace explain the region. Even the pursuit of an explanation, in its breadth, depth, and volume, is unusual.

We have not attempted to name the journals, magazines, and public spaces dedicated to the Civil War and the Confederacy. Or to regional personalities, like Bubba and good ol' boys. Or to public icons, like Margaret Mitchell, Elvis Presley, B. B. King, and Eudora Welty. Or to Dixie's less attractive personalities—white segregation groups, Southern nationalists, and militant survivalists. It is representative of an inward scrutiny and identity fascination that we do not believe can be found elsewhere. Midwestern reenactors? The Center of Rocky Mountain Food? An Institute for Northeastern Studies? *Northwest Living*? So many historians and sociologists crafting research agendas on regional distinctiveness elsewhere? We could not find them.

A Slice of Southern Culture

Although there were already differences between the South and the rest of the nation prior to the Civil War (Taylor 1961; Fredrickson 1965; Coclanis 2000; Appleby 2000), the events between 1861 and 1865 were important in ways that other shared experiences were not. Harwell (1964) and Grantham (1994) point out that the war created a sense of solidarity among the men who fought for the Confederacy, a social bond that transcended the immediate experience of the war itself and that validated both their sense of separateness from Union soldiers and their distinctiveness as valiant warriors. Sectionalism, rather than being something to extinguish, became a badge of honor.

"The primary difference between the South and the rest of the nation," according to Fox-Genovese (1993), "has been its anguished, and occasionally violent, struggle with the consequences of its history" (65). Distinctions before the war were grounded in a climate, geography, and economy hospitable to a social system and culture based on race-based slavery. After the war, Southerners coalesced around resistance to modernity. They spurned industrialization and economic advancement in deference to traditional values and ordained roles, sustained by a narrative of fallen, yet valiant, heroes. Like Don Quixotes, Southerners tilted at windmills and vouchsafed the virtues of their Dulcineas. During the late nineteenth century, as it had been earlier, culture was defined through conformity to values held by white males (Wyatt-Brown 2001). Men below the Mason-Dixon Line did not welcome ideas, behaviors, and people that they considered foreign.

The Civil War contributed to a new and somewhat different solidarity among upper-class Southern women, many of whom had been recently widowed or whose husbands were no longer able to provide for or protect them. The old patriarchal order associated with a master and his manor disappeared. It was replaced by a plantation myth celebrating a hierarchy dominated by a privileged, paternalistic few. After 1865 many Southern women needed and sought jobs to sustain their families, yet proper ladies did not willingly give up their special status. To differentiate themselves from more common laborers, they turned to women's clubs and good works as a means to make visible that separation (Edwards 2000). Directly and indirectly, they constructed sociocultural barriers that separated them from other women in the region, barriers validating the chivalrous narratives of their men. Women were or aspired to be pedestal ladies. Men were dashing rogues who loved their mothers and eventually settled down with a good girl. A critique of traditional gender roles came late to the region and lacked the forcefulness that characterized criticisms of patriarchy elsewhere.

Sustaining, then deepening, the distinctions between the South and the rest of the nation was the economic collapse of the region in the 1860s. Before the war, the states below the Potomac had been prosperous, although the fruits of that prosperity were inequitably distributed. After Gettysburg, the South entered a period of prolonged and steep decline, so that by 1900 the region was arguably even more distinct than it had been in 1861. Few of the new, late nineteenth-century immigrants came south. Less than one-fifth of the population lived in cities. While the North and northern Midwest were being transformed into the industrial giants of the world, only 10 percent of Southerners worked in manufacturing (Coclanis 2000). Slaves had been replaced by sharecroppers and tenant farmers, alternative forms of economic servitude. They came without a master's abiding economic interest in the health and well-being of those men and women who tilled his soil. Agriculturally, the region was underdeveloped. It eschewed mechanization for less-productive human labor and became increasingly dependent on Northern-owned extraction industries.

By the end of the nineteenth century, a Southerner was less likely to be described as a cavalier, a gentleman, or a lady, and more likely to be identified by epithets that are still found in our national lexicon. A Southern was an Arkie, cracker, hillbilly, peckerwood, hick, poor white trash, ridge-runner, cottonhead, linthead, clay-eater, or wool hat. Collectively, Southerners were rednecks, an indication of the primacy of males. (There are few women described casually as rednecks but, in the minds of some outsiders, many Southern men wear the label.) Huber (1995) and Cobb (1999) argue persuasively that Southern men have reclaimed the term *redneck* and now use it with pride. Yet, for all Billy Carter's assertions about being a redneck and proud of it, in spite of songs like David Allen Coe's "Long-haired Redneck," Ronnie Milsap's "I'm Just a Redneck at Heart," the Charley Daniels Band's "What This World Needs Is a Few More Rednecks," and John Schneider's "A Redneck Is the Backbone of America," redneck chic has more a regional than a national following. Few Yankees yearn to grow up to be one, let alone encourage their daughters to marry one.

Rednecks wear jeans with a back-pocket circle imprint from their chewing tobacco tins. Their heads sport a John Deere or Bubba Bar-B-Q baseball hat. Their trucks are well traveled, have Confederate flag bumper stickers, and sport a shotgun in the rear window. Their political views barely got off Noah's ark and their racial opinions are to the right of bigotry.[2] Rednecks are Southern, working-class males, hot-blooded, idle, mean-spirited, ignorant good ol' boys spoiling for a fight.

Southerners have a reputation for violence. It is a region that has been and continues to be obsessed with uniforms, military schools, guns, and the martial arts (Vandiver 1964; Franklin 1964). Civil War battle simulations are popular weekend and vacation activities. Southerners reside in the nation's regional murder capital (Reed 1993). A recent study conducted by the Justice Policy Institute (2003) found that Southern states have higher incarceration rates than the United States as a whole (526 per 100,000 people as opposed to 470).[3] Louisiana and Mississippi, if considered as separate entities, lead the world in the proportion of their population in prison. There are a number of different ways to read such statistics. A whole lot of crime is happening down South, affirming a general tendency to lawlessness. Or, Southern states might be particularly energetic defenders of public peace, enforcing prison sentences in lieu of parole or probation. Then again, Southerners might simply be keeping their criminals locked up longer. However one looks at such numbers, though, they confirm that there is an unusual amount of criminal behavior in Dixie. Southerners do not want anyone messing with their stuff or their people. They will jail those people who do or risk jail themselves to address transgressors of the "do not mess" law.

Even recreational activities in the region are tinged with violence. Southerners make up the "core audience" for professional wrestling (Kyriakoudes and Coclanis 1997, 9). They are more likely to celebrate certain holidays or events with fireworks than are non-Southerners (60 percent to 24 percent). They are four times more likely to welcome the New Year by shooting a gun (Reed 1996). The South invented stock-car racing, whose origins are in dodging revenue agents. Dirt tracks are a countryside staple. The region elevated football to a semisacred community meeting. One can still find, in certain corners of the South, cock fights drawing a crowd on a Saturday night. Southern men are attuned to hunting seasons; "opening day" does not refer to schools. The Southern inclination to violent displays, when combined with a regional loyalty to family and place, manifests itself in hyperpatriotism. A disproportionate number of Southerners march to war, whenever the nation decides to move in that direction. They have a long history of rallying around flags.

Nisbett and Cohen (1996) attribute the South's propensity for violence to habits of mind developed during its founding and frontier days, when families made their living as herders and socialized their children to expect the world to be violent and cruel. Most Southern men were not patricians. They did not have the power—financial, political, or social—to exercise domination organizationally. They worked for a boss man; they could only boss their wives and children. To compensate, to demonstrate their manliness, working-class Southerners took refuge in fighting, blood sports, drinking, and acting the role of autocrat at home (Blackwelder 1991, 106).

Popular music of the South challenges bourgeois notions of appropriate aspirations and behavior; country musicians—suspicious of hierarchy, individualistic to its core, because making a living is killing them—tell boss men to shove jobs.[4] Songs celebrate Saturday nights, honky-tonks, beer, outlaws, railroads, mama, good times, and jail time. They are, simultaneously, lyrical rebellions against class exploitation and declarations of masculine independence (Smith and Rogers 1995). Country boys are hunters, drinkers, lovers, and fighters. They keep good dogs, have bass boats, and two-step in time to the music. Country girls are loyal, with an unfortunate tendency to attach themselves to wayward drifters, low-down husbands, and two-timing men.

Dolly Parton attributed the popularity of country music to lyrics. "It's just stories told by ordinary people" (quoted in Tichi 1994, 7). The South is filled with storytellers, from local tale-spinners to novelists. The National Storytelling Festival is held in Tennessee. Many stories are cautionary tales, culminating in personal catastrophe punctuated by individual acts of violence. Others are tall tales, stories about bragging rights. Still others recount the times that the dispossessed got the better of someone. Southerners, in spite of a rich literary tradition, are not voracious readers—but they are good listeners.

Edgar Allan Poe, nineteenth-century exemplar of Southern Gothic, has been joined in the twentieth century by authors adept at crafting masterpieces of disaster (almost anything by Faulkner), devising small moments of poignant and deadly confrontations (Tennessee Williams's *Cat on a Hot Tin Roof*), exploring the banality of evil (Flannery O'Connor's killer in "A Good Man Is Hard to Find"), or detailing real, but exotic, crime stories (John Berendt's *Midnight in the Garden of Good and Evil*). Anne Rice mixes together a devilish brew of Creole and vampires in New Orleans. Even if natives talk stories more than read them, a rich tradition of literature in the second half of the twentieth century builds on that pervasive oral tradition.

John Shelton Reed (1993), a sociologist whose scholarly agenda includes a broad-based interest in the region, delights in pointing out all things Southern and unique. Kudzu grows only in the South. So does illiteracy, to a greater extent than elsewhere in the country. Dixie periodically votes against the grain, going for Al Smith in 1928, Strom Thurmond in 1948, Adlai Stevenson in 1952 and 1956, Barry Goldwater in 1964, and George Wallace in 1968. Home to a disproportionate number of African Americans, it is the region in which African Americans were most likely to encounter lynch mobs. In 1980, of the eleven states with the highest number of houses without complete plumbing, nine were in the South. In 1982, all but one of the states with the fewest dentists per capita were in the South. Southern states have the most Baptists. The states most often mentioned in country music songs are south of the Mason-Dixon Line.

Southerners have a justifiable reputation for being polite. They are more likely to use polite forms of address when speaking to an adult than residents of other parts of the nation (Reed 1995). They are nearly twice as likely as their non-Southern counterparts, mountain states excluded, to have lived at some point in their lives in a mobile home—almost 40 percent of them have. More than half of all new houses in the South are some variety of manufactured housing. In *Devil's Dream*, novelist Lee Smith invented the lyrics to a country-music song that contained the line "on a double bed in a double-wide with a double shot of gin." When she got her proofs back, an editor had asked in the margin "A double-wide what?" No true Southerner would have had to ask (Reed 1997, 112).

According to the Odem Institute's spring 2000 Focus on the South survey, Southerners are more likely to have a meal at home. They are more likely to go to church with their children, say grace before eating, attend church regularly, believe religious faith is important, be Protestant, and identify as fundamentalists or Pentecostals. They are less likely to drink alcohol, live in a metropolitan area, or identify, if they are white, as a Democrat. White Southerners are considerably more likely to self-identify as political conservatives. Southerners believe that relationships between men and women have grown worse over time; non-Southerners believe that they have improved. Clear gender roles persist in the South with regard to household responsibilities. Women prepare the meals; men fix things around the house. Women do the laundry; men make the most mess. Women do the housework; men work in the yard.

Southerners value the idea of home, of a particular place from which one came and to which one continues to belong, even after moving away. Harry Crews (1995), writing about his youth in southern Georgia, captures its importance in *A Childhood: The Biography of a Place*.

> I come from people who believe the *home place* [italics in original] is as vital and necessary as the beating of your own heart. It is that single house where you were born, where you lived out your childhood, where you grew into young manhood. It is your anchor in the world, that place, along with the memory of your kinsmen at the long supper table every night and the knowledge that it would always exist, if nowhere but in memory. (16)

Home meant kin, meant "my people." As Crews writes, "a large family was the only thing a man could be sure of having. Nothing else was certain" (16). A family marked one's spot on the earth. Who someone was, to whom that person was related, and where he or she lived served as social anchors in a hostile world.

In one of his many good ol' boy roles, Burt Reynolds plays a Southern policeman in *Sharky's Machine*. When he finally confronts the film's antagonist, he lists the three things he has against him. He is fooling around with Reynolds's city; he is "walkin' over people" as though he owns them; and, "the worst part," the sin of sins, because he was "from out of state." Paul Escott (1991) claims that personalism characterizes Southern social interactions and contributes to a natural rift between insiders and outsiders. Southerners are more likely to do business with people that they know than with people they don't know. "It takes a long time to be accepted" is a truth that even long-time residents encounter (4).

Social conventions like small talk are crucial factors in establishing a level of belonging. Southerners became accustomed to communicating indirectly, partially as a way to deal with those men, the landowners whose land they worked as sharecroppers or tenant farmers or the mill owners in whose factories they worked as laborers, who had power over them. They learned to avoid open conflict, preferring silence or apparent agreement to a clear, declarative no. "Courtesy, tact, and indirection," according to one commentator, "helped a deeply divided society to function, and they still ease social intercourse today" (Escott 1991, 12). Courtesy and indirection are polite words for dissembling.

Like families and particular communities, churches were stabilizing institutions in the South. Rural churches combined fatalism, bombast, and emotion in powerful ways. "Hell was at the center of any sermon I had ever heard" (Crews 1995, 70). Christine Heyrman (1997) traced the beginnings of Southern evangelicalism to the early antebellum period, showing how Methodists and Baptists recast their messages in ways that aligned them with regional beliefs about family, patriarchy, place, and masculine honor. These churches "tailored their teachings to uphold . . . the authority of male heads of household" (160). What began in the late eighteenth century as a religious movement that promised a degree of emancipation for subordinate groups became, by the mid-nineteenth century, institutions that "invested their energies in upholding the equality and honor of all white men" (254–55). Positions of authority went to middle-aged, married, majority-race males. Rigid division of gender roles and its explicit hierarchy (men lead and women follow) characterized Southern churches throughout the twentieth century.

Connections between fire and brimstone, between damnation and wrong living, have long been part of Southern experience. In the South, religion is connected to politics, both of which are individual in nature and conservative in content (Carter 1999). At his revivals Billy Graham regularly condemned godless communism. Adopting positions staked out earlier by organizations like the Christian Anti-Communist Crusade and the Church League of America, which had Southern connections, contemporary televangelists use the airwaves to bolster financial bottom lines as well as broadcast political pronouncements. Pat Robertson is based in Virginia. Bob Jones University is in South Carolina. Oral Roberts set up shop in Oklahoma. Jerry Falwell established Liberty University in Lynchburg, Virginia. Before their fall, Jim and Tammy Bakker broadcast from outside Charlotte, North Carolina, where they also built a Christian theme park. The religious home of Franklin Graham, Billy's son and heir apparent, is in Boone, North Carolina. Jimmy Swaggart got his start in Baton Rouge, Louisiana. The region is the home of both the Christian Coalition and the Moral Majority. Between 1970 and 1985, the Southern Baptist Convention added over two million members to its ranks, the largest growth in both absolute and relative terms for any American denomination during those years. A greater proportion of Southerners watch televised religious programming than do residents in any other region (Wuthnow 1988).

Southern Baptists remain the largest religious denomination in the region. In spite of demographic changes that have brought Catholics, Jews, and Muslims southward, as well as various underrepresented Protestant denominations, Dixie's brand of Protestantism separates it from the rest of the nation. It is the Center of Born Again. It has been "created and recreated—so many times. Some people joke that the South is really Hindu because it can reincarnate" (Kenneth Sanchagin, quoted in Murray n.d., 2).

Some observers believe that the South is being "northernized" at last. Urbanization, industrialization, demographic shifts, travel, the media, and education are eroding a belief system built upon outdated agrarianism. The preservation of strict (natural) boundaries between and among people is being successfully challenged. For the past two decades, the South's economy has boomed relative to most of the rest of the nation. Poverty has declined. Income is up (Armas 2002). Rather than being indolent loafers, Southerners now average about the same number of hours at work as the rest of the nation (forty-four hours per week) and are more likely to work in the evening or on weekends (Odem Institute n.d.). Contemporary Southern writers satirize once sacred southernisms (Gray 1999). Today, Lost Cause fanaticism is the subject of farce. Confederate statues are picturesque, not sacrosanct.

One can almost chart the Americanization of the region by looking at three films, each representative of a perspective frozen in time. D. W. Griffin's 1915 release, *Birth of a Nation*, glorified night riders. It justified racist attitudes and policies, demonized blacks, and condoned violence on behalf of honor. *Gone with the Wind*, which appeared in 1939, provided its Depression-era viewers with a grand Southern romance of belles and beaux, chivalry and charm, ennobled loss and lost tomorrows. Northerners were vile and villainous, threatening women and burning Atlanta. The South was not so much evil as misunderstood. When *To Kill a Mockingbird* made it to the silver screen in 1962, it played before an audience whose views of Southern segregation were less influenced by magnolia-scented memories of old times too long forgotten. About a lawyer defending a wrongly accused black man, it portrayed some Southerners as racists and others as striving to overcome the prejudices of the region's bloody past. Overtures of reconciliation were palpable. The films show the South on a journey from one world to another, moving one reel at a time.

The possibility of a gradual convergence with Northern or national beliefs, aspirations, and attributes would have been unthinkable to early twentieth-century critics of the South. To them, the region was a barren wasteland. H. L. Mencken (1920) condemned it as "the Sahara of the Bozart," a land without the letters and arts that define a civilization. Carl Carmer, a Northerner who journeyed below the Potomac in the 1930s, declared "the Congo is not more different from Massachusetts or Kansas or California" (quoted in Griffin 1995, 10). Native son W. J. Cash ([1941] 1969) claimed that there really was no New South. It "is a tree with many age rings, with its limbs and trunk bent and twisted by all the winds of the years, but with its tap root in the Old

South" (x). Writing at the time of the Civil Rights Movement, Howard Zinn (1964) concluded that the South remained "a freak . . . a stranger to the nation" (217).

The South might have come a long way from the parochialism that caught Mencken's attention, but there were "enduring" differences between the South and the rest of the nation (Reed 1986). More than six decades ago, Cash ([1941] 1969) found the region schizophrenic.

> Proud, brave, honorable by its lights, courteous, personally generous, loyal, swift to act, often too swift, but signally effective, sometimes terrible, in its action—such was the South at its best. And such at its best it remains today. . . . Violence, intolerance, aversion and suspicion toward new ideas, an incapacity for analysis, an inclination to act from feeling rather than from thought, an exaggerated individualism and a too narrow concept of social responsibility, attachment to fictions and false values, above all too great attachment to racial values and a tendency to justify cruelty and injustice in the name of those values, sentimentality . . . these have been its characteristic vices in the past. And, despite changes for the better, they remain its characteristic vices today. (439–40)

Southerners are anti-institutional, suspicious of central government in any guise, and prone "to redress grievances privately, which sometimes means violently" (Reed 1993, 59). The region has retained cultural elements of its agrarian past, including a politics that encourages the persistence of class divisions and that limits mobility (Carlton 1995). Southerners view their world as local and familial. They are, for example, more likely to name family members or religious leaders to most admired lists than non-Southerners (Reed 1993). Although a winner in recent boom times, the South remains poor relative to other regions. Between 2000 and 2001, the South's increase in number and proportion of people classified as poor was greater than in any other region (Proctor and Dalaker 2002). Although the South has closed the educational gap that once separated it from other states, the dropout rates in its high schools remain the highest in the country (National Center for Education Statistics 2000b).

Other observers acknowledge that differences do, indeed, exist on opposite sides of the Mason-Dixon Line. However, they contend that they are trivial in nature and tend to be quaint rather than substantive. As they become more like their fellow Americans, Southerners "grope for and fondle its fading distinctions" (Yoder 1964, 40). Films like *Fried Green Tomatoes*, *Driving Miss Daisy*, and *Crimes of the Heart* emphasize amusing eccentricities or characters. They have about them a sense of time long ago, when female solidarity and racial rapprochement helped marginalized people support one another and resist prevailing expectations about proper place and conduct. There is, according to Eric Bates of *Southern Exposure*, a danger of "fetishization of a false past" (quoted in Cobb 1999, 136). It is all too easy to disguise the darker side of the South's past and present: racial segregation, cross and church burnings, Leo Frank, labor exploitation, mill villages, violence, pellagra, hookworm, ignorance, and the excesses of parochial religion. The warts do show up on the wide screen, giving viewers a different side of the region. *Mississippi Burning*, *Paris Trout*, and *The Prince of Tides* reflect the erotic violence that Cash claimed was an unfortunate part of the Southern landscape. But in popular culture the South is often a place of either/or, of *Steel Magnolias* or *Deliverance*. Normal is located in another place.

Historians, like Larry Griffin (1995), have pointed to the persistent use of the South as an oppositional culture by which we gauge our national character. Northern codification of particular myths, like those associated with crackers, demagogues, white supremacists, or the insane, provide constructs of what the nation is not. The South developed countermyths of the War of Northern Aggression, honor codes, and damsels in distress to shape their self-image in contrast to the crass, greedy, materialistic Northern industrialist. Each region needed and needs the other to complete its portrait.

Another way of looking at the region is that the nation as a whole is moving south, is becoming "southernized" (Carter 1999). According to Malcolm X, admittedly in a different context, "Mississippi is anywhere south of the Canadian border" (1965, 417). Culture follows money and money is migrating from Rust Belt to Sunbelt (Harvey 1995). The South has become what James Cobb (1990) describes as "a conservative capitalist's dream come true" (39). Not only are jobs relocating to the part of the country with the lowest union memberships and the cheapest labor costs but they are entering friendly political territory too.

The formation of black majority congressional districts has diminished Democratic voting strength throughout the South and diluted affirmative action programs. According to Applebome (1997), "what the South has really done is redefine the political center of gravity from center-left to center-right" (348). Values once associated with Dixie are now national values. Once solidly segregationist Democrat, the electorate, following Nixon's southern strategy, is now divided into white Republicans and black Democrats, into conservatives and misbegotten liberals. The Republican Party, the current political home of white males, the party of Strom Thurmond, Jesse Helms, Trent Lott, Tom Delay, George Bush, and Newt Gingrich, is now the South's dominant political organization. From that party organization come the men who head the federal government too. In 2004 Republicans control both houses of Congress and the White House. Majority leaders in the House of Representatives and the Senate are from the South (Texas and Tennessee respectively). The president is a Texan and he follows a two-term native of Arkansas. Southern politics are now national politics.

David Potter (1972) calls the South a "sphinx on the American land." He had earlier written about it as an "enigma" (1961). Southerners "could not bear either to abandon the patterns of the Old South or to forego the material gains of modern America" (Potter 1964, 460). Applebome points out that the South has managed to hang on to a distinctive identity while simultaneously "putting its fingerprints on almost every aspect of the nation's soul, from race, to politics, to culture, to values" (22).

Gender and the South

Antebellum Southern ladies developed what Joan Cashin (1996) called a sisterly "culture of resignation" that distinguished them from Northern women. Deciding that gender inequities were a permanent part of their world, they retreated to a female-dominated private sphere in which they shared their frustrations about the limited opportunities afforded members of their sex. They conformed to the conventions expected of white women in their society, eschewing challenges to the status quo and seeking solace in the company of like-minded and similarly constrained companions. They did not march, sign many petitions, or agitate in unseemly fashion.

Their struggle intensified on the geographic frontiers of early nineteenth-century Southern society, where gender conventions lost the ameliorating effects of classical paternalism. Second sons sought their fortunes in non-seaboard states. Freed of dependence on their fathers, they embraced what Cashin labeled a "new masculinity" that enhanced the dependency of their women. Once in the new southwest (today's Deep South), they defined "manly independence" as a "daredevil masculinity" that emphasized "prodigious drinking, gambling, [and] skill with a gun." Their obligations to wife and children "became more tenuous" (102). Ritualized and random violence proliferated. "Women reacted with fear, bewilderment, and anger to these changes." Now far removed from extended families and friends, set psychologically adrift in a hostile environment that demanded of them more labor and less stability, they "became more dependent on men" (108).

Dependency did not mean that Southern women became shrinking violets. Behind whatever façade of genteel fragility they could maintain was a lifetime of work. Even Southern ladies, mistresses of large manors, worked.[5] "Gentlewomen played an essential part in elite social life" and did not necessarily go quietly into the parlor (Kilbride 2000, 583). For them, the growing division of private and public spheres so aptly described by Douglas (1977) signaled a decline in their status that they were reluctant to accept.

Following the Civil War, gender roles, North and South, diverged partially because of the persistence of rural communities and poverty in the latter region and partially because of the South's elevation of white female moral purity as a rationale for the political suppression of former slaves. Southern men may have failed in their 1860s push for independence, but they would not fail in their defense of idealized womanhood thereafter. As a consequence, social codes for women proliferated. Good women, women of breeding, moral women were expected to dress and act a certain way. For women of privilege, feminine refinement and the mastery of ornamental arts were important. They were raised to be courteous flatterers of their male protectors. They were Melanies, not Scarletts, in an era of "chivalric sexual oppression" that continued into the twentieth century (Blackwelder 1991, 100). Whereas Northern women of a certain economic status went to college, Southern women were educated for romance and marriage.

Education for romance has never gone out of fashion in the South. Holland and Eisenhart (1990), in a multiyear study of women in two Southern colleges conducted during the 1980s, found that within two years high-aspiration women shifted their energies from academia to peer groups and romance.[6] They were, as the title of their book so aptly puts it, *Educated in Romance*. "Campus peer society and culture was the major purveyor of male privilege." It "emerges as one of the major sites of reproduction of the patriarchal gender hierarchy" (220). Admittedly, women at the millennium were less likely to fall into marriage-trap thinking. But for the women in our study, the pressures that sent some previously high-achieving women into academic tailspins were the ones that they encountered when they began their college educations.

Being demure was important. Appearance counted. Beauty pageants are to some Southern women what hunting or football are to their men. Double-name Southern women have as much a penchant for winning Miss America titles as their men have of playing professional football. Both neighbors and family members enforced rules of public decorum. Trudier Harris (1996) remembers being sprawled on her front porch, legs wide apart, only to be told by a local woman to "sit according to your family." In other words, sit like the lady your family raised you to be. Where, but in the South, is wearing white after Labor Day considered a social faux pas of sufficient magnitude to warrant luncheon conversation?

Many girls learned their Southern belle lessons vicariously, through the print or film versions of *Gone with the Wind* (Mitchell 1936). All Southern belles were expected to grow up to be ladies and for Margaret Mitchell, that meant becoming Ellen Robillard O'Hara. She well knew the obligations of a mistress-in-training. "Before marriage, young girls must be, above all other things, sweet, gentle, beautiful and ornamental, but after marriage, they were expected to manage households" (60). Her

> life was not easy, nor was it happy, but she did not expect life to be easy, and, if it was not happy, that was a woman's lot. It was a man's world, and she accepted it as such. The man owned the property, and the woman managed it. The man took the credit for the management, and the woman praised his cleverness. The man roared like a bull when a splinter was in his finger, and the woman muffled the moans of childbirth, lest she disturb him. Men were rough of speech and often drunk. Women ignored the lapses of speech and put the drunkards to bed without bitter words. Men were rude and outspoken, women were always kind, gracious and forgiving. (61)

Ladies knew a thing or two about toting barges, but they did it with grace. They had "a steely quality" hidden among their various other charms (43).

Because "the first duty of a girl was to get married," Southern women mastered the art of dissembling, of meeting expectations (61). One must, for example, "appear demure, pliable and scatterbrained," rather than intelligent (63). It was the role of Southern ladies to "make those about them feel at ease and pleased with themselves," a "conspiracy" they enacted so well that it was what "made Southern society . . . pleasant" (156).

One reason for the popularity of *Gone with the Wind* was that it resonated with the plantation ideal that already existed in the American consciousness outside Dixie and in the wish-it-could-be fantasies of Southerners. Frank Owsley (1936) recounted a World War I train trip that he made with some young women from the Midwest to Alabama. Their expectations of the exotic land to which they were bound included white columns and happy workers tending cotton fields. Red clay, sharecropper shanties, and deserted mansions were not quite what they had in mind, although that is what they found. The ideal that emerged in the antebellum period continued through Mitchell's novel and into the formative years of the women in our study. Southern women were expected to be "beautiful, graceful, accomplished in social charm, bewitching in coquetry, yet strangely steadfast in soul" (Gaines, quoted in Tindall 1964, 4).

Southern women, according to Blackwelder (1991), come in only two basic models: flirtatious belle or competent and caring saint. "Both presuppose a rigidly patriarchal society and sufficient material well-being to permit 'refined' behavior" (96). With luck, belles became ladies when they married. In the real South, for the whole of the nineteenth and much of the twentieth century, few women enjoyed the luxuries of Tara. Most females labored as part of the working poor or were, by virtue of race, confined to a life of servitude, first as slaves and then as victims of social segregation.

Class exacerbated the effects of sexism. A spate of recent memoirs confirms that being female and being poor meant there were two barriers to hurtle (Allison 1992; Flowers 1992; Karr 1995, 2000; Ray 1999). Add race and a person is living in a sea of discrimination (Bolton 1994; Greene 1992). Linda Flowers (1992) describes growing up the daughter of a sharecropper in eastern Carolina. Her story is one of poor children whose teachers felt they could not learn, whose new jobs (after they left the land) disappeared when companies closed, and whose dreams shriveled, as Langston Hughes (1995) foretold, like raisins in the sun. "Fairness," Flowers writes, "is something only little children any longer much expect" (210). If one is poor, getting by is less about ideological positions with regard to gender or race and more about the next meal, the rent next month, the broken transmission on the decade-old car.

Class barriers persist; the dreams of poor people remain deferred or require extraordinary skills and persistence. In the mountains, though, most people got by rather than prospered—a condition that continued until the 1960s. Our sample comes from families that were at least working middle class. None of them came from wealthy homes; a few of them were from families that struggled periodically. For them, being from humble economic circumstances was not a deterrent to knocking eventually on the door of economic and social advancement.

"Paternalism was an integral feature of life in the New South, pervading relations between classes, races, and sexes, as well as employers and employees" (Newby 1989, 262). Social conventions glorified faithful homebodies. Church conventions reinforced traditional gender roles, affirming that a woman's first responsibility was to her domestic vocation.

Poor women, plain folk, and women who found themselves on the borders of Southern society, adrift from kin and dependent upon their men, were well aware of the challenges inherent in rural life. Harry Crews recalled that the stories told by his relatives, male and female, "were full of violence, sickness, and death." But there was one telling difference. "It was the women whose stories were unrelieved by humor and filled with apocalyptic vision. . . . The stories were as stark and cold as legend or myth" (1995, 100–1).

The Institute for Women's Policy Research conducts regular comprehensive reviews of how women are faring politically, economically, and socially. In a 2002 report, it found that Southern women were least likely to participate in politics, a composite finding based on voter registration, voter turnout, representation in elected office, and institutional resources. Southern women fared somewhat better economically. Nevertheless, overall earnings were the lowest for Southeastern women. In a review of women's health insurance, education, business ownership, and poverty rates (the variables included in the social and economic autonomy composite index), the South placed eleven states in the bottom third of the rating scale. The reproductive rights composite is an index of nine factors. Eight Southern states are in the bottom third, three in the middle third, and only North Carolina ranks in the top third, and that barely at number seventeen. The pattern continues on the health and well-being index. Ten of them are in the bottom third and only three are in the middle third. Of the nine "worst states" in terms of overall status of women, six are in the South.

In spite of the South's backwardness in meeting the needs of women, Blackwelder (1991) sees the idealized images of the belle and the Southern lady as "merged into a single symbol" and fast fading in importance. Getting ahead is now a Southern pastime too. Prosperity has led to new opportunities; opportunities create options. What constitutes being a Southern woman has changed, even though "girls growing up in Southern families today still inherit and learn traditional gender roles that are rooted in an older society in which both women and blacks held secondary status" (105). Social traditions encouraged ambitious women to exercise restraint in their pursuit of a more fulfilling life.

In *Daughters of Canaan* (1995), Margaret Wolfe claims that the radical feminists found few allies in the states below the Mason-Dixon line. Southern women "never renounced their femininity" (204). No friend of lesbians, no enemy of make-up and fashionable clothes, and no believer in patriarchal conspiracy theories, Southern feminists, according to Wolfe, embraced the implications of biological and psychological difference and the special considerations that women required as a result of such difference. Most females "adjusted themselves to the prescribed feminine roles of service and sacrifice" (205). Another reason for the softer public face of the women's rights movement below the Mason-Dixon Line was the presence and continuing influence of angry white Southern men exemplified by the popularity of regional writers like Lewis Grizzard. To him, all feminists were "hairy-legged Yankee women," ultimate outsiders (quoted in Applebome 1997, 331). The patriarchy that Mitchell described with broad and often exaggerated strokes has weakened in the South, but it is still central to mapping the vagaries of gender. Men control the power structure and women still access it at their pleasure.

Conversely, Jane DeHart (1997) contends that feminism did exist in the South, but it showed its face later there than elsewhere. Most Southern women associated with second-wave feminism are middle class, educated, less parochial than their neighbors, more inclined toward liberal politics, and less likely to be affiliated with fundamental or evangelical religious groups. They are employed in professional fields, have parents who were themselves educated, and engaged in civic discourse. Affiliated with like-minded professional or issue-oriented organizations, they reached adulthood in the 1960s. Because they lived in communities in which there were African American and poor white working women, their political activism was played out against a backdrop of overt prejudices other than sexism. Southern women were less likely to focus exclusively (even primarily) on gender discrimination. Biases based on race and/or poverty appeared more profound and lasting and it was toward their amelioration that these activists turned their initial attention. Gender consciousness, according to DeHart, took a somewhat different road in Dixie.

According to a 1992 poll, both Southern and non-Southern men and women thought Southern women were "friendlier, less career oriented, less feminist, more strong-willed, less self-centered, less independent, and less assertive than American women in general" (Reed 1994, 125). Although Southern men were more likely to see Southern women as independent and strong-willed, they were less likely than non-Southerners to see them as career-minded and feminist. Within that contradiction was a space through which independent women could claim the right to challenge a glass ceiling.

Ann Jones (1996) points to the cultural coerciveness of gender constructions found in the South, reinforced by a more general American belief that power is masculine. In reviewing the work of Southern Renaissance writers, she argues that, although women found the image of the "New Woman" a model for liberation, men saw her as considerably less attractive. The early and mid-twentieth-century Southern canon read by most of the people in our sample was masculine in orientation, describing the problems and challenges of the South from a white male perspective. The women of William Faulkner and Tennessee Williams, for example, disappear into tragic corners, are dominated and dependent, or conspire, sometimes unknowingly, in the downfall of their men. They were more like Shakespeare's Ophelia than either his Kate or Portia.[7] Silenced entirely were the voices of serious women writers and African Americans.

Carolyn Heilbrun (1988) once noted that "it is a hard thing to make up stories to live by. We can only retell and live by the stories we have read or heard. We live our lives through texts" (37). For Southern women of a certain age, the generation we studied, the stories they heard and read did not give them many realistic examples of strong women. Yet they came of age as regional popular fiction added to its collection portraits that had been missing. First the generation of Eudora Welty and then that of Lee Smith crafted stories of aspiring women. They wrote not of the imaginary ladies of Margaret Mitchell's South, but of gritty commoners pushing cultural walls to claim their own places at the table. That change was a harbinger of larger cultural shifts.

A Note on Race, Gender, and the South

Julia Blackwelder (1991), in her study of the New South, observes that, "In the South, race and gender twisted together like vines of wisteria, ensuring that the rights of Southern blacks could not be advanced entirely in isolation from the rights of women" (95). Southern women—black and white—shared stories of subjugation.[8] For that reason and because, except by its absence, race does not play a significant part in our study, it receives less attention here than gender. The dynamics of suppression and resistance take different forms. Despite those differences, when one marginalized group finds ways to reduce its outsider status, the members are preparing, deliberately or unintentionally, the ground for other groups to follow them. For example, when the barrier of geographic outsiderness falls, it makes possible overcoming the barrier of gender. That action, in turn, makes conceivable challenging exclusion on the basis of race.

From the colonial period onward, Southerners structured, initially unconsciously and then with a willful deliberateness, a white man's country (Jordan 1973). The South's "peculiar institution," defended by ideologues and scripture, laid the foundation for centuries of segregation and inequities based on race. Slavery was an oppressive institution that demeaned both master and slave, creating the conditions that led to the South's economic plummet after the Civil War. By the twentieth century, Jim Crow laws made separation legitimate, perpetuating the racist idea that former slaves and their children were morally and intellectually inferior. Legal subordination and political exclusion ensured the maintenance of white economic and social privilege.[9]

Challenges by African Americans were met with intimidation and violence. For example, when Republicans and Populists in North Carolina gained control of the state government in 1894, they tried to ameliorate conditions for the working poor, both white and black. In response, the Democratic Party, purged of race sympathizers, swept into office on a platform of racial purity and low taxation. By 1897, when Democrats began their return to political supremacy, they did so with a vengeance. In response to an editorial in the *Wilmington Record*, a mob of the city's "best" citizens (businessmen and professionals alike) initiated a rampage in 1898 that resulted in the death and injury of black citizens, the destruction of their property, including business establishments, and the forced departure of Republican sympathizers. The state's main newspaper, the *Raleigh News and Observer*, ran as its headline "Negro Rule Is at an End in North Carolina" (Applebome 1997, 221–22). Returned to power, Democrats worked to disenfranchise blacks. Segregation remained the law for over half a century.

Black second-class status was as clear as crystal glass in the South. Pauli Murray recalled growing up in piedmont North Carolina.

> Our seedy, run-down school told us that if we had any place at all in the scheme of things it was a separate place. . . . We were bottled up and labeled and set aside. . . . We came to understand that no matter how neat and clean, how law abiding, submissive and polite, how studious in school, how churchgoing and moral, how scrupulous in paying our bills and taxes we were, it made no . . . difference in our place. (Quoted in Crow, Escott, and Hatley 1992, 118)

"There were only two kinds of people in the world—*They* and *We*." There were only insiders and outsiders, the privileged and the dispossessed.

Black feminists found themselves in a quandary as the Civil Rights Movement advanced. Long active in antilynching initiatives and early suffrage efforts in the South, they played important roles in desegregation efforts. A 1982 Harris poll noted that African American women were the ERA's greatest supporters in North Carolina. In the midst of struggle for gender equality, black women were also engaged in an effort to end the differences that race generated. At precisely that time, the Moynihan Report (1965) on the African American family blamed the socioeconomic difficulties of black Americans partially on a disproportionate number of female-headed households. Accused of trying to emasculate their men, these women were confronted by conflicting expectations. To struggle for gender equity appeared to reinforce negative consequences of racial separation. They could be feminists or they could be black activist; to be both was problematic. Racial solidarity meant underplaying gender claims. Minority women could be followers or uppity leaders; most of the time they opted to be the latter.

How did African Americans cope with a rigid system of exclusion, defended with arms and the threat of violence? According to Cowie, a character in Mark Steadman's *Angel Child* (1987), "Colored folks can't treat white people straight out. We haven't had time enough for that yet" (211). They dissembled, adopting behaviors that preserved for them physical, emotional, and social space, in the company of whites. They built vibrant African American communities in piedmont and coastal towns. They left the state in the "Great Migration." They subsisted, living hard on tenant farms. In some mountain counties, they disappeared. Ethel Mills, an African American principal of a Transylvania County school, was probably correct in her assessment of typical mountaineer knowledge of their African American neighbors. "Some white people don't think we know A from bull feet. They think Blacks are dumb enough to try to throw an elephant, but it's pure, unadulterated ignorance. . . . They've had no experience with Negroes" (quoted in B. Reed 2000, 91).

Southern Ceilings Reprised

In 2003 the Deep South Regional Humanities Center, located at Tulane University, sponsored an essay contest for high school students in Alabama, Arkansas, Louisiana, Mississippi, and Tennessee on the topic of Southern identity.[10] It received approximately 450 entries and recognized seventeen winners. Those essays were reproduced on the center's Internet site and provide a contemporary glimpse at how native and nonnative Southern young people view themselves and their region.

They tell us:

1. church and family are key institutions (many students mentioned extended families and place-situated knowledge of people);
2. home-cooked food is a distinctive and important signifier of what is good about the South (greens, fried chicken, mashed potatoes, catfish, po'boys, watermelon, biscuits, grits, peanuts, iced sweet tea, and lemonade);
3. Sunday gatherings, particularly after church and around a meal, are a common ritual;
4. the ability to sit and visit is a crucial social skill (the pace of life is slower; people are hospitable, polite, and friendly; talk is important);
5. communities come together regularly (football games, church picnics, county fairs, Resurrection Days, parades);
6. gender divisions persist (mom is at home and dad outside, women lunch together and men hunt, "I am a twentieth-century Southern belle and I love it.");
7. the past is not forgotten ("love our traditions and our heritage"), most references fell into what Gretlund (1999) described as "devotional, certifying, and celebratory," but several students expressed regret about the South's history); and
8. the majority of pop culture icons are male (rednecks, cowboys, and planters).

One author concluded that "the land is steeped in stories, good and bad. You can't have the one without the other."

Ayers (1996) described a survey of 300 undergraduates at the University of Virginia that included respondents from over thirty-three countries and from diverse ethnicities. Of those who considered themselves Southern (less than half), there was an evident pride in claiming regional identity. That pride was most evident in responses from women and from African Americans. Asked to rate twenty-eight traits in terms of "Southernness," they reached relative consensus on several of the same attributes that appeared in the high school essays. Speech, courtesy, hospitality, a sense of history, and the natural beauty of place set the South apart. In 1971 Jonathan Yardley wrote that Southerners had a "love for and closeness to the land; a strong and intimate sense of family; an awareness of the past and its hard lessons; genuine hospitality, civility, and courtliness; perhaps most of all, a sense of community" (quoted in Applebome 1997, 351). Whether the New South can retain those qualities is another matter.

Appalachia

Defining Appalachia raises more difficulties than does defining the South. As John Williams (2002) observes, "one problem with attempting to view the region is that Appalachia has no agreed-upon boundaries—nothing comparable to the Mason-Dixon Line." A Minnesota newspaper in 1861 labeled the area Alleghenia and included counties in Virginia, Kentucky, Tennessee, Alabama, Georgia, and the two Carolinas, areas "of Corn and Cattle, not Cotton" (9). In 1895 William Frost, president of Berea College, said it encompassed 194 counties, 33 more than the Minnesota editors listed (Williams 2002, 11–12). Horace Kephart (1913) focused his attention on the people living along the North Carolina and Tennessee state lines, in the Smoky and Unaka Mountains; they were his highlanders. James Still, a poet, calls Appalachia a "mythical region," but its heart is "the hills of Eastern Kentucky" (Drake 2001, vii). Henry Shapiro (1978) claims it is a construct invented by Northern travelers.

Geographic Appalachia is vast indeed. Extending from southern New York to the northeast corner of Mississippi, it passes through fourteen states and encompasses five regions—the Piedmont, Blue Ridge, Great Valley, Allegheny (Cumberland) Mountains, and the Appalachian Plateau. It takes in a great spine of uplands from the coastal plains on the east to the beginning of the heartland plains in the west.[11] But is the geographic Appalachia the same as cultural Appalachia? Is economic Appalachia only those counties that had extraction industries or is it the region defined by the Appalachian Regional Commission? Williams offers a postmodern definition in *Appalachia: A History*, noting that natural (geographic) and artificial (political) boundaries are arbitrary definitions (2002, 12).

Below, we consider only the mountain counties in Virginia, Tennessee, North Carolina, and Georgia and with particular attention to comments by and/or about the counties we studied. Because many of the characteristics of Southern culture are common in the region's uplands or mountains, our overview is shorter than the one we provided for the South. It emphasizes those cultural patterns that appear to be important in shaping the cultural consciousness of our informants and the people for whom they work.

Distinctive Appalachia

Casual and formal students of Appalachia have been penning descriptions of the region and its inhabitants for over a century. Appalachians are, according to Powell (1966), "a simple people" (7). "They made themselves independent of the outside world, not by choice, but by force of circumstances" (25). Mountain people are resourceful, also by necessity. Like Southerners in general, they embrace opportunities to defend their country, are fond of sports, and treasure their families. In 1873, *Lippincott's Magazine* published a piece by Will Wallace Harney entitled "A Strange Land and Peculiar People," setting the tone for later authors. Horace Kephart (1913), perhaps the most influential of the early twentieth-century commentators, called the place "the back of beyond" (28). *Our Southern Highlanders* describes the land and people in and around what would become the Smoky Mountain National Park. "Time has lingered in Appalachia. The mountain folk still live in the eighteenth century" (18). "Our highlanders are a sly, suspicious, and secretive folk" (279). "As a class, they have great restless energy" (290). Despite unhealthy conditions, "the hill folk remain a rugged and hardy people" (304).

Writing from Polk County, Margaret Morley (1913) preceded Kephart to the mountains. There is no hurry in the uplands. According to Morley, "the ancient and honorable art of 'setting around' has been cultivated until it has grown into an integral part of life" (10). People are close to the soil and share an intimacy with the land. They are "simple and kindly," have "quaint speech," and live a "primitive life" (108). "The principal recreation . . . is visiting" (167). Cecil Sharp came through the region in 1915, collecting songs. He found families that "have for a hundred years or more been completely isolated and cut off from all traffic with the rest of the world." "They are leisurely, cheery people in their quiet way." "They are strong and of good stature, though usually spare in figure" (quoted in Sheppard 1915, 138–39). John Campbell, in *The Southern Highlander and His Homeland* (1921), saw them as "tall, lean, clear-eyed, self-reliant, never taken by surprise, and of great endurance" (72). The mountaineer was "an extreme individualist" (91). Campbell speculated that the danger of "romantic appeal . . . in some of the darker aspects of mountain life," led several writers to characterize erroneously the region's inhabitants as "feudists and moonshiners" (149).

Muriel Sheppard's (1935) *Cabins in the Laurel* was one of the most popular of the early books on Carolina's highlanders. It was accompanied by over one hundred photographs of the region and its people by Bayard Wootten. Set along the Toe River, which includes portions of Yancey and Mitchell Counties, the book mixed folklore, legends, and observations together. Her mountaineers were hospitable and lacked self-consciousness. "Hill people enjoy an audience" (140). They are industrious when the need to be so presents itself and intensely loyal.

Olive Dargan, a socialist and a feminist, lived for two decades in Swain County. *From My Highest Hills* (1998), originally published as *Highland Annals* in 1925, is a fictionalized account of her experiences. Like Sheppard's book, it too includes a collection of Wooten photographs. As a consequence, often to outsiders the face of Appalachia was literally the face of a North Carolinian. The narrator of her stories sets up housekeeping in the mountains and chronicles the changing lives of her neighbors. Chided by a friend for writing about mountaineers who "will not have even a fossilized survival" and are unworthy of her pen, she sets out to demonstrate that life "in a *cul de sac*, a pocket of society" deserves a chronicler (59, italics in the original). Dargan, attuned to the coming economic exploitation of the region, juxtaposes the consequences of salaried work and living off the land. Mountain people who do public work "won't take the time to look up at you passin'" (170). They have lost their sense of humor and zest for community in pursuit of a dollar. Change was moving up the hills as relentlessly as trees green up in springtime. Clocks tick forward, but not back. "These fine old mountaineers are passing . . . passing," among the last words in the book, read like a benediction on a way of life (221).

Mountain clergy were "hostile to 'book larnin'" (Kephart 1913, 345). Religion was evangelical. Pentecostal and personal, it emphasized the wages of sin and possibility of redemption, more of the former than the latter. Churches promoted virtues like modesty and humility, independence, love of and responsibility for family, and social hierarchy (L. Jones 1999). Small, they held congregations and generations close. The threat of being put out of church, of community ostracism, was real and powerful. Even in the 1950s and 1960s, some churches exercised discipline on their congregation, enforcing gender roles and local codes of conduct (Morgan 2002). Although the Appalachian religion is unique (McCauley 1995), its culture, like religion in the greater South, stresses the centrality of saving grace and Christian fundamentalism.[12] It validates, rather than disturbs, traditional definitions of gender difference and appropriate authority.

Life in the uplands was, until recently, physically challenging, contributing to a pioneering spirit that persists even though technology has altered the conditions that once necessitated it. Malone (1993) compares mountaineers to cowboys, stressing their "freedom and independence," and "their fearlessness" (73–74). Highlanders have an "appetite for land." They readily "stand up calmly under fire" (Powell 1966, 23, 27). They believe in the central roles of family, kinship, and continuity. Blevins (1995), an African American and an Appalachian, recalls that her "people were arrogant, individualistic, isolation-prone, violent, scare-with-words folks" who were disinclined to share their space with people who did not "live around here" (533).

By the time our informants were beginning their professional careers, life had changed in the backcountry. In Asheville, around large tourist destinations, and in some of the towns, it had changed even earlier. Appalachian observers concentrated their gaze on small communities, perpetuating the fading image of a strange land and a peculiar people. Whereas places that modernized looked like the South as a whole, remote valleys were depicted as still being in the early stages of transition in the 1950s and 1960s.

The Carolina mountain communities that Hicks (1976) and Beaver (1986) studied were similar to or the ones with which our sample of educational leaders were familiar.[13] Among their findings were:

1. The core of community is the preservation of family and kinship ties. There is a belief in the importance of generational continuity and a nostalgia for the land, particularly property associated with the original settlement of a family in a particular area.
2. A suspicion of outsiders, particularly newcomers who purchase property but lack the community values associated with it, continues. "These Floridy people come in here and buy a little patch of land and stick no trespassing signs all over it" (quoted in Hicks 1976, 53). Outsiders do not share the same ethic of neighborliness, built upon a tradition of mutual aid and social norms that bound settlements together.
3. Outsiders "stood off" from their neighbors, which transgressed another mountain value: egalitarianism. Mountain people were "just plain folks." Customs that ensured that residents did not step over the egalitarian line include gossip, exclusion, and condemnation as "uppity." Upland egalitarianism preserves a modicum of conformity and serves as a leveler, restraining aspirations of people who "rise up" in unseemly fashion.
4. Joined with an abiding belief in equality is adherence to an ethic of self-reliance and independence. Although a degree of neighborly dependency was necessary to persevere in the mountains, a Highlander dislike for external imposition ran deep.
5. As much as independent and egalitarian, worthiness describes a good person (Beaver 1986, 140–41, 154–60). To be worth something means to be responsible for one's actions and to exercise common sense. To be "worthless" is to join the dregs of society.
6. Highlanders resent negative images of themselves and their land. Southern Appalachians resent being demeaned and insulted. They dislike being underestimated, although they sometimes use that to their advantage. "You can't treat mountaineers like that. They'll quit. They just won't take it"

(quoted in Hicks 1976, 32). "It gets old after so long a time, to be pictured as a 'hillbilly' who goes around barefoot, shooting at revenuers and stealing chickens" (quoted in Hicks 1976, 29).

7. An ethic of neutrality (Hicks 1976, 90–91) describes much of mountaineer behavior. Uplands residents believe in minding their business and avoiding controversy or arguments. They do not value calling attention to one's self or people who make demands by assuming authority over them.
8. Concern about the consequences of change is palpable. World War II "just about ruined this whole country. It wasn't just a lot of us going out and learning things we never would have got up here, but nothing seems right any more. It just ain't as good a place as it used to be" (quoted in Hicks 1976, 15).

Hicks, when he returned to the site of his fieldwork twenty years after his original visit, found the attitudes and values of local residents the same, albeit faded. "The firm cement of place and history is rapidly loosening" (60).

Gender and Appalachia

Descriptions of mountain life before the roads came through emphasize the deleterious effects that work had on the region's women.

> Many of the women are pretty in youth; but hard toil in house and field, early marriage, frequent child-bearing with shockingly poor attention, and ignorance or defiance of the plainest necessities of hygiene, soon warp and age them. At thirty or thirty-five a mountain woman is apt to have a worn and faded look. (Kephart 1913, 288–89)

Morley (1913) concurs. "The pretty girls too often become old women at the age of thirty" (164). Routinely dismissed as drudges, women did not sit at the dinner table but stood and waited on their men.

> There is no conscious discourtesy in such customs; but they betoken an indifference to woman's weakness, a disregard for her finer nature, a denial of her proper rank, that are real and deep-seated in the mountaineer. To him she is little more than a sort of superior domestic animal. The chivalric regard for women . . . is altogether lacking in the habits of the backwoodsman of Appalachia. (Kephart 1913, 331–32)

Why did women put up with that treatment? Kephart claimed that women rarely complained about their lot. "She knows no other. . . . Indeed she would scarce respect her husband if he did not lord it over her and cast upon her the menial tasks. It is 'manners' for a woman to drudge and obey. All respectable wives do that" (332).

Gender roles remain distinct, although lines have blurred more during the last two decades. Hicks (1976) found that there were long-standing and deeply held, sex-segregated expectations for public behavior. Men took leading roles and women supported them. Behavioral constraints for males were more flexible than those for females, who remained on a shorter social leash. Even in the 1970s some mountaineers believed that women did not need too much formal education because they were expected to marry, raise a family, and take care of a home. Men could drink and curse; good women did neither.

"Sex role differentiation begins at birth" (Beaver 1986). That is true for all of us, but what differs is degree and type. For Beaver's Appalachian women, outside work is the province of men, who also exercise primary authority within the family. Boys are freer than girls, whose restricted independence is coupled with the expectation that they shoulder a portion of the household labor. "The husband is the public spokesman for the family among other men. . . . The wife rarely interrupts or contradicts her husband in public" (97). Patriarchy was (is) entrenched and rarely challenged.[14]

Despite economic exploitation of women in the public labor market, working-class consciousness is only "slowly emerging, particularly among women. A strong sense of rootedness in place, identification with and reliance on extended-family ties, as well as a sense of history in the community combine with a sense of purpose and role in the family and community" (114). Beaver notes that the introduction of public work began to alter the roles women played in families and community. Their initial introduction into the rural labor market was usually employment in low-wage, low-autonomy, and low-status jobs. They were "second-class citizens in the wider industrial world" (113). But they also encountered different women in public work, women with different levels of education, expectations, and experiences. Once introduced into the world outside the home, they could not be kept from surveying the entire range of options available.

Appalachian communities socialized most of our study participants. Their cultural curriculum prescribed behavior patterns that benefited men seeking leadership positions and disadvantaged women. Females were challenged in three ways: (a) the culture as a whole expected them to follow rather than lead, (b) men were socialized not to follow them, and (c) they were socialized not to lead. Yet there coexisted with those norms contradictory standards that provided a wedge in nearly closed doors, a wedge of sufficient room to gain entry, particularly if their behavior did not pose direct challenges to men. Beaver writes about the "strong sense of personal identity" that mountain women possessed and the general "recognition of the importance of women's contribution to home, family, and community" (1986, 114). Reed (1994) notes that Southern women are perceived as "more strong-willed" (125), an attribute that Beaver claims grows with age in the mountains. Appalachian women come into more familial and community power as they age, whereas the reverse is true for men (1986, 102–4).

Moreover, there exists a history of women leading missionary, settlement, and folk schools in Appalachia, even in the most remote communities. There exists a tradition of outsider and female educational leadership in Southern Appalachia (Arthur 1914; Morgan and LeGette 1958; Painter 1996; Searles 1995; Sloop 1953; Stoddart 1997; Van Noppen and Van Noppen 1973). Recent historians have tended to view their participation in the region as complicit with the economic and cultural exploitation of the native population (Eller 1981; Whisnant 1983). Deborah Blackwell (1998), in an exploration of the role of gender in reform efforts in Appalachia between 1890 and 1935, disagrees. Looking at the reform biographies of five women, four of whom were formally associated with educational work (the fifth founded the Frontier Nursing Service and construed a significant part of her job as educational), she argues that their performance transcended simple narratives about either outsider exploiter or secular sainthood. It was "a complex amalgam of social-control and benevolent impulses saturated with contradictions, negotiations, and accommodations" (198). It was also a model of female school leadership that made the idea conceivable.

In Madison County, the Dorland-Bell Institute was overseen by Julia Phillips (1895–1914), Lucy Shafer (1914–1923), and Ruth Taylor (1927–1942). In Mitchell County, Lucy Morgan helped first with her brother's Episcopal mountain school, then converted it to an adult-education facility specializing in local handicrafts. Penland, now an internationally known arts and crafts school, continues to operate today. Farm extension agents, such as Velma Moore in Clay County, began educational services in the region in the 1920s (Smith 1997). Mary Martin Sloop, a physician, founded a mountain school and, with her husband, a hospital in Mitchell County. John Campbell's wife stayed in the region after his death, establishing a folk school named in his honor on the border of Clay and Cherokee Counties. It, too, continues to operate. Florence Stephenson was head of the Asheville Home Industrial School, one of three schools whose merger eventually resulted in Warren Wilson College.

Additionally, the first female county superintendent in the state, Ethel Terrell, secured that position in 1919 in Buncombe County. Many of the region's early teacher supervisors were women, as were (are) curriculum and instruction directors and assistant/associate superintendents. There were female high school principals in remote counties before their ostensibly more enlightened piedmont counterparts moved in that direction. Given that in many mountain counties there are few secondary schools, the appointment of a woman was a significant achievement.

Small but important historical and cultural spaces, combined with years of practice at successful dissembling, provide the platform from which the females in our study extended their reach and succeeded in securing and exercising power. They have done so in proportions that exceed the their downstate sisters and in a part of North Carolina that retains a reputation for being parochial and conservative.

Southern Appalachia Reprised

In 2003 a regional magazine, *Blue Ridge*, conducted a readers' poll of favorites. They dutifully responded with their choices of "Best Fishing Lake," "Best Biking Trail," "Best Stretch of the Appalachian Trail," and the like (Best of the Blue Ridge Region). Among the superlatives was a category entitled "Person of the Region You'd Most Like to Meet." Tied for first place were Billy Graham and Dolly Parton, whose connections with the region conveniently bookend the counties we studied. Graham lives in Black Mountain, a small town to the east of Asheville in Buncombe County. Parton grew up in Sevier County, Tennessee, whose border extends through the Smoky Mountain National Park to the North Carolina line in Swain County.

Could there be a more disparate couple selected? Yes and no. Graham is an internationally known evangelist. Parton is probably equally well known as a country singer. Both write. Graham composes sermons and Parton songs. Both are God-fearing. It is Graham's business. Parton has included gospel music on her albums, acknowledges its influence, and started singing in a small, local church. Graham's children are in the religion business. Some of Parton's siblings sing for their living. Graham established a Baptist retreat and training center in Buncombe County. Parton set up Dollywood as the first of several entertainment centers in Sevier County. They take care of their family and neighbors. Billy Graham does good works, counseling presidents and other leaders in need of his ministry. Parton has established scholarship and literacy programs in her home county. Both maintain deep ties to the place and acknowledge its influence on keeping themselves centered.

Whereas Graham has a reputation for conservatism, Parton is flamboyant. Graham's demeanor and dress are somber; Parton's appearance is almost a caricature and her dress purposefully reveals as much as it conceals. Graham is convinced that there are limits on individual conduct and he is not reluctant to share them. Parton lives and is content to let others live, too. She comes close to being a social libertarian. He is the stern, authoritarian father. She is Daisy Mae with a generous bank account and feet made for dancing.

Tied for second place are Doc Watson, a blind bluegrass musician from the Carolina foothills, and Hugh Morton, the owner of Grandfather Mountain in Carolina's northern mountains. Watson represents the joy of picking and singing, the tragedy of losing a playing partner/son, the stoicism of moving on and overcoming, and cultural continuity with the region's storytelling past. Morton operates a nature conservatory, helped reinvigorate the region's Highland Games, and has recently published a collection of photographs.

Taken together, the four of them represent the yin and yang of the Southern Appalachians, of its layers and complexities and of its common bond to a special place. Self-reliant, independent, generous, respectful of the land, its people, and traditions, and yet different, they are part of a region in transition. That a woman tied for first on a platform with Billy Graham and that she is the author of that feminist anthem "9 to 5" is a clear signal that gender divisions so neatly described at the beginning of the twentieth century are far less applicable today. Dolly Parton is no Southern belle but an Appalachian Steel Magnolia with spice.

North Carolina's Southern Highlands Today

The Setting[15]

Fifteen counties in the Carolina's southern mountains, chosen because they fall within the area considered Appalachia and because they are located in one of the state's former educational service regions, are the setting for our study.[16] Within those counties are sixteen school districts. North Carolina's legislature has attempted, with considerable success, to make district and county lines congruent, encouraging city systems to surrender their separate charters and merge with county systems. There are only a handful of city districts remaining, only one of which, Asheville City Schools, is within the geographic boundaries that we studied.

The fifteen counties range in size from Buncombe at nearly 660 square miles to three counties under 300 square miles (Clay at 220.8, Mitchell at 221.81, and Polk at 238.6). They range in average height, with considerable internal variability, from Yancey (2,817 feet in elevation) to Polk County (1,145 feet). Nine counties average over 2,000 feet high. The counties in the far west, where the mountains gentle down, and in the east, as they begin to rise, account for the lowest averages. Nine counties contain parts of the Blue

Ridge Parkway, which often follows the ridgelines that divide one county from another. The highest mountain east of the Mississippi River is in Mitchell County; most of the peaks over 6,000 feet in the East can be found in Carolina's Southern Highlands.

The education levels of the adult population in the region rank below the state average. In North Carolina, 78.1 percent of adults have attained at least a high school education or its equivalent and 22.5 percent have completed a college undergraduate program. In the Southern mountains, the highest high school completion percentage can be found in Henderson County (76.2 percent) and the highest college completion percentage is in neighboring Polk County (20.07 percent). Places with the highest levels of education tend to be those that have attracted a comparatively larger proportion of non-Carolinians, either as permanent or summer residents. The top seven counties on each list (Buncombe, Haywood, Henderson, Jackson, Macon, Polk, and Transylvania) are the same, although the order varies slightly. All seven serve retirement populations. Five are home to a two or four-year college.

Those counties with the lowest rates of college completion have fewer people and are in the more remote sections of the region, away from easy access to a four-year institution. There are some unexpected but explicable variations in educational attainment. For example, Madison County ranks fourteenth out of fifteen counties in high school completion rates, but is ninth in college degrees. It is the site of Mars Hill College, the presence of whose residential faculty serves to skew its college completion rating. Cherokee County is last in college completion, but tenth in high school degrees. It is the county furthest from a four-year state institution.

Geography is both an economic asset and a challenge. Tourism thrives in the summer and fall, as hikers, campers, and day-trippers flood the region to take advantage of the Smoky Mountain National Park and numerous national forests. The Appalachian Trail has a long section through this part of North Carolina and there are towns that maintain active trail service centers for thru-hikers.[17] Additionally, there are several white-water rivers, all of which have rafting companies that operate during the warm months. Outdoor opportunities (mountain climbing, mountain biking, distance and endurance racing, lake and river fishing, hunting) bring visitors to the area. Motorcyclists—alone, in pairs, or in caravans—are attracted to the winding, up and down rides possible on the Blue Ridge Parkway and Cherohalla Skyway.

George Vanderbilt's Biltmore, located in Asheville, is the largest privately owned home open to tourists. Carl Sandburg's last home, near the old resort town of Flat Rock, is a national historic site. A new state arboretum is located off the Parkway in Buncombe County. The Eastern Band of the Cherokee maintains an indoor museum open throughout the year and an outdoor living museum open during the summer. The tribe produces *Unto These Hills*, an outdoor drama about the beginning of the Trail of Tears. Its casino is the most-frequented attraction in the state. A tourist train operates out of Jackson County. In the summer, professional and community theater abounds, as do concerts, adult and youth programs at the area's colleges and universities, and camps. There is a vital, year-round arts and crafts community whose members live and work in the region.

It is no wonder, then, that in eight counties in our sample the largest percentage of employed workers are in the service sector. Swain County, which includes a large part of the national park, Lake Fontana, and a rafting river, ranks the highest, with 55.1 percent of its people working in such jobs. Traditionally, service sector positions are seasonal and low paying. White-water rafting, for example, is not commercially viable here during winter months. Rafting primarily employs the young, the healthy, and the unencumbered. It is a way for river aficionados to earn a modicum of money and continue to practice their skills; it is rarely a career. Given the relatively mild winters in the South, even in the mountains, cold weather recreation options, such as skiing, are economic gambles. Although there is a smattering of snow-based activities in the uplands, none of them is a certain moneymaker.

Geography influences economic opportunities in other ways, too. There are few extensive flat fields for commercial agriculture, but there are increasing numbers of small commercial farms specializing in niche crops or organic produce and meat products for local markets. Henderson County has a number of commercial orchards. One can find mountain tomato farms in several counties as well as trout farms. Local farmers grow Christmas trees for a national market.

Manufacturing employment ranges from a high of 47.3 percent of the working population in McDowell County, whose county seat is located immediately off Interstate 40, to a low of 3.4 percent in Swain County, which has no outlet to the direct west. It has only one four-lane road and it does not extend to a readily accessible major highway. The manufacturing plants that remain in counties like Swain are small and employ few people.

In McDowell County, Baxter Healthcare, a pharmaceutical maker, employs over 2,400 people. In 2000 the county had six other enterprises employing 400 or more workers. Henderson County is home to eight companies that employ over 400 people, including a General Electric plant with 1,000 workers. Most of the companies that have been in the region the longest are engaged in some sort of textile or furniture work. A few paper plants, once one of the area's manufacturing mainstays, remain, but most have been shuttered. Champion ended its affiliation with the largest paper mill, located in Haywood County, several years ago, putting the jobs of its 1,300 employees in jeopardy. The plant remains open today only because of a worker buyout. If there is a manufacturing trend in Carolina's southern mountains, it is the loss of jobs. Almost all counties in the region have experienced the loss of at least one manufacturer in the past five years. Several of them have permanently lost many of their highest paying jobs.

Proximity to transportation is an important variable in industrial size and relative strength. McDowell, Buncombe, Haywood, and Henderson, the counties intersected by interstates (either I-40 east and west or I-26 north and south), have the largest companies and the most people in manufacturing jobs. An extension of I-26 into Tennessee opened in Madison County in the late summer of this year. Local developers hope that it will encourage job production there. Only one commercially viable airport is located in the area. It sits between Asheville and the Henderson County line, off I-26. There is a fairly abbreviated manufacturing corridor in the uplands. Transportation remains problematic for more remote counties.

Several counties are classified as economically depressed. On three of the more common measures of economic health (average weekly wages, per capita income, and median family income), a majority rank in the bottom half of the state (eleventh on two indices and tenth on the other index). Six of them are in the bottom quartile on two indices and seven on the income per capita list. Mitchell County ranks 98 out of 100 counties in weekly wage income, Swain ranks 98 in per capita income, and Yancey comes in 99 on the median family income scale.

In a composite ranking of the three indicators, the counties at the bottom of the list (Clay, Mitchell, Swain, Yancey, and Graham) are small, distant from interstates, and have few permanent and low numbers of summer and retirement residents. Those in the top third of that list (Buncombe, Henderson, Transylvania, McDowell, and Macon) have more people, are more likely to be larger in size, have better access to transportation, and house residential areas that cater to second-home owners and retirees. Unemployment in the region ranges from 12.7 percent (Yancey) to 3.4 percent (Henderson County). Counties with low rankings on other economic features (few banks, distant from transportation hubs, low weekly salaries, many service or seasonal and few manufacturing sector jobs) have high levels of unemployment. The highest unemployment percentages are found in Yancey, Swain, Mitchell, and Graham Counties, whereas Henderson, Buncombe, and Macon are among the bottom four counties in unemployment.

In spite of economic disadvantages and pockets of poverty, there is relatively little crime in the region. No county comes close to the overall, violent, or property crime indices covered by the State Bureau of Investigation's Uniform Crime Report. The overall index for the state in 2002 was 4,771 crimes per 100,000 people. The highest incidence of crime was in Buncombe County (3,905). Madison County reported an overall incident rate of 887. In that year, violent crime for North Carolina averaged 474 incidents per 100,000 people. Buncombe County was again high on the region's list with 370.3 crimes; Macon recorded only 53. Property crimes came in at an average of 4,297 for the state, but at 3,535 for Buncombe County and 513 for Yancey County.

One of the initial reasons for early outsider travel to the southern mountains was its reputation for a healthful climate. Places like Highlands, Hot Springs, and Asheville became centers for the treatment of lung diseases, particularly tuberculosis. Asheville continues to be a medical center, with over 650 physicians located in Buncombe County. Access to health care varies widely, depending on proximity to Asheville and other area hospitals. There are only four doctors in Graham County and three in Clay; citizens in those communities travel to Cherokee County for hospital care. The number of dentists, another health indicator, is likewise variable. In Buncombe County one can find a dentist for every 1,910 people; in Madison County there is one dentist for every 9,818 residents. Medical practices in outlying counties often maintain office space and hours in more than one location to facilitate access for distant patients.

There are five notable political trends in the region. In a few instances, local politics are personal, even cranky, or linked to remote, violent memories of past transgressions. That principally appears to be the case in low-population counties in which there are very uneven registration patterns, very small differences between registrations, or in counties with unfortunate political histories. In Clay County, for example, there is only a 100-voter spread between the two parties. Madison County was once known as Bloody Madison because of the Shelton Laurel Massacre.[18] Candidates, be they Republican or Democrat, are almost all clustered near the conservative and libertarian ends of the political spectrum.

Recent voting patterns favor Republicans, in spite of registration patterns. Currently, the region is represented in Congress by a Republican and tends to vote Republican in federal and some statewide races. There is a western residence for the governor in Asheville, but its presence has not eliminated the sense on the part of longtime residents that events that occur at the state capital in Raleigh, four hours away on good traffic days, favor citizens in the populous Piedmont and closer coastal plains than they do the mountains. Finally, reflective of a regional independent streak, nine counties have a percentage of undeclared registered voters that is higher than the state average. Over 20 percent of the registrants in five counties have declined to affiliate with either of the major parties.

Again because of geography, some areas of the region are more linked to the cultural, medical, economic, and political centers in surrounding states than with similar institutions in North Carolina. For example, it is 118 miles from Murphy, the Cherokee County seat, to Atlanta, Georgia, but 359 miles to Raleigh. Murphy residents are closer to Birmingham, Alabama, which is only 238 miles away; Chattanooga, Tennessee, is a mere 94 miles to the west. Even Asheville residents, several hours by car to the east of Murphy, can get to Atlanta in 207 miles, whereas they must travel 251 miles to their state capital. Sylva, in the center of the region and Jackson's county seat, is only 150 miles from Atlanta, 195 miles from Columbia, South Carolina, and 272 miles away from Nashville, Tennessee. It is 296 miles to Raleigh.

There is only one regional television station, an ABC affiliate out of Asheville. The other major networks broadcast from a neighboring state. Geography limits access to television and radio signals, necessitating the use of satellite or cable systems for the former and a number of transponders for the latter. In a few instances, the mountain hollows are too steep to permit the use of a satellite dish and residents there are unlikely to have cable television. There is only one large daily newspaper, the Asheville *Citizen-Times*. Most counties have local newspapers that publish one to three times a week. Several counties have, at various times in the last century, been without a local newspaper altogether. Being "off the grid" is easy here. Some people have opted for that level of self-sufficiency.

Although variability characterizes the region, there are commonalities. The place is mostly rural. People born here are likely to stay or come back. It is increasingly a retirement and second-home destination. The population is still relatively homogeneous racially. Transportation remains a challenge. Unemployment is higher than the state average, as is the poverty rate. Wages, on average, are approximately 90 percent of the state average, as is per capita income. Some employment is seasonal and dependent on tourism, which is likely to become an even larger part of the region's economy in the future. Over the past decade, a number of industries have closed their plants in the region, leaving former employees who want to remain in the region without well-paying alternatives. Temporary or workday out-migration for employment continues to be part of the local economic vocabulary. There are sizeable and increasing differences between rich and poor, with clusters of geographic outsiders at the high end and clusters of locally born residents on the low side.

The People

There are, relative to the rest of the state, few people in the Carolina uplands except in Buncombe County. The entire mountain region, both north and south, approximately one-fourth of the state geographically, is home to only 12 percent of North Carolina's population. Our fifteen counties are only half of that area. (There is a northern mountain region.) Population growth is, on average, below that of the state as a whole and is, again on average, slightly older.

With one notable exception, there are few minorities in these counties. That one exception is the presence of the Eastern Band of the Cherokee Nation, whose main reservation land is located in Swain and Jackson Counties. Swain's Native American population is nearly 30 percent of its total; Jackson's population is a little over 10 percent. The Snowbird Cherokee reside in the mountains of Graham County, where Native Americans constitute 8.8 percent of its population. In comparison, the next largest Cherokee presence is in Cherokee County and makes up only 1.6 percent of its residents. There are approximately 12,500 enrolled members of the tribe, many of whom live within the Qualla Boundary, the reservation located in Swain and Jackson Counties. Cherokees have the option of attending federal reservation or regular public schools in the counties in which they live. Because Cherokee schools are operated apart from state institutions, have their own administration and administrative policies and procedures, and tell a very different story of privilege, we have excluded them from our study.

Compared to the rest of the state, other minorities are underrepresented. Whereas North Carolina is approximately 21.6 percent African American, the county with the largest proportion in our study is Buncombe, with only 7.48 percent. Asheville, however, is an exception. Its population is 78 percent white, 17.6 percent black, nearly 1 percent Asian, and slightly over 3.7 percent Hispanic. Asheville's percentages would rank them first in the southern mountain region, if it were listed separately from Buncombe, on rating scales in each of those racial or ethnicity categories.

Like the state's proportion of African Americans, that in the southern mountains has decreased over time. In 1850, census figures indicate that 52 percent of North Carolina's inhabitants were black. At the end of Reconstruction, in the 1880 census, the percentage had declined to 38 and steadily decreased as a proportion of total population, a result of black departures, white arrivals, and natural increase. The same pattern holds true both in proportion and in some cases in actual numbers for other counties in the region.

On the 2000 census, considerably less than 1 percent of the population was listed as African American in five counties: Graham, Mitchell, Yancey, Clay, and Madison. There were no African Americans in Graham County on census lists for 1910, 1960, 1970, and 1980. There were only five counties with percentages above 3: Buncombe, Polk, Transylvania, McDowell, and Henderson. Proportionately, the African American presence in the region declined, but geographically it retained patterns set nearly 150 years ago. Counties with the highest numbers and percentages of blacks then have the highest numbers and percentages today.

As elsewhere in the United States, there is a growing Latino presence in the area. North Carolina is among those states experiencing the highest rate of increase in Spanish-speaking residents. In the 1990 census, only Henderson County, whose farmers used migrant labor in their apple orchards, registered over 1 percent of its population as Hispanic. In the latest census, all the counties in our sample with the exception of Clay (0.83 percent) and Graham (0.75 percent) have a Hispanic proportion of total population over 1 percent. Henderson County remains the one with the highest percentage, with nearly 5.5 percent of its population listed as Hispanic in the 2000 census. No other single minority group tops 1 percent proportion of the population in any county.

Most western Carolinians live in valley areas, in counties with swatches of flat land, and in places on or near interstates. With the exception of Asheville (a 2001 population of 69,837), there are no cities to be found here. The next largest town is Hendersonville, the county seat of Henderson, with a population of nearly 11,000, followed by Waynesville (population 9,328), the county seat of Haywood, followed by Brevard (6,758), the county seat of Transylvania, and Marion (4,980), the county seat of McDowell. Populations drop precipitously from that point onward. Hayesville, the county seat of Clay, is home to 465 people; Bakersville, the county seat of Mitchell, houses only 361 residents.

There is a wide range of populations within the region, from Buncombe County, which has nearly 213,000 people to Graham County, which has slightly over 8,000. Henderson and Haywood Counties rank second and third in population, with 93,033 and 55,299 people respectively. In most counties the largest town is also the county seat. The exceptions are Madison, Mitchell, and Polk, but even their largest towns are small (Mars Hill, 1,767; Spruce Pine, 2,050; and Tryon, 1,794). Of the fifteen counties in our study, twelve of them rank in the lower half in population for the state; seven of them are in the bottom quartile. Of 100 counties, Clay is 96 and Graham is 97 in year-round residents.

Cracker-Barrel Wisdom

Given the presence of McDonalds, Wal-Marts, cable and satellite television, and the World Wide Web, can any region of the country retain its distinctiveness? Grantham (1994) believes that a unique Southern identity persists, agreeing with Reed (1993) that it is grounded in attachment to place, to kinship ties, and to church. In an earlier book, Reed (1986) notes that some of the statistics that once distinguished the South from other regions, such as its ruralness and poverty, are disappearing, but that a sense of Southern identity and culture is not simply persisting but actually increasing. Carlton (2001) attributed its staying power to an ability to adapt to change, to accommodate in ways that retained certain core values and institutions. When Loyal Jones (1994) compiled a coffee-table book about Appalachian values, his chapter titles reflect our findings: religion, independence, self-reliance, pride, neighborliness, familism, personalism, humility and modesty, love of place, patriotism, sense of beauty, and a sense of humor.

Margaret Mitchell (1936) believed that ladies knew how to keep their men happy and themselves provisioned.

> Women knew that a land where men were contented, uncontradicted and safe in possession of unpunctured vanity was likely to be a very pleasant place for women to live. So, from the cradle to the grave, women strove to make men pleased with themselves, and the satisfied men repaid lavishly with gallantry and adoration. In fact, men willingly gave the ladies everything in the world except credit for having intelligence. (156)

When cable television's country music station solicited a list of the 100 most influential country and western songs, Tammy Wynette's "Stand by Your Man" came in first. In 1998, John Reed (2001) selected a panel of broadly representative men and women who were familiar with, and had commented on, the South, its history, and culture, to choose a list of the twenty most influential Southerners in the twentieth-century, they found only two women worthy of inclusion: Margaret Mitchell (she was the first split-vote choice at number seven) and Rosa Parks (she came in at number nineteen). Mitchell was not the only cultural representative, nor even the only writer. William Faulkner, Elvis Presley, Louis Armstrong, Muhammad Ali, Hank Williams, Tennessee Williams, and Michael Jordan also made the final twenty. Parks is the only person whose achievements included only one "significant action." The other representatives had sustained careers.[19] Reed's list seems eminently Southern. It includes the woman who gave us the holy grails of Southern belle (Scarlett far too much of the time) and Southern lady (Scarlett's mother, Ellen, always; Melanie most of the time; and Scarlett rarely). She is paired with a woman whose chosen form of resistance is modest, thereby Southern, by design.

In her aptly titled book *Belonging in America: Reading between the Lines*, Constance Perin (1988) points to the cultural complexity of the United States. Rather than being neat and tidy, orderly and clear, it is filled with "incoherencies, confusions, contradictions, enigmas, paradoxes, and conflicts." Yet with all of those conundrums, "social orders both endure and change" (6). As Edward Leach (1976) points out, "boundaries become dirty by definition" (61). The categories we have proposed are smudgy. They provide us with a semblance of orderliness, line drawings to serve as social anchors. They are also useful in describing what was, as well as what is, in the process of departing. Culture is a form of "social memory," a way to explore the connections between identity and history by looking at the boundaries groups construct and the meanings implicit in those constructions (French 1995).

The following are cultural expectations, attitudes, and/or norms that distinguished the two regions that we have described. They are germane to the selection and conduct of senior-level educational leaders in Southern Appalachia, and, to one degree or another, can be found in the first years of the twenty-first century in the Carolina highlands. They are overlapping, connected, and flexible.

1. Experience with outsiders as well as being negatively perceived as an outsider or "the other" contribute to a regional suspicion of people who are not born and raised in the area. The question "Who are your people?" is an important one, determining initial levels of trust and allegiance. Familial or kinship connections are particularly strong. Knowing people counts.
2. Patriarchy is rarely overtly challenged. Gender roles persisted here after they had begun to blur elsewhere. They are now fading. Challenges to gender roles assume a more feminine than feminist guise, with the persistence of forms of deference based on gender, social status, "worthiness," and age. At one time, and whenever possible, regional leaders were male in those institutions that mattered: the family, the church, the school, the business place or market square, and the political arena. That has begun to change.
3. Race privilege persisted in standards of strict segregation legitimized by both law and custom. Challenges to race privilege trailed modern challenges to gender hegemony. Regional leadership was white. In Jim Crow Southern Appalachia, blacks rose to positions of power only within their separate, rarely economically equal, institutions. Patriarchy was not so clearly ascribed in African American communities, although males maintained a semiblurred level of privilege. All of those conditions are in flux, most evidently in those pockets within the region in which there is a minority population of sufficient size to challenge white hegemony.
4. Fundamental, evangelical religious beliefs elevate individual salvation above social justice, reinforcing an emphasis on kinship and neighborhood loyalties at the expense of more abstract ideals about responsibilities to others. They affirm the ideal of individual resolution to social problems, contributing to an unwillingness to fund public institutions and their employees well. Religion once validated ideas about gender and race that placed power in the hands of some individuals and denied it to others.

Churches blessed certain ways of being and, by cloaking them with the mantle of "the sacred," made challenges difficult and the pace of any change slow. However, change is part of today's mountain culture. In the 1970s a Yancey County resident complained that "a man don't hardly know where he stands no more; there don't seem to be anything steady" (Hicks 1976, 15). Even the church cannot hold steady in these times.

5. Long reliance on subsistence or for-profit agriculture and the attitudes associated with an agrarian or traditional mind-set make land and land ownership important. A sense of place as well as a love for the land still keep people close to their geographic origins and encourage a homogeneity that feeds egalitarianism. It also promotes parochialism and conformity.
6. Progress as a product of technological innovation and science remains, for some people, an unproven proposition. Although New South advocates adopted and pushed eastern, urban ideas about progressive change, particularly in economics, there remained believers in the idea that if something is not "broke," there is little reason to change it. Even today one hears people complain about a younger generation member who "has got above her raisin's" in ways that let the listener know that is never a good thing. For many things, the "good old ways" are still "the best ways."
7. Civility persists in the form of customs related to greetings, to valuing small talk, to teaching social lessons through stories rather than debate or logic, to honoring predecessors and continuing traditions. It masks areas of disagreement, makes loyalty a virtue, and displaces contentiousness in ways that make resolutions of conflicts difficult and the likelihood of violent resolutions higher than might otherwise be the case. Regional culture, in the words of Genovese (1994, 21) remains one of "folk and feeling." School leaders must be able to negotiate an ethic of neutrality.

·3·

GOOD OL' BOYS AND GIRLS

The Professional Context

If, as we contend, educational leadership selection and behavior were (are) shaped by cultural norms, then individuals who sat in district superinten dent's seats in Southern Appalachia generally fit the bill. They met understood personal and political assumptions. Because of a past relatively untroubled by outsiders, a persistent homogeneity reinforced by geographic isolation, and national norms about race and gender that were not successfully challenged until recently, expectations remained untroubled far into the twentieth century. Cultural barriers, while permeable, were high. For the past two decades, however, they have visibly shifted, expanding to include individuals hitherto unconsidered as candidates for administration positions.

At first, white, "worthwhile" men filled the chairs reserved for the region's superintendents. Good ol' boys, in the Southern sense of that phrase, they were, more often than not, locally born and raised. True believers of the Protestant gospel, they subscribed to the politics in favor in a particular county. Although party affiliation varied in the Carolina uplands, political positions were predictably conservative and, until late in the twentieth century, likely to reflect racial biases grounded in segregation. Yet, in at least one way, these school leaders were considered progressive. Like local businessmen and politicians, they were intent upon encouraging conditions that advanced the economic interests of their region and its citizens. They had a highlander version of the "right stuff." They were forceful in an unassuming way; skillful at getting along with other men; mindful of local standards and interests; solicitous of mountaineer dignity; and attentive to building bigger and, therefore, better school systems. As will become clear in part two (chapters 4–8), they have now been joined by several good ol' girls, women who have some of the same "right stuff," with a feminine twist.

In this chapter we address an additional factor in educational administrator selection and behavior. As high as the mountains rise, there is always a path through them. The world writ large intrudes almost everywhere, more so now than in the past. Notwithstanding the picturesque images of a place that time forgot, the ideas of the world without were a part of life in the uplands even before the twentieth century began. Appalachian otherness was never quite as exotic or whole as visitors imagined. Because Carolina's public education is primarily state funded, there have been statewide expectations for educator conduct and schools from the nineteenth century onward. As compulsory schooling grew and became more centralized, a mandated system of credentialing educators layered an additional set of attributes and skills upon local requirements. They formed an external picture of professional right stuff to which administrator and teacher candidates subscribe in order to secure a license to practice.

Formal preparation programs subscribed to some professional standards and not others, because they, too, aspired to external validation through state, regional, and, in some disciplines, national accreditation. Even in their nascent stages, colleges and normal schools tried to guarantee that what they taught was Kansas City up-to-date. Using summer schools for teachers, certification sticks and salary carrots, encouragement of professional organizations, the bully pulpit, statewide magazines and meetings, regulations, tighter supervision, and a growing body of legislation, state school leaders defined and encouraged certain expectations and behaviors. By mid-twentieth century, candidates for the state-funded school positions in Clay County or Asheville had to meet the same minimum criteria as candidates in Raleigh or Charlotte.

Those criteria, codified in certification (licensure) requirements, were considered necessary for competent practice. How an administrator should behave, then, necessarily extended beyond local expectations and norms to those held by individuals in statewide positions of power. In education, as in so many other fields from the late nineteenth century onward, people who influenced policymaking were, or were guided by, experts. A claim to expertise came, increasingly, to depend on formal education that culminated in another set of credentials, a degree. That piece of paper certified that its holder was judged competent to perform certain tasks.

Robert Wiebe (1967) considers the ascendancy of professional experts one element in our national search for order as modernity swept agrarian assumptions aside. Into the chaos of what Karl Polanyi (1944) calls "the great transformation" came sociopolitical efforts to tame the consequences of industrialization. Wiebe labels the resultant order creation "rationalization." It is a way of making rapid changes that challenge long-held community truths both understandable and acceptable. The growing importance of expertise and modern professionals is a result of that process. Another is the gathering together of experts into specialized associations, which then became the arbiters of disciplinary truth (Haskell 2000). Their truth was the curriculum taught in colleges and universities to professional wannabes.

Rationalization is akin to Kuhn's description of the transition from pre-science to science. Initially, all truth is personal and local. Lacking independent criteria and systems of communicating, testing, debating, and revising reality claims, knowledge is constantly rediscovered and affirmed. Consequently, it fails to serve as a foundation and benchmark for investigation, for doing normal science. Pre-science is, in many ways, intellectual cacophony. It is an unstable framework upon which to predict, to make, and to make sense of new discoveries. Moving from a state of pre-science to science is a process of rationalization, of bringing order to a process.

Over the course of the last two hundred years, rationalization came to U.S. public schooling. Keeping school was once an individualized, local enterprise, often involving but a single educator. Gradually, as formal education became a prerequisite for success in a modern nation and as experts understood more about the processes governing effective teaching, keeping school became a public and state responsibility. Whereas once teaching might have been considered an art, by the twentieth century it was moving from being a craft to a science. By the twenty-first century, at least to some practitioners and policy-makers, both teaching and educational administration were considered professions. The possession of an approved body of knowledge and skills was considered a prerequisite to successful practice.[1]

It is to a survey of changing ideas about the specifics of that package of knowledge, skills, and attributes that we now turn. Individuals had to meet certain local cultural and social expectations to be considered for positions of educational leadership (and they did). They had to perform in those roles in ways that met certain local expectations (and they did). They also had to demonstrate, particularly in recent decades, that they met minimal professional standards. Although it may have been possible in the nineteenth century to be a district school superintendent, particularly in the Carolina mountains, without a college degree from an accredited institution, it would be impossible today. Even today, when state legislatures are inclined to open the superintendency to individuals with compensatory life experiences rather than formal certification, they are reluctant to remove all formal barriers. Some standards remain. Candidates must possess at least a modicum of formal education and have proven leadership experiences. In most states, individuals who hope to contend for a superintendency have generally completed at least one or, more often, two graduate degree programs, taught, administered at the building and/or system level, and demonstrated academic competence on some form of externally scored examination.

What did they learn in that process about administering school districts? How were they intellectually prepared for leadership? In what ways were they acculturated on the job or on the way to the job? What did the professional culture, often outside the communities in which they worked, expect them to do? What was the professional "right stuff"? How did its definition change over time? Did those changes make more likely the introduction of other voices in senior-level district leadership positions?

Professional socialization is a set of nested expectations, somewhat like the wooden dolls tourists purchase in and around Russia. At the center is an individual, with a unique complement of eccentricities, talents, and limitations. That person rests within another doll, one that represents the predispositions and experiences associated with family and neighborhood. It is, in turn, contained within the social and cultural expectations of a particular locality, community, or region. Enveloping them is yet another set of norms, including state and national standards for professional competence and conduct.

Professional expectations exert their influence in several ways. By condoning specific constructions of "good" leadership, experts determine the language that frames practice. Expectations govern the credentialing process through establishment and enforcement of licensure and accreditation standards. Those standards shape the content (sometimes even the delivery) of formal preparation programs. They define practice that is professional and distinguish it from practice that is bogus, serving a gatekeeping function. Academics influence directions scholarship can take by controlling research through oversight of its funding, publication, and reception. We look at two ways the profession itself influences expectations. First, we describe those leadership constructions that carried the most weight in this particular part of the country. Second, we look briefly at texts on district leadership in the regional institution from which most of our informants took the coursework necessary to qualify for an administration license.

The profession does not function alone in setting access and behavior boundaries. The state supports the position financially and legislates the responsibilities that it entails. So, we also describe how the definition of county superintendent changed over time in North Carolina. A third element of professional culture, one potentially more powerful than any other in candidate socialization, is experience. How do effective administrators do what they do? Educational leaders in the field model behaviors that prospective administrators observe, evaluate, and choose to emulate, modify, or ignore. Sometimes they serve as formal mentors; sometimes their influence goes unrecognized. Occasionally, their behaviors become exemplars of conduct to avoid. But if leaders are well received by their peers, subordinates, board members, and community patrons, if they serve long and productive tenures, then they become influential in shaping the behaviors of their subordinates, of the individuals who come after them, and of the community as a whole.

Preprofessional Practice

Before there were educational bureaucracies in need of experts, there were individual and then clusters of small, autonomous schools. Early educational leaders were secular evangelicals. They placed their worldly hopes in schools as portals to a successful temporal life in much the same way they placed their sacred hopes in churches as a doorway to a heavenly, rather than a hellish, eternity. Tyack and Hansot (1982) call these men members of an "aristocracy of character" to distinguish them from their twentieth-century successors, whose approach to school administration fell within the tradition of scientific management. Early education advocates wielded power benevolently on behalf of the people they wanted to help. They did so also, and sometimes with more fervor, on behalf of their vision of a well-ordered, moral commonweal whose behavior was guided by Protestant precepts. They worked in a preindustrial world in which local communities routinely trumped the state in setting school policies.

Charisma is an elusive quality. It, like art, seems to be a gestalt rather than a combination of discrete, easily explicable parts. Conger and Kanungo (1988) found that modern charismatic leaders are future-oriented, self-confident advocates of radical change. They are able to articulate a vision in ways that make it desirable to others. They possess a set of personal qualities (strength, persistence, focus, a willingness to take risks) that facilitates pursuit of their goal. Included therein and requisite to being perceived as a leader is an ability to motivate others to join in the pursuit. Followers do not perceive them as custodians of the present but as ushers to the future. Charismatic leaders are attuned to their environment, almost intuitively able to recognize the resources it contains that will assist them in reaching their goals.

There are numerous historical examples of charismatic leaders. America's founding fathers led a revolution that established a form of government independent of inherited nobility. Abraham Lincoln refused to consider a nation divided as an option. Martin Luther King's dream of a new nation captured the imagination of integrationists and the conscience of a nation. Individuals who started successful religious movements often qualify as charismatic. Jesus, Mohammed, and Buddha rejected the status quo, proposed an attractive alternative, gathered a band of followers, and left a sufficiently compelling legacy for their ideas to take root and grow.

Robert E. Lee and Stonewall Jackson are remembered as charismatic, although their vision of loyalty to home states and family is a more limiting vision than Lincoln's desire to have a nation whole and unencumbered by slavery. Charisma does not require scruples. Morally bankrupt leaders like Hitler can have a message, communicate it all too well at a time when potential followers are ready to heed it, and manipulate skillfully the resources at hand. Jim Jones, Charles Manson, and David Koresh are versions of charismatic leadership gone badly awry.[2] Elvis Presley, whose vision was less about politics and more about personal freedom, had it, as did the Beatles as a group and several members individually.

The word "charisma" is a Greek derivative and originally meant a gift of God's grace. *Webster*'s first definition is theological. Charisma is a "divinely inspired gift . . . or talent" (Guralnik 1970, 240). Someone either has it or does not. As a gift, it can neither be learned nor earned. Personality, complemented by grace, assisted by opportunity, produces a charismatic leader. The stories societies tell revolve around these people. Homer's Odysseus, Virgil's Aeneas, Beowulf, the men and women of the Icelandic sagas, King Arthur and his knights are guideposts to right living and destiny on course. Early histories served the same purpose. Catalogues of great men (rarely, for so long a time, great women), they defined leadership by deed and daring. The hero, notes Joseph Campbell (1949), hears a call, transcends his temporal limitations, is somehow transfigured, and returns to renew or redeem his followers with a new message. There is a call (the problem), barriers (the status quo), transformation (the message), and renewal (the deeds). Modern heroes, according to Campbell, are not the giants that once strode the Earth.

> The democratic ideal of the self-determining individual, the invention of the power-driven machine, and the development of the scientific method of research, have so transformed human life that the long-inherited, timeless universe of symbols has collapsed. . . . It is not only that there is no hiding place for the gods from the searching telescope and microscope; there is no such society any more as the gods once supported. The social unit is not a carrier of religious content, but an economic-political organization. (387)

The heroic ideal might have collapsed, but the notion that a great man will take the stage at the last moment and save the day is part of our national psyche. Shane will ride in, triumphant, and, in the final reel, ride off into the sunset. Joe Clark purges the schools of undesirables. Jaime Escalante teaches everyone calculus. Arnold Schwarzenegger terminates California's debt. Someone throws the rascals out. Happiness reigns over the land.

Charisma is artistic leadership for people whom the gods have graced. People so blessed rise up, gather a crowd, and try to change, fix, enhance, establish, or amend something. They do not maintain. There are few charismatic leaders in any generation. Evangelists, modest messengers bringing good news, do the heavy lifting. Horace Mann shaped the common school message and for the rest of the nineteenth century various local, state, and regional leaders sought out converts. In North Carolina, Charles Wiley is credited with accepting Mann's challenge and pushing the agenda of common schooling to Tar Heels. The first state superintendent of schools, Wiley saw his efforts flounder as the South first drifted, then headed with deliberate speed toward war. The credentials of Carolina's first educational leader were typical of men in those positions. He was only thirty-three years old when he was appointed to the position; like Mann, he was a member of the legislature that did the appointing. He had graduated from college and was a lawyer. A student of the humanities, he wrote novels. Noble (1930) claims that Wiley "was thrilled at the possibilities before him, and with joy in his heart he went about his task with a hope and enthusiasm that never left him." And well he should, since "so much was dark, dreary, and uninviting" (136). How Noble was able to discern Wiley's inner spirit is a mystery, but it is instructive to consider the way he described it.

Wiley's sense of mission inspired many of the early schoolmen. Schooling, they felt, would save the body politic and make America whole. There was a messianic quality to the messages of these educators. In his Tenth Report, Horace Mann (1951/1846) alluded to the Pilgrim Fathers of Massachusetts. They had, he wrote, "two divine ideas . . . their duty to God and to posterity. For the one they built the church, for the other they opened the school" (163). When the Masons of Selma, Alabama, sought a headmaster for their new school, they wanted a man who "should be a finished scholar; have experience teaching—be industrious and energetic, have a good temper, . . . above all exception in his moral character" (Sewell 1951, 167). "Educate the rising generation . . . and the nation and the world would reach the millennium within one hundred years," proclaimed a U.S. Senator in 1882 (quoted in Tyack and Hansot 1982, 15). George Atkinson, an educator in the Pacific Northwest, wrote in the 1870s that the office of county superintendent "can be the radiant light . . . or the center of darkness" (42).

The men and women—there were a few females like Mary Lyons, Catherine Beecher, and Emma Willard championing education—who carried the torch for common schooling throughout the country knew each other's work.

They exchanged letters, encouraged one another, collaborated, commiserated about the laggardly South, and proselytized on behalf of their cause whenever possible. What held them together was not a formal organization but the messianic quality of their messages and their faith in its power.

Over the course of the nineteenth century, their calling changed to fit the times. Tyack and Hansot (1982) write of "the bureaucratization of redemption" in their history of public school leadership. Francis Parker, whose work as superintendent of the Quincy, Massachusetts, school system brought him national attention, attributed his professional enthusiasm to his "intense desire to see mind and soul grow" (quoted in Cremin 1964, 129). Parker and his fellow pedagogical pioneers, Lawrence Cremin's term for them, were among the last of America's educational prophets. Their fervor was domesticated by industrialization and the evolution of schools into systems. If leadership continued to rely exclusively on charisma, it would have no place in a modern landscape, whose measure was calculated by science.

Cognizant of the vagaries of local prejudices, animated by a belief in the secular benefits gained from formal education, and attuned to the new social sciences, men who made careers in education recognized the need for a new organization and governance structure. They saw advantages in uniformity and centralization. The regulation of modern factories held promise for social institutions as well. Efficiencies of scale awaited the science of management. More students being taught in more buildings, each housing more classrooms, would save money, increase productivity, and root out the parochial incompetence possible in one-room schools. Common schools could become truly common, slicing through geographic and class barriers. A few progressive educators even dared to suggest extending the benefits of common schools across racial and gender lines. Educational leaders became advocates for a new profession, educational administration.

Professional Practice: A Caveat

Given the need for many administrators and more than a few leaders in large, complex societies, it is inevitable that charisma's charm faded. God's gifts are not necessarily programmed for human, on-time delivery. Bureaucracies require active and prospective administrators to know how to do their work effectively. Into that vacuum step scribblers and academics.[3] They use standard texts written specifically for educational administration preparation programs, books on such topics as school law, finance, curriculum and instruction, the principalship, facilities, organization theory, and supervision. They also recommend and sometimes require readings from other allied fields, such as business administration. Course syllabi and best-seller lists direct students to volumes on managing in one minute (Blanchard and Johnson 1983), thriving in the midst of chaos (Peters 1987), cultivating seven essential habits (Covey 1989), and moving cheese (Johnson 1998). Leaders can be enlightened (Oakley and Krug 1991), principle centered (Covey 1992), constructivist (Lambert et al. 1995), and intuitive (Dyer and Carothers 2000). They can put into practice "the warrior's edge" (Alexander, Groller, and Morris 1990), Sun Tzu's "art of war" (1971), a variation of Lao Tzu's *Tao Te Ching* (Heider 1986), strategies from ancient China (Yuan 1991) or advice from a seventeenth-century Jesuit priest (Kaye 1992). Given that North Carolina is ACC basketball country, local school leaders might seek advice from coaches John Wooden (1988, 2003; Biro 2001), Dean Smith (Chadwick 1999) and Mike Krzyzewski (2000), or from female coaching great Pat Summitt (1998). Former mayor Rudolph Giuliani (2002), the richest retailer in the world, Sam Walton (1992), and Fortune 500 CEO Jack Welch (2001; Slater 1998) also want to share their leadership secrets.

A cursory review of relevant "how to" work in the field shows the leadership literature to be large, diverse, and overlapping. It incorporates advice from multiple disciplines by authors at home and abroad who are in or out of the school business. What works in one organizational context has, these authors tell us, applicability to another. Writers distinguish between management and leadership or leadership and administration, but distinctions sometimes blur and definitions merge. Lessons for mid-level administrators are applicable, at least some of the time, to senior-level leaders. Advice for the CEO provides insight for the aspirant. There is situational leadership, transactional leadership, transformational leadership, constructivist leadership, feminist leadership, and postmodern leadership from which to choose. Leaders can strive for effectiveness, excellence, or quality, depending on the authority of the moment. Sometimes leadership is leadership is leadership, except when it's not.

Some of that advice comes from research studies. More lessons are derived from anecdote and example.[4] That is an inevitable result of working with an ever-changing set of unique people embedded in a complex and altering world with differing views of organizational missions. It is also testimony to the elusiveness of the concept. In the field of educational administration, finding a grand theory, a leadership silver bullet, is as likely to prove successful as Sisyphus is to succeed in rolling his rock up a hill.

Educational theories, like the residents of George Orwell's *Animal Farm*, are all equal, but some are more equal than others. At certain times, specific constructions of educational leaders have been ascendant. Popularized by traveling consultants, school leadership pundits, and professors, they become the professional vocabulary of preparation programs, scholarship, and experts.

They frame leadership discourse and are the building blocks of stories educators tell one another. They provide the backdrop of professional socialization and essential to the position's transition from a pre-science pursuit to a profession resting on a contested, somewhat ill-defined knowledge base. They also guide policymakers, who are less attuned to theories removed from their experience. For that reason, we are paying particular attention to scientific management and its descendents. It resonated in two ways with mainstream America. It was draped with the mantle of science and was measurable. It looked familiar. School organizations began to resemble businesses by the turn of the last century and businessmen were among the most desirable of the early candidate for school board positions.

Scientific Managers

Frederick Winslow Taylor is usually the first stop in a survey of classical theory development in administration. Famed for introducing time management to the manufacturing world, he began the studies that led to *Principles of Scientific Management* (1911) at the Midvale and Bethlehem Steel Companies in Pennsylvania. Convinced that workers were not as productive as they could be and that industrial processes were operating at less than capacity, Taylor, in true Robert Wiebe fashion, sought to rationalize them. He wanted to make them more orderly and, therefore, more efficient. The goals of scientific management were enhancement of productivity, elimination of wastefulness, and maximization of profits.

The push for orderliness in education did not begin with Taylor. John Philbrick, author of *City School Systems in the United States*, an 1885 publication, pointed out that industrialization pushed modern civilization toward uniformity. "The best is the best everywhere" (quoted in Tyack 1974, 40). Taylor articulated, in plain and well-publicized terms, that sentiment by introducing a set of principles designed to promote standardization as a means of enhancing quality. He was to the beginning of the past century what men like Peter Drucker and Tom Peters were to its closing decades. A number of different fields adopted his ideas. Taylor attracted acolytes who believed that they had come upon a panacea for all that troubled their particular worksites. His ideas were popularized by the media and taught in the best universities. By 1910 the Taylor System was part of the curriculum of the Harvard Business School (Callahan 1962, 22).

Businessmen wanted a method to lower costs, step up production, and increase profits. Taylor called for detailed studies to determine the most efficient and, he assumed, effective way to do a job. He produced processes that could be determined with mathematical specificity. Once found, one best way became the standard against which all similar performances were measured. People who met the production standard were rewarded while workers who fell short of that goal were penalized. Supervision was necessary to ensure compliance, so administrators divided work into small, repetitive segments. Specialists were more efficient than generalists. Overseeing the entire process was a planning department staffed with experts, whose tasks included monitoring the system, improving the tools workers used, and enhancing worker skills. Workers themselves were to leave the thinking to the planners.

Taylor designed for what became the modern factory system, a hierarchical bureaucracy in which a profitable bottom line signaled success. It required mid-level and senior managers, as well as professional planners. Their cost was balanced by the increased productivity of line workers, which actually lowered the number of people necessary to generate products. Supervision was the key to better factories. Increasingly, school reformers thought it was the key to better schools.

The application of Taylorism to public schooling came quickly. In 1911 the World Book Company began publication of a school efficiency series. In 1912 an engineer gave a lecture to high school principals in New York on the application of scientific management to their institutions. Joseph Rice, who had authored an influential series of articles critical of urban schools two decades earlier, published a collection of essays entitled *Scientific Management in Education* (1914). Raymond Callahan (1962), a student of the application of efficiency principles to public schools, concluded that Taylor's "ideas were adopted, interpreted, and applied chiefly by administrators." They had their "greatest impact upon administration, the administrator, and the professional training programs of administration" (41). The popular response to the outbreak of school criticism that arose in the early 1910s was the application of Taylor principles to educational settings. Schools had become wasteful. They were, according to the title of an article in *Saturday Evening Post*, using "Medieval Methods for Modern Children" (Warren 1912, 11). Critics blamed a variety of social problems on the perceived poor performance of the public schools.

In 1913 Frank Spaulding, an urban superintendent and later a member of the Yale University faculty, told the annual meeting of the National Education Association that the time had come to apply scientific methods to the operation of schools. He boasted of quantifying quality in the Newton, New Jersey, schools. He spoke of plants, products, and investment per pupil. The establishment of educational factories was the way to quell public criticism. To gain control over the budget, superintendents must merge the financial and the educational functions of their districts.[5] These functions, he stated, were inseparable. The former addressed the efficiency of an organization and the latter, its effectiveness. Both were the responsibility of the district leader, who was expected to be a competent businessman with financial expertise. School finance became an area of specialized study in preparation programs for prospective leaders. By the time someone reviewed the curricula of 1930s college programs, it was ranked first among topics about which an educational administrator should be knowledgeable (Callahan 1962, 201).

As scientific managers, school superintendents oversaw factories (schools), foremen (principals), and, sometimes indirectly, workers (teachers). They provided tools (teaching supplies and texts) and supervision in a process that involved the conversion of educational raw materials (students) into viable products (graduates) at the lowest possible cost. The conversion of raw material to finished product was to be systematic and orderly. An early adapter, Frank Rigler, superintendent of Portland, Oregon, schools could tell any interested visitor from what page and in what book each teacher was instructing at any particular hour on any particular day of the academic year (Tyack 1974, 48).

According to Beck and Murphy (1993), 1920s administrators were "energized by a zeal for education and guided by principles of scientific management." They combined nineteenth-century redemption aspirations with Frederick Taylor. Their work was "linked with absolute, spiritual truths and values" and they were "expected to be a social leader in the community" (14). Their professional practice consisted of "the best of modern methods and discoveries to create and manage an efficient and productive school" (15). These school leaders saw no conflict in the two sets of expectations. They should be models of virtue and exemplars of the latest business methods. Tyack and Hansot (1982) believe that 1920s administrators were comfortable mixing "small-town pietism and science" (114). From their churches, they took the values of "hard work, duty, order, thrift in time and money." They had an "imperative to set the world straight." From Taylor and his advocates they gained an admiration of "efficient organization, 'scientific' facts . . . [and] methodological planning" (116).

Prior to the late nineteenth century, there were no formal textbooks on how to supervise school systems or administer schools.[6] There were no professional schools where prospective candidates obtained the requisite skills and knowledge to do the job scientifically. By the early 1920s, when Ellwood Cubberley (1924), one of the pioneers in the professional preparation of school administrators, contributed a chapter on his field for a book surveying the past twenty-five years in American education, that condition had changed profoundly. He described the period as one of great creativity, resulting in the design of a specialized study for prospective school and system leaders. Specific college divisions or departments introduced programs in the management of educational institutions. Cubberley applauded the application of statistical methods to the study of education and to the assessment of schools, systems, and personnel, pointing with pride to the design and increased use of comprehensive surveys by progressive districts.[7]

Taylorism as a shaper of educational administrator behavior is alive and exceedingly well today. In the 1980s, in response to *Nation at Risk* criticism, North Carolina policymakers legislated a "one best way" to teach, making a six-step lesson plan the template against which evaluators were to measure teacher performance. An evaluation system was standardized and implemented statewide. Used to make continuing contract decisions and establish grounds for dismissal based on poor performance, it ostensibly brought quality control to public schools. However, when standardizing teaching failed to produce desired results, Carolina school reformers, like those in many other states, turned their attention to outcomes. They adopted a standard curriculum that included lists of competencies that all students must demonstrate before graduating.

By the 1990s, scientific management ideas set the organizational tone of Carolina's schools. The organization itself is hierarchical with layers of supervisors. Teachers are divided by discipline and/or grade and charged with performing specialized tasks. Generally they do the same task each academic year, be it teaching third grade or sophomore English. Where and what they teach, often even how and when it is done, are prescribed. Policymakers use measured outcomes from annual external assessments as benchmarks for school effectiveness. They tie rewards (bonuses) and sanctions (humiliation when school results are made public) to results. Principals of poor-performing schools can lose their jobs. Superintendents in poor-performing districts cannot count on a renewed contract.

Education governors make their reputations on the adoption of ambitious, outcomes-based, accountability programs. In 2001 an education president proposed requiring some variation of that model in every state. No child should be left behind. Supplementing state sanctions, there are now national report cards. Thinking—at least, that creative mental activity involved in task definition, assessment, and general implementation—is done somewhere else. The role for educational administrators is local oversight. In addition to business sense and fiscal skills, they need to know the state curriculum, the accountability measures by which their district will be judged, and strategies helpful in maximizing performance on the assessments. They may choose to include local requirements to the state system, which must now comply with national guidelines. It is a process that they cannot disavow. They are legislatively bound to an educational bottom line that, like a proverbial dog's tail, wags the system.

Social Engineers

Planning to meet set goals, employing the right people for specific jobs, providing them with the appropriate tools, deploying them efficiently, supervising them, and holding the organization accountable for results are generic administrative tasks. In *New Demands in Education*, Franklin Munroe (1912), a member of the University of Chicago faculty, argued for "'educational engineers' to study this huge business of preparing youth for life" (10). In an article on the history and status of educational measurement, published six years later, Leonard Ayers noted that "knowledge is replacing opinion, and evidence is supplanting guess-work in education as in every field of human activity" (quoted in Knight and Hall 1951, 749). In 1913 Franklin Bobbitt comfortably asserted that "education is a shaping process as much as the manufacture of steel rails" (quoted in Callahan 1962, 81). Nearly one hundred years ago, Bobbitt, also on the faculty of the University of Chicago, sounded like some critics of today's public schools. He believed in quantifiable standards of performance, frequent testing, rigorous teacher training, and holding teachers to specific expectations about the work they were to do and the methods they were to use. Bobbitt invited business people to develop the goals schools should meet. He reserved for educators the responsibility of determining how to reach them, but the specifications of the product they were to produce was determined elsewhere, independent of local variation in needs, desires, and barriers. Goals were communicated through central offices to production floors.

The more the work of education resembled private businesses, the more the image of its leaders became that of a businessman. As schools adopted science as their guide, leaders were expected to be familiar with it and its handmaiden, mathematics, both areas of study generally reserved for men. In the nineteenth century, redemptive work was routinely done by women. They served as missionaries, settlement house and school leaders, social workers, temperance leaders, and frontier nurses. Associated with sentimentality and romanticism, they threatened to feminize America (Douglas 1977). It was not the image that policymakers had for the twentieth century.

By the end of World War I, educators were as enthusiastic about the prospects of progress as was Sinclair Lewis's title character in *Babbitt*, a novel that made its first appearance in 1922. Babbitt's modernity signifiers were gadgets. He loved machines, the promise of technology. In a Chamber of Commerce speech celebrating the election of a business candidate over a reform alternative, Babbitt brags about the things that make his hometown, Zenith, "forward-looking." The schools are "complete plants." They have "the finest school-ventilating system in the country." Their students, at least their male students, are in the process of becoming "our Standardized Citizen[s]." Leading Zenith to future heights are its regular, busy, out and about, up and doing, businessmen. "Here's [sic] the specifications of the Standardized American Citizen! Here's the new generation of Americans: fellows with hair on their chests and smiles in their eyes and adding machines in their offices." Zenith is the home of "manly men and womanly women" that are "setting the pace for a civilization that shall endure" (1922, 148–54). Babbitt reserves, as did most men of his generation, public space for men (hairy-chested fellows) and home to women. Setting the pace for educators as scientifically enlightened businessmen were professors and sitting superintendents. They worked in preparation programs, authored administration texts, dominated the public discourse, and held positions of power in organizations dedicated to school and district leadership.

In the 1930s Jesse Newlon did a content analysis of educational administration program texts as part of his doctoral dissertation. Fully 80 percent of the over eight thousand pages he reviewed addressed the "executive, organizational, and legal aspects of administration." None of the books explored the theoretical foundations of the field, nor did they consider the implications of various approaches to administration. They were technician oriented. In 1933 the Commission on Educational Leadership, affiliated with the National Education Association, published the results of a survey of courses available in preparation programs. They emphasized skills, the "how to do it" aspects of the job. Asel Murphy's 1931 dissertation asked experts in the profession (superintendents and professors) to rank the importance of various administrative tasks. School finance came in first overall. It was followed by business administration; organization and administration of supervision; organization and administration of curriculum; and administration of teaching personnel, in that order. The development of curriculum, consideration of school purposes and missions, and educational philosophy did not make the top eighteen topics. Human beings are reduced to tasks (School Officials, Functions, Duties—number twelve on the list) or outside the educational setting proper (Public Relations and Publicity—number six). Professional ethics came in number fifteen. Newlon uncovered 290 theses produced in educational administration between 1910 and 1933. Fifty-five of them addressed fiscal issues. Thirty-four concerned business administration. They, too, suggested that educational leadership was a business task, requiring many of the same attributes and skills that a leader of industry would need (Callahan 1962, 200–3).

According to Beck and Murphy (1993), the three dominant values of the 1930s were "the discovery of 'truth through research';" "the application of 'truth' through scientific management;" and "the realization of truth in objective educational outcomes" (27). By the Depression era, the language of redemption had lost to the language of business. The principal's task was "administrative, not instructional. She or he is considered to be an executive within the school" (23). Organization and supervision are the key tasks of school administrators. Joseph Rost (1993), after reviewing 587 books, chapters, and articles about leadership written between 1900 and 1990, found 221 definitions of the term.[8] Definitions from the classical period (1900–1930) emphasized "control and centralization of power." Leadership is "the ability to impress the will of the leader on those led and induce obedience, respect, loyalty, and cooperation" (quoted in Rost 1993, 47).

By the mid-1930s, performance expectations involved maintaining order and control and designing schools to eliminate the unnecessary and accentuate productivity. Embedded within that search for effective efficiency, for the production of Babbitt's standardized citizen, was a belief that what one was engineering was not simply a system, but a society. Charisma never disappeared. There was still a preference for the appearance (ideally the actions) of strength. The hopefulness of schooling's redemptive qualities had been replaced by a belief in its ability to shape workers for a modern work.[9] In a 1925 speech, Calvin Coolidge claimed that "the chief business of the American people is business" (Bartlett 1980, 736). By that time it had become the school's primary business, too.

Ameliorating Influences

The early important influences on the construction of educational leadership came from the business arena, science, and engineering. Empirical investigation quickly became the one proper way to conduct research. Science became the guiding light in a wilderness of superstition, old wives' tales, and urban myths. Wiebe (1967) concludes that as "the bureaucratic ideal" became an intimate part of social and economic life, it transformed "yeoman into yokel" (147). In a region striving to gain a piece of the newly evolving industrial pie, the mantle of science elevated ideas to incontestable heights. Its emphasis on doing rather than thinking, on measurable products rather than more amorphous outcomes, fit hand in glove with the perceived educational needs of a remote, rural region. Schooling, done well and right, meant a ticket to a better tomorrow. Pushing for centralized services, the consolidation of community schools, and curricula patterned on what was available in towns and cities became the primary tasks of county school leaders. Its measure was in buildings constructed, enrollment and graduation rates, and accreditation.

By the mid-1920s, the deepening depression sullied the image of business. Efficiency at all costs lost its luster and strict reliance on the mathematical precision of the natural sciences loosened. John Dewey was critical of professors whose promises exceeded the possibilities of their methodologies. He led a movement to consider systematically what happened in the field, in real classrooms with real students (Curti 1974). By the 1930s, a second generation of schoolmen entered university teaching, turning to the social, rather than the natural, sciences for guidance. The work of Elton Mayo and his colleagues at the General Electric's Hawthorne Works in Illinois demonstrated in dramatic fashion the influence of groups on individual behavior. The studies ended in the early 1930s with the conclusion that human factors are important in organizational processes. Workers do the work. To focus exclusively on processes or tasks to the exclusion of the people who enact those procedures limits productivity. To improve output, a manager or administrator paid attention to both.

The human costs of the 1930s and the toll of fascism in the 1940s further stimulated a movement away from exclusive task orientation. The profession turned its attention to more democratic practices. There had always been alternative voices in the school business. Ella Flagg Young, superintendent of Chicago Schools and a friend of Dewey, emphasized the need for participatory leadership in the early 1900s. A friend of teachers, she condemned initiatives that made them "mere workers at the treadmill" (quoted in Tyack and Hansot 1982, 181). Flagg advocated democratic management practices. Margaret Haley challenged male domination of the National Education Association, at a time when the association was led by professors and superintendents. Beginning in 1920, Mary Parker Follett published a series of books on business administration that advocated a human relations approach to leadership. "One person should not give orders to another person, but both should agree to take their orders from the situation" (quoted in Pugh, Hickson, and Hinings 1964, 48). She anticipated a body of work on situational leadership influential later in the century and underscored the importance of moving from a technical approach to leadership to a human one. Follett was one of the original advocates for a "power with" rather than a "power over" administrative orientation.

In the 1930s and 1940s, new school administration scholars, like Arthur Moehlman and John Sears, grounded their work in the social sciences and the importance of settings. Moehlman particularly emphasized the role of culture in administrative behavior. Public education does not, Moehlman (1951) argued, take place in isolation. It is buffeted by cultural forces both without and within, necessitating that administrators pay attention to what they ought to do. Their actions should be congruent with democratic ideals. If Americans value democracy, then their public schools must reflect participatory values.

Following World War II, the profession entered another stage of energetic theory building, stimulated in part by the 1947 founding of the National Conference of Professors of Educational Administration (NCPEA) and the Kellogg

Foundation's sponsorship of the Cooperative Program in Educational Administration (CPEA). In the 1950s, the University Council for Educational Administration (UCEA) became an active promoter of the development of an administrative science. *Administrative Science Quarterly* popularized the new emphasis on theory and by the mid-1960s the profession circulated ideas in *Journal of Educational Administration* and the *Educational Administration Quarterly*. Begun in 1915 as the National Association of Directors of Research, the American Educational Research Association became another vehicle for discussing and disseminating administrative theories.

In 1959 Daniel Griffiths's *Administrative Theory* advocated replacing a prescience reliance on practicality with a scientific approach to theory building. After an examination of the reasons the profession rejected theory, Griffiths advocated moving leadership into the twentieth century through proper development and explication of theories. He argued that administration is found in "all human organizations." It is the process "of directing and controlling life in a social organization" through utilization of the "decision-making process in the most effective manner possible." Administrators work with and within groups, so it is behavior with and within groups that must be the focus of study and action (91).

By the end of the 1950s, there had already been one full, albeit modified, swing of the ideological pendulum. Beginning with nineteenth-century managers whose orientation was philosophical rather than scientific, the profession moved toward a technical perspective imbued with Taylorism and business rhetoric. That orientation smothered fledgling challenges by women like Young and Follett, although the idea of human relations caught organizational fire of sufficient heat to modify the language of school administration. It began to advance behaviors grounded in democratic or participatory governance. By the 1950s, the language of science once again took center stage, at least for the research community. A more human and sensitive approach to theory construction became the core of preparation programs. Normative ideals associated with men like Moehlman were replaced by elaborate descriptions of what school and district leaders did and the processes best designed for performing effectively.

A sense of the changing emphases given to senior leadership performance can be gleaned by looking at how textbooks used in the preparation of professionals construed the job. Cubberley (1922) emphasized the need for male board members who were successful businessmen. Such men are "usually wide awake, sane, and progressive; not afraid to spend money intelligently; are in the habit of depending upon experts for advice" (124). The experts to whom they turn are formally trained in the new profession of school supervision. They are men, "clean, both in person and mind," who are temperate, "honest and square," with good time-management skills, neither "flabby or weak," and "able to get things done" (137–38). Both statesmen and businessmen, Cubberley's educational administrators perform as can-do, modest, efficient members of the community.

Bolton, Cole, and Jessup (1939), writing a generation later, emphasized that no idea in public school life was "more important than that of democracy" (1). Superintendents must be aware that schools were not factories in the business of grinding out students, but institutions in the business of developing citizens. In them "all must become homogeneous in ideals, aspirations and service in a common quest for the perpetuity of this land of opportunity and freedom" (15). As chilling as that statement might be when critically examined (homogeneity as a defense of freedom?), its intent is to reorient school leaders from an emphasis on training workers to a focus on preparing students for citizenship. Superintendents lead democratically. Adopting Cubberley's statesmanship language, Bolton, Cole and Jessup decried authoritarian attitudes and practice. They emphasized building relationships and remaining open-minded to new ideas. District leaders were experts, guides, coworkers, community participants, and doers. The authors did not recommend dumping efficiency; instead, they wanted to humanize it. Their book, *The Beginning Superintendent*, contains pages upon pages of practical advice, supported by the testimonials that Griffiths and his colleagues criticized. Their arguments are also bolstered by the type of bottom-line efficiency statistics that make business managers proud.

Hagman (1951) stressed the importance of working within a democratic context. With widening expectations of schools to extend and facilitate opportunities for all students, senior educational leaders were urged to extend the roles of their institutions to include the community. Leadership cannot be imposed, but emerges from a group. Real authority cannot rest on legal or positional power, but is granted by the group. Superintendents are accountable, responsible, and moral. They are neither above nor outside the group, but a part of it. Conversely, Graff and Street (1956) illustrate the influence of Griffiths and the theory movement. Writing only five years later, they propose a competency pattern that, if adopted by leaders, enhances productivity and intelligent practice. Working with the framework of the NCPEA and CPEA, they suggest that "democratic cooperation is a slogan," not a theory (5). Noting recent attempts to capture occupational performance in mathematical formulas, they guide prospective administrators through a systematic process that leads to competence. Competent behaviors force scientific behaviors, and the individual and the organization are the better for it.

Graff and Street note that the tasks with which an administrator is concerned fall into seven domains: organization, finance and business management, student personnel, curriculum and instruction, staff personnel, facilities, and transportation. Their list is not all that different from the ones that Newlon had compiled nearly thirty years earlier. The Educational Policies Commission (1965) defined the role of district leader as "bringing out the best in community and staff" (3). The modest swing away from the science and attempted precision of systems theory and other models that came from the application of social sciences to administration towards human relations and democracy reflects the mood of a country enmeshed in several civil rights movements. A superintendent in the 1960s is "a stimulator and a cooperator, not a commander" (5). He is a "teacher, politician, philosopher, student of life, public relations counselor, and businessman" (7). He embodies the philosophy of the nineteenth-century humanists, the efficiency of business, the human relations skills of the social sciences, and the political acumen of a skilled public servant.

Blumberg (1985), himself a former superintendent, noted that what changed for administrators over the decades were the size and contentiousness of the position. District leaders "play in larger, more ill-defined, and, in many respects, quite different ball parks" from their professional colleagues in classrooms and schools (3). Sports metaphors were not the only ways that the profession remained gender-coded. Blumberg's wife contributed a chapter to his book. She wrote about her role in his career, stressing the helpmate services of the good wife. Spouses must meet community expectations about conduct and dress, too. Wives become, like their professional husbands, "public property" (184). Blumberg did capture the growing political forces that impinged upon their conduct as administrators, while retaining the masculine orientation that prompted the work of earlier colleagues.

Later texts stress the myriad of contradictory political pressures that come with the job of leading districts. Norton, Webb, Dlugosh, and Sybouts (1996), for example, include on their list of tasks at which leaders must be proficient addressing local politics, working with school boards, governance through policy development, and public relations. They join the standard list of administrative responsibilities: organizational structure, planning, legal issues, fiscal management, facilities, curriculum and instruction, and human resources. Added to the ability to function as a businessman and an educational statesman was talent at living in the midst of conflict. District leaders apply a little science, some artfulness, and strategic stagecraft to get their jobs done.

Although texts like Norton et al. remain on the market and in libraries, the profession itself has become more, not less, unsure about how to construct leadership and prepare prospective administrators for today's school districts. That does not mean that it knows less about what leaders do and how they do it; they know more. It does, however, suggest that any compromise between theories grounded in science and skills in working with people lacks consensus from the academic community. In the 1990s, as Leithwood and Drake (1999) point out, formal theorists have turned their attention to normative practice. Rather than focusing on how a leader performs, recent scholars have explored how they should act. Their concern is on the values leaders bring to, and embody on, the job. Authority comes from the strength and viability of their convictions. Moral leadership (Hodgkinson 1991), servant leadership (Greenfield and Ribbins 1993; Greenfield 1991), and symbolic leadership (Slater 1994) are approaches that are value laden. Leaders perform the principles they hold. If participation in a democratic, just society is desirable, educational leaders are advocates for marginalized and silenced voices. They promote social justice ends with democratic means. In an era in which fuzzy logic and complexity characterize not only human interactions but also the natural sciences, administrators must do more than manage. But have they the space within which to do it?

While the academic side of the educational leadership house continues to explore diverse constructions of what administrators do or should do, individuals in central offices address an often contradictory constellation of mundane and eccentric obligations. Without a coherent voice, the profession's hold on expectations has loosened everywhere but the academy. Policymakers, politicians, and businessmen are currently leading occupation construction through legislation and white papers. University experts write increasingly for each other, rather than for practitioners whose practice is again subject to external rationalization by individuals with almost unlimited faith in numbers.

Given the cacophony that seems to characterize what the profession thinks, it is no wonder that two other factors shape professional performance locally probably more than theoretical foundations discussed in college classrooms. The first is how the position is perceived by the state. What role do senior administrators have in custom, law, and regulation? The second is how the role is modeled, how people interpret their legal responsibilities at a local level. We turn to the evolution of the profession in North Carolina and a survey of how leaders in one system, Buncombe County, performed the role of public school district leader.

North Carolina's District Superintendents

Leaders hold certain standards for their performances, some of which are a function of their past experiences, innate abilities, and personal dispositions. Their families, both immediate and extended, influence who they are and what they aspire to be. Their community sets certain expectations, not simply for people in particular positions but also for people who live within its geographic boundaries. If they hope to hold professional positions, they master an accepted body of knowledge. They attend school. They spend time as interns with practitioners of the profession in which they aspire to work. If their chosen field is public education, they also learn from watching. They have been in classrooms of one sort or another since they were five years of age, first as students and then as practitioners themselves. They have seen teachers teach, principals administer, and, occasionally, senior-level administrators manage, delegate, and lead.

How teachers practice in classrooms is partially a function of the experiences they themselves have had with teachers. In spite of what educators learn in formal preparation programs, they sometimes rely on what they learned from all those years observing. Teachers teach as they were taught. That instinct holds true for first-time school leaders. They, too, return to the lessons of the real world, to the advice of a colleague or mentor, to what seemed to work when they were followers. They lead as they have been led. For that reason, we turn from the more abstract world of formal theory building and textbooks to the stage upon which our informants do their work.

Changing Expectations for County Superintendents

How did district superintendents practice in the southern mountains? As elsewhere, the superintendency, as it is now constructed, is of relatively recent origin.[10] North Carolina adopted a statewide system of common schools for white children in 1839, overseen by county boards. In 1853 it had its first state superintendent, Charles Wiley, who used his position as a bully pulpit from which to advocate for the advancement of free schooling, better teachers, libraries, teachers' organizations, and the establishment of an education journal for the state. Wiley thought of public education as a crusade, not a vocation.

The Civil War destroyed that fledgling system. The office of state superintendent was abolished from 1865–1868, then filled by a Massachusetts carpetbagger, whose assistant was the Reverend James Hood. A black man, Hood's primary duty was the supervision of services to North Carolina's African American children. During Reconstruction most white children stayed home. The legislature gave only meager resources to the reconstituted common school system. Local governance remained in the hands of local citizens. In 1872 North Carolina passed legislation authorizing the establishment of a county board of education from the old board of commissioners charged with overseeing the public schools. The legislature appointed a county examiner, whose duties included visiting schools and interviewing teachers to ensure that they met minimum levels of competence. According to Alexander McIver, then state superintendent, the first requirement for the state's educators was that they be of "good moral character" (quoted in Noble 1930, 362). Only after that criterion was met did a county official need to concern himself with the candidate's familiarity with the various branches of learning and training in the act of teaching.

When the Democrats resumed control of the state in 1877, they established the governance system in place, with occasional revisions, through 1930. Like other Southern states, it was centralized. After the legislature, at the top of the governance hierarchy was the State Board of Education. Each county also had a board of education as well as district school committees, county examiners, and teachers. Counties were divided into separate, quasi-independent districts under the direct supervision of committees, each of which had three members. Every district committee sought its own teachers and was responsible for the soundness of the local school. Districts were community-sensitive. Committees did not hesitate to appoint local residents, friends, or relatives to teacher positions. There were two countywide officials. The superintendent's responsibilities were primarily clerical while the examiner visited buildings, observed teachers, and issued licenses. Neither position was particularly powerful.

In 1881 the position of examiner was abolished and replaced with that of county superintendent. The only requirement for office was selection by a joint meeting of the county board of education and the county boards of magistrates and residency. The superintendent was now responsible for examining candidates for teaching positions and issuing appropriate teaching certificates. Superintendents were also responsible for the condition of schools. They were expected to visit them at least once a year, a not insignificant task on mountainous roads in counties with many schools. Their other obligations included fostering attendance, limiting the addition of more local districts, and encouraging the merger of districts whenever practical.

Two years later the state legislature limited the role of the county superintendent, reduced and capped his salary, and limited travel expenses. In 1885, it restored responsibilities and salary to the office. The legislature became explicit about the requirements for holding the office. Superintendents were to be "of good moral character, liberal education . . . [with] due regard being given to experience in teaching." In that same year, the county board of education assumed responsibility for the overall administration of the public schools, a responsibility shared with county commissions. The commissioners retained control over the local budget, which included the schools. So, although superintendents were charged with preparing the annual budget and local boards of education were obliged to approve it, the money did not flow until another political body also approved it. The multiple-tiered system was (and continues to be) subject to partisanship and contradictory priorities. The state also tried to bring some order to the boards themselves. They were to be elected by the justices of the peace and county commissioners biennially, reside in the county in which they worked, and "be qualified by education and experience to specially further . . . public school interests" (Noble 1930, 393). Local superintendents served three masters. They performed those duties designated by the local board; they met obligations set by the state superintendent, who was charged with implementing state school laws; and they prepared budgets acceptable to local county commissioners. Additionally, local superintendents had responsibility for two systems, one for white children and one for black children.

At the same time that legislators designed a common governance system for the state's public schools, the movement for graded schools accelerated, particularly in urban areas. During the nineteenth century, district superintendents in towns, as well as principals of town high schools, had greater status and higher salaries than did county superintendents. With a quickening of the secondary school movement, counties included both rural or county schools and town districts. County superintendents had responsibility only for the former. Status and money were more likely to accompany men working in the latter.

At the beginning of the last century, Charles B. Aycock came to the office dedicated to improving the public schools of North Carolina. Newspapers promoted education, as did local ministers from their pulpits. In 1902 a public conference adjourned after issuing a declaration against illiteracy and urging every citizen to join in a campaign to elevate the state's educational facilities. Grand juries, already responsible for inspecting county jails and homes for the indigent, were encouraged to inspect school buildings. In 1907 the state's supreme court affirmed the right of individual counties to levy supplemental taxes to state allotments. The purpose of the taxes was the improvement of schools. Between 1900 and 1910, almost 3,000 schools were added to those already in use. The office of the state superintendent became more powerful. Responsible now for regular bulletins touting progress and best practices, it established statewide communication systems ensuring that local educational leaders shared a common vocabulary and knew about successful practices elsewhere. Those bulletins served to solidify a sense of group identity among district leaders. The powers of the state superintendent to supervise what went on in schools increased, as did his staff. The academic year was lengthened, attendance made compulsory, preparation programs started at normal schools throughout the state, and provisions made to improve public high schools.

In 1917 certification of teachers became a state, rather than a district, function. That simple switch had unintended consequences. Promoted to improve the quality of teaching, to remove political partisanship from the process (certification and employment were sometimes matters of local patronage rather than merit), and to standardize credentialing, it also centralized power. Local autonomy declined, setting the stage for subsequent power shifts. A prerequisite to professionalizing education and designed to improve the quality of teachers, the costs of state licensure included the diminution of community influence. The schools became less a part of the neighborhood and more one of many state institutions.

Through midcentury, legislated changes gradually transferred more authority to Raleigh. The office and functions of the State Department of Public Instruction expanded with the adoption of consistent teacher and administrator certification requirements, development of departments of educational administration in colleges and universities, and the design of preparation program accreditation standards. Educators were now licensed practitioners, certified experts in their fields. The state superintendent became a member of the governor's cabinet. He was now an elected rather than appointed official, giving him some independence from the governor's office and the legislature. State superintendents ran on particular platforms. Their elections, they claimed, represented popular approval of the directions they believed that education should take. Yet they, too, were always subject to policies determined by the State Board of Education and laws passed by the legislature. They never controlled the size of their budget. Because the electoral clout of the mountain counties is a faint shadow of the number of votes available in the piedmont and coastal counties, state policies popular elsewhere became, independent of local aspirations and desires, required policies in the uplands.

The legislature abolished all but grandfathered town and city districts in counties. It provided financial incentives to the remaining charter systems to merge.[11] With that change, the role and status of county superintendents increased. They now oversaw consolidated units without district trustees (their positions were abolished) and separate urban systems. Gradually, more students attended more months of school, so that by the 1950s twelve grades of public education were available to all North Carolina children, who were required to be in attendance at least through the age of sixteen. By the 1950s, what had once been a position of dubious influence and limited power had become, for many counties, the top education job. In the southern mountains, by 1952, nine districts were countywide. The exceptions were Buncombe, Cherokee, Haywood, Henderson, McDowell, and Polk Counties. They each retained town districts.[12] All of them were gone by 1990 except Asheville and Hendersonville, the two largest towns in the region. Only Asheville remains today.

By the 1920s and 1930s, good roads legislation, the country life movement, and school mergers changed the nature of rural districts. Scattered one-room schools closed, replaced by newer, much larger, centrally located, consolidated schools. The county superintendent's office reflected the growing complexity and expectations that the state and its citizens had for public education. The introduction and expansion of vocational education meant someone was needed to direct that program. By the 1940s, baby boomers crowded into classrooms, precipitating a building boom. The 1950s comprehensive high school movement put pressure on districts to centralize secondary education.[13] Merging smaller, community schools into larger ones also centralized administrative power. Responsibility for getting children to their classrooms, for housing them in safe and inviting physical environments, and providing them with decent meals during school hours meant even more duties fell to the county superintendent. In the aftermath of the successful launching of Sputnik came a spate of educational reforms. Responsibility for consistent implementation fell to the superintendent's office, which expanded its curriculum and instruction functions. School desegregation began, albeit slowly, eliminating the state's old dual systems. The central office oversaw the enforcement of court orders and preparation of students and staff for the end of segregation. By the late 1960s, expanding services for students with special needs necessitated oversight of that program. Title IX extended athletic programs to women, swelling sports schedules and increasing the need for supervision in that arena. Central office staffs increased in number and responsibilities. County school districts came to resemble corporate headquarters, with centralized planning and oversight in one location and actual production in scattered, albeit large, other locations.

By the end of the administration of Governor Terry Sanford (1961–1965), most schools were under the supervision of a county superintendent who met state-designated licensure standards based on successful completion of approved preparation programs. They were Carolina men whose professional profiles corresponded roughly to national norms. From rural or small towns, married, white, middle-aged, Protestant and church-going, moderately conservative in outlook and politics, former teachers, often coaches, routinely principals, and in large systems central office assistant or associate superintendents, they were the local educational experts toward which professors like Ellwood Cubberley and George Strayer had begun to move the profession at the beginning of the twentieth century. Although there were only one or two women in superintendencies from the early 1950s through the late 1980s, beginning in 1966 there were a string of years in which no female headed a school district.

National and state administration organizations were vehicles that brought together senior-level school leaders to exchange information, discuss issues, and issue reports on the state of their profession. Administrators throughout the state slowly built a collective identity, a sense of themselves as a group. They recommended colleagues for jobs, traded information about teachers, and occasionally shared resources. In North Carolina, professional affiliation was reinforced by regular statewide and regional meetings sponsored by the state's Department of Public Instruction. The five-term, activist administration of one of their own, Craig Phillips, state superintendent from 1968 to 1988, created a powerful central bureaucracy at the state level that pushed for greater standardization of schools, schooling, and personnel. His administration represents the heyday of the county superintendency in North Carolina.

By the late 1970s and early 1980s, professional organizations solidified membership and purpose. They became adept at lobbying, advocating for their particular slice of the educational budget and the interests of the people they represented. Superintendent mobility increased. Rather than staying in one county throughout a career, or at least in one region, small county systems became stepping stones to larger districts. Size was correlated to salary. Not only would a superintendent's pay increase on the state scale but larger districts also had the tax base to enrich the compensation package with salary supplements and fringe benefits. Like business executives, who migrated from one company to another as they gained more experience, central office leaders began to travel. Perceived expertise and past experience within an organization were considered more important in some places than local roots. It was during this period that most of our study's informants came of age professionally.

The southern mountain counties have yet to experience the same degree of professional mobility that occurs downstate. By the early 1980s, though, a few upwardly mobile administrators looked to the west for starter superintendencies. For a brief period of time Polk County seemed particularly amenable to outsider candidates. Three downstate district leaders got their start or spent a portion of their career there. Central office strivers usually moved from small to larger systems and from rural to more urban districts. In North Carolina they also went from the mountains or coastal plains to center of the state. Downstate superintendents rarely left districts there for the uplands. For mobile district leaders, mountain counties were where one began a career, not where one finished it. That trend changed somewhat in the 1990s. A Durham County superintendent moved to Buncombe County. The superintendent of Orange County came to Henderson. The Guilford County superintendent moved briefly to Asheville. More recently, there has been mobility among superintendencies in South and North Carolina affecting mountain districts. In our sample was the head of the state education agency in Mississippi, now a county superintendent in the Carolina uplands.

For a longer time, there has been some internal or regional mobility. Sometimes at the assistant or associate ranks an administrator will move from county to county in the same position (Henderson to Polk), from a subordinate role to the head position in a neighboring county (Clay to Graham), and from superintending one rural system to another in the same area (Haywood to Jackson). Again, it was less mobility than one finds in more the populous systems downstate. Most local administrator aspirants stay home, working their ways up local ranks and biding their time. That trend provides a measure of stability, knowledge of the place and its people, and connections to regional networks. At the same time it reinforces existing ideas about schools and schooling and it takes a long time for certain administrative positions to open.

System leaders led within legislated and customary boundaries. By the mid-1960s senior educational leaders were, at least in North Carolina, well positioned to exercise authority. The superintendency had grown into an influential office with a myriad of responsibilities and challenges. In small and/or rural systems it was filled disproportionately with sly good ol' boys. Well educated by state standards, they hid their book learning behind a veneer of back slapping, jokes, and sports stories when it served their purposes. Often a politician or a newcomer to education politics would misconstrue their aw-shucks demeanor as a sign of timidity, and a lack of intellectual depth, only to lose more than a battle or two. These were men who used their perceived lack of guile with remarkable shrewdness. They knew the territory and they knew each other. They had coached together or on opposing sides of a sports field, ascended similar local leadership ladders, worked collaboratively in professional organizations, gathered together for meetings, and often attended the same graduate school classes. They wore ties, played golf, were North Carolinians, stayed close to home in seeking jobs, joined the Rotary Club or the Lions, rarely missed Friday night football games at a local high school, hired men to run their schools, and paid particular attention to facilities, finance, high schools, desegregation, and local legislators.[14]

Yet by the late 1970s their ascendancy was starting to change. The cohesiveness that Craig Phillips had nurtured began to fray. Large systems, both county and city, recruited superintendent candidates from outside the state. Mobility for all administrator ranks increased. Senior-leader loyalty transitioned from a place to a profession. African Americans served as principals in desegregated schools. Some of them moved into upper-level administrative positions locally, at the state level, and within professional organizations. Educational administration programs became larger, added doctoral degrees, and recruited faculty known more for their research skills rather than for their experience in public schools. Women moved into elementary school principalships; a few secured secondary school principalships. There were more women in central offices, particularly in food services, special education, elementary education, and curriculum.

By the 1980s, political changes foreshadowed alterations in school governance. Phillips presided over a confederacy of county and city systems. He built a centralized service center at the Department of Public Instruction (DPI) and started outreach programs at regional centers. The department provided staff development programs, curriculum consultation, and model curricula. It oversaw accreditation of teacher and administrator preparation programs. DPI issued licenses for certified personnel. Although Phillips transformed the state superintendency into a politically powerful office and his department into a large, comprehensive bureaucracy, district-level leadership retained considerable autonomy.

In the wake of the 1983 Bell Commission report, politicians scrambled aboard education reform bandwagons, criticized school efficiency and effectiveness, and hunted for villains. When duplicitous scoundrels proved in short supply, they looked for scapegoats. Bureaucrats were particularly subject to political scrutiny. To create the lithe and lean educational machines that state educational woes appeared to need, political leaders looked for places to trim budgets and send more money to schools. In North Carolina, they began to replace the loose confederation of local systems served and supervised by DPI. In its place was a smaller, increasingly less powerful state department; a gradually more activist state board; a politically divisive legislature; a divided professional education community; and a general demand for greater accountability.

Recession limited funds. Richard Nixon's southern strategy began to take hold, creating viable two-party systems in what had been a solidly Democratic South. Power migrated toward Republicans. They were disinclined to spend money on state programs, less receptive to teacher organizations, often attuned to the wishes of the business community, and allied with social conservatives. North Carolina elected a Republican governor in 1984, beginning a period of ideological realignment. Democrat Terry Sanford, a friend of education, lost his Senate seat. Republicans gained seats in the state legislature and picked up slots in the state's federal delegation. Accountability entered educational debates and alliances alternated, as teacher and administrator groups split over funding priorities.

As a result of fiscal necessity, then ideological purity, control over professional practice gradually moved from practitioners to policymakers. The Department of Public Instruction saw its budget cut repeatedly. Its staff was reduced. Regional centers disappeared or were supported by regional coalitions. Money for professional development reverted to local districts. Policies regarding curriculum and testing that once provided local latitude became more prescriptive. Minimum competency tests for high school graduation morphed into a comprehensive testing program that included state-determined gateway scores for promotion at certain grades. Tests originally designed to provide teacher feedback about student mastery became high school final exams factored into course grades. Local autonomy existed in determining how one met narrowly defined goals, but there was scant negotiation space about the goals, the indicators of mastery, the curriculum and its sequence, and the resources available.

At the beginning of the twenty-first century, access to district-level leadership positions is no longer restricted to candidates who have completed professional preparation programs. The legislature provides a loophole for local school boards that want to reach outside the profession's box for someone to lead their district. Although no system has exercised that option, it signals a temporary end to confidence in professional credentials, at least in the field of public education. Tenure for principals no longer exists. If test scores for a particular school are too low (if it fails to meet production goals), then its leader can handily be replaced. Job security increasingly rests on student performance, driving a system of test preparation and narrowed focus on a standardized curriculum. The annual report cards issued by the state on the basis of test performance and other outcome indicators, such as measures of safety and attendance, generate public recriminations or applause.

Weber's bureaucratic cage is wrapped tight around Carolinians in educational organizations. Today, local leaders exercise authority within confined and generic space. Ironically, as governance moves from practitioner expertise toward noneducator policymakers allied with business interests, the individuals who enter the profession are more likely to be experts. The superintendency was initially a position of limited authority. It became, with consolidation and legislated policies, one of local autonomy and power. Once a political patronage reward, it was transformed over time into the position of chief education officer. Expectations of who should do it evolved from moral males to technical experts. Currently, circumstances are altering the role again. The superintendency is less the job of a professional able to exercise judgment and more the job of a technician able to follow a policy manual. Education is not the only publicly sponsored arena to lose practitioner power to nonexpert politicians. Compulsory sentencing laws, for example, limit a judge's ability to judge. As its power diminishes, the superintendency becomes less attractive a position at the very time the people ready to enter it are the most formally prepared prospective leaders that we have had.

Buncombe County, 1881–1935

Of all the socialization influences on practitioners, probably none is more powerful than local exemplars of what one hopes to practice. To understand how North Carolina Appalachians enacted district leadership roles, we turned to a case study of the superintendency in one district. We selected Buncombe

County for its size (the largest system in the region),[15] for its central location (close to most of the region's counties), for its demographic and cultural fluidity (contains Asheville), and the likelihood that leaders therein would exercise a disproportionate influence on surrounding systems. We looked at the superintendency only through 1969, by which time most of our sample had launched their professional careers and a model for superintendent behavior was set.

In Leonard Miller's 1965 history of Buncombe County schools, there are photographs of the first fourteen county system superintendents. With one exception they are male. The first eight, serving various terms from 1881 to 1905, look appropriately stern. They are, their portraits suggest, serious men. Four look directly back at the camera, four glance slightly off to the side. Each of them, as was the fashion of the day, appears with a mustache, beard, or both. Three wear wire-rimmed glasses. All of them are dressed in dark suits, white shirts, and ties.

When the Reverend James Atkins was appointed county superintendent in 1881, there were seventy-two white and sixteen "colored" school districts in the county. Three local committeemen governed each district. The system was not so much a system as a ragtag collection of small, rural schools. There were 264 supervisors, none of whom had to be versed in education. Indeed, none of them had to be literate. Teachers, often neighbors or relatives of committeemen, were usually young women responsible for presenting a basic set of reading, writing, and arithmetic skills to a class of multiage students. When the fourteenth superintendent left office not quite ninety years later, there was a single board of education responsible for a centralized, multifaceted, regionally accredited organization administered by a professionally credentialed hierarchy of educators. Of the last six superintendents that Miller profiled, there is, in addition to an absence of facial hair, a more congenial appearance and, on the faces of five of them, a smile.

Only a few of the first superintendents were professional educators. The Buncombe County superintendency was a political appointment granted to a middle-aged, white, male community member who had some knowledge about the place and schooling. His strongest credential was a reputation for moral rectitude. Education was rarely the profession for which he trained nor was it his only job. The first eight superintendents, those bewhiskered men, served terms of relatively short duration. With the exception of Julius Martin, who served less than one month, their average tenure was slightly more than three years of service. The normal contract term was two years. Again with the exception of Martin, these men served variations of that (one for six years, three for four years, and three for two years). Martin marks a turning point in access qualifications. He was chair of the county board of education when he was named to the superintendency and he held the position only until the first of the modern superintendents, A. C. Reynolds, accepted the office. Before Martin, county leaders were gentlemen superintendents; after him, they were professional experts.

Of the first eight district leaders, two were born in another state and at least three others were born elsewhere in North Carolina. The backcountry of North Carolina was relatively sparsely populated compared to downstate sections. It was still a beginner's place, an area where a man might move and make his way. Because the county seat, Asheville, was a tourist and health destination, Buncombe had more demographic mobility than that found in more rural and remote counties in the region. All of the first eight superintendents were Southerners. Three of them had Civil War experience. Of the one about whom there is no birth record, there is ample evidence that he had been in the county for some time and was familiar with its schools. The last six district leaders were closely linked to Carolina's mountains. Three were born in the county, two in neighboring counties, and only the one with the shortest tenure remains a cipher in terms of place of birth. Being from elsewhere became a disadvantage.

Among the first eight superintendents were a minister, a merchant, two lawyers and a law student, two engineers who did surveying, and a lumber mill owner. Buncombe's first superintendent was more a religious leader than a school administrator. A Methodist minister and graduate of Emory and Henry College, James Atkins came into the Carolina mountains from Tennessee to preach. In 1879 he was made president of Asheville Female College, a role he continued to perform while overseeing the public schools. He was appointed county superintendent in 1881. Atkins became president of his alma mater, Emory and Henry, in 1889 and moved to Virginia. In 1894 he was back leading Asheville Female College for two years. Atkins then moved away from the mountains to pursue Sunday School publications and ministerial work, originating the Bible Teachers Sunday School. He epitomized the typical nineteenth-century combination of churchman and entrepreneurial educator.

John Starnes (1883–89) spent several years teaching and serving as a principal, both in public and private schools. He saw the wisdom of affiliation with professional colleagues and was an early leader of the North Carolina Teachers' Assembly, serving as its second president. Charles Way (1889–93), born a Mississippian, moved to Texas in the antebellum period. He came to Asheville in 1889 for his health. A lawyer, former legislator, and judge in Texas, his ascent to the county superintendency came within a year of his move to Asheville. Way's appointment attests to the relatively low status associated with the post, its usefulness as an initial step on local political ladders, and his ability to make the right connections rapidly. Within a short time he moved on, holding other county appointments, and eventually securing a judgeship.

Andrew Felmet (1893–97), another Methodist who "served his church with ardent fervor and gave liberally to all worthy causes," added the position to his long list of civic contributions. Although it was not his only source of income, he did have teaching experience, "changing from time to time to various schools in the county" (Miller 1965, 121). The owner of a lumber mill, he was at one time a tax collector and the Asheville treasurer. Like Way, Felmet's tenure as superintendent was one of several local political appointments he held in the county. David Ellis (1897–99) was the first Peabody graduate of the group. A man specifically trained to be an educator, he taught and served as principal in various schools in Tennessee, North Carolina, and Florida. His two-year term in the middle of fifty-two years of educational experience is further testimony to the dubious status of the job. Samuel Venable (1899–1903) was a church elder, an engineer, and a sometimes teacher in a private academy. He died in April 1903. His absence did not hasten board deliberations about a replacement. The system went for three months without a superintendent, not hiring his replacement until July.

James Reagan took Venable's place in 1903 for a two-year term. A Buncombe County native, he earned his degrees from Weaverville College, where he taught mathematics for twenty-five years, including the time that he superintended the Buncombe County Schools.[16] Once his tenure as superintendent ended, Reagan moved into civil engineering and surveying, which he pursued for the next three decades with only occasional stints as a teacher of mathematics. In 1905 he was followed by the school board chair, Julius Martin, a lawyer and local politician. Martin held the position for only two weeks, before surrendering it to Reynolds and a new set of system administrators.

These early superintendents had in common a Protestant faith, a reputation as men of the community, political friends in high places, at least a casual interest in education, and other vocational pursuits in which they occasionally engaged at the very time they were working as a district superintendent. They had sufficient business acumen to work within the constraints of a decentralized, erratically funded, disparate, and diverse system of schools. They fought or were loyal to the "right" side during the Civil War. The tasks they did fit under the category of "good works" as much as they did "education." They were not visionaries, but men who followed patterns established in tradition, local custom, and the politics of state education that began with the election of Charles Aycock. They were there to ensure that money was not misspent, that schools opened and closed on time, that they were staffed with warm and hopefully competent bodies, and that there were sufficient buildings in which to house students. Their chief qualifications for their positions came "not so much by professional training as by church membership and a shared earnestness" (Tyack 1976, 258). Their administrative tasks were vaguely and variously defined as the job waxed and waned in legislated importance. Their mission was more distinct: to ensure the moral uplift of local children.

The biographies of the second generation of district leaders were relatively alike. Their roles, qualifications for performing them, and educational mission reflected changing times. They were not active, independent agents pushing communities toward some ideal good, but self-aware professionals, socialized through training and practice to view themselves as managers of complex organizations. Robert Wiebe (1967) describes the adoption of a "bureaucratic orientation" as the transition from "essences to actions" (148). Educational leaders began to tame a sometimes discordant, decentralized, chaotic set of schools operating within the same county lines into a coherent single system. They became less the moral aristocrat and more the rational bureaucrat.

In 1905, when A. C. Reynolds moved from the presidency of Rutherford College to the superintendency of the Buncombe County Schools, there were 103 schools in the district, of which 95 were one-room and the rest two-room structures. Ten of them included instruction in high school subjects. No student was enrolled in the last grade of high school. Of the total student enrollment of 7,698, only 2,244 students were promoted to the next grade. His primary task was changing those statistics. He wanted fewer, but bigger, schools serving more students. Reynolds also wanted students staying longer in schools and he wanted more young people to graduate from high school.

A Buncombe County native, Reynolds attended local schools, then earned an undergraduate degree at Peabody College. A teacher in the county from the age of eighteen, after graduating from Peabody, he became principal of Camp Academy. In 1901 Reynolds left the county for the presidency of Rutherford College. In 1902, he was elected superintendent of Burke County Schools, where the college was located, and worked both jobs until 1905. At that time, the head of the Asheville *Citizen-Times* encouraged him to apply for the newly opened superintendency in his home county. His first tenure in that position lasted eight years and brought stability to the post.

Reynolds made education his career. It was the focus of his college education and it encompassed more than an occasional job paired with other vocational pursuits. From his first superintendency in Buncombe, he traveled to Jackson County where he served as president of Cullowhee Normal and Industrial School. He then became superintendent of Haywood County Schools. After a brief tenure as a high school principal (1924–26), he began his second term in Buncombe. It lasted from 1926 to 1933. Reynolds left that position for the presidency of Biltmore College from which he retired in 1936.

He was persuaded to come out of retirement to help the local public schools, ending his career with two more high school principalships.

The ease with which he slipped in and out of county superintendencies, sometimes while holding another position, indicates the limited responsibilities of the office. Its prestige and that of small, regional colleges were relatively on par through the early 1930s, testimony to the lowly estate of the colleges more than the elevated state of county schools. High school principalships, particularly of larger secondary schools, were considered as important a role until the 1950s when consolidation changed power dynamics. A doctorate or advanced degree was not yet a prerequisite for work either at the college or the county level, nor were specific administrator credentials and training required for leadership positions. The boundaries among various school positions and levels were relatively permeable, particularly in the South, which was playing educational catch-up with the rest of the nation. Prior to Reynolds, county superintendents usually had some college preparation, an inclination toward the profession, the right character, and connections. During the Reynolds period, though, that compass shifted.

Like his predecessors, Reynolds was a churchman. An Asheville editorialist found him a "rugged, strong-willed and persevering" man. He was a "teacher, builder and Christian." The Asheville *Citizen*, keeping the Civil War as a marker of approbation, likened him to Robert E. Lee. He was a warrior for schooling. In character, he had much in common with his predecessors (Miller 1965, 126). He was, like most system leaders of the period, a practitioner who administered schools in the state of his birth. He was white, male, and Protestant, a son of rural America whose beliefs mirrored those of the Southern Appalachian communities in which he worked.[17]

In his first term in office Reynolds campaigned for and got tax increases in many of his local districts. With that money, the county funded additional months of schooling, built better facilities, and improved the curriculum. During his tenure, Reynolds convinced the county board to champion secondary education and he established several high schools in the county. Additionally, he provided the beginning of educational consistency throughout the county through summer teacher-training programs. In 1912 he expanded his central office staff by adding the position of business manager. Reynolds believed that his duties included rallying the public to the cause of formal education. Usually reserving Mondays for paperwork and meetings, he spent the rest of the week touring the county and visiting schools. When far from home, a none too unusual occurrence given the conditions of travel at the time, he stayed the night with community patrons, urging them over dinner to support longer academic years, more proficient teachers, and better provisioned buildings. When he first left the office of superintendent, there were still over 100 schools, few students reached high school, the length of terms varied, and absenteeism continued to be a problem.

However, Reynolds readied the audience for the next superintendent, William Handy Hipps, who began his six years as district head in 1913. Mountain-born, although in Madison County, immediately north of Buncombe, Hipps grew up on a farm. The son of a Baptist minister, he attended Baptist-sponsored Mars Hill Academy and graduated from another Baptist school, Wake Forest. After completing a law degree there, he returned to the mountains as principal of a Buncombe County high school before accepting the position of principal of Asheville's Biltmore High School. A joiner, he associated with local civic and business leaders in organizations like the Rotary Club. At the age of twenty-seven, he was selected as county superintendent and aggressively built upon Reynolds' work.

Hipps raised local tax support for county schools, oversaw the addition of high schools, increased the number of teachers employed, and expanded by nearly a factor of five the tax valuation of school property. He pushed for a longer school term, fewer local districts, more oversight of teaching, and better buildings. During his tenure the system's first attendance officer was hired. He initiated efforts to secure transportation for students, a prerequisite for continued consolidation. Hipps set up a regular summer program for county teachers in collaboration with Asheville Normal School. During his administration the school system began a comprehensive adult education program that eventually received national attention and started a formal vocational education initiative. Central office staff increased to include a rural supervisor and a director of the countywide literacy program. Although reappointed for a fourth two-year term, Hipps resigned to accept the superintendency of Johnston County. He left education in 1922 at the age of thirty-seven, returning to Buncombe County to practice law and engage in civic work both there and in Madison County. He was the last Buncombe County superintendent to leave education midcareer in something unaffiliated with schooling.

When Hipps resigned, the board had difficulty filling his unexpired term and turned not to a local man, but to someone whose work and family they knew well—the county's rural supervisor. What made the selection unusual was that the supervisor was, as were many people in that position, a female. The first and so far the only female to serve as Buncombe County superintendent, Ethel Terrell was the daughter of a Methodist minister. Born in Cherokee County, she graduated from a Methodist college, Davenport, in 1906. Over the course of the next thirteen years, Terrell completed additional coursework at the University of Tennessee, the North Carolina College for Women in Greensboro, and the University of North Carolina. Well educated for the time, single, familiar with the county and the district's schools, she had occupied the county supervisor position a scant three months when she was tapped to be its superintendent. She was touted as "the first woman south of the Mason-Dixon line to become superintendent of a public school system" (Asheville *Times*, 2 April 1969, 14). Terrell's selection was not without precedent in the region. Although no female had headed a public school district, there were several women who led educational enterprises in the region.

Given the direction in which county schools were moving (from decentralized, poorly funded, understaffed, and locally governed to a more centralized system with a fledgling bureaucracy) and the aggressive work of Hipps, the selection of a woman might be construed as a signal that gender was no longer a criterion for ascension to positions of educational power. However, the way in which the selection was made suggests a temporary lull in the modernization of the system itself, rather than a change in direction and a scattering of early twentieth-century glass ceilings. The board did not even consult Terrell before making its choice, indicating that they were confident that she would accept the position. The board, all male, that chose Terrell was not new. They had been together since 1913, had approved Terrell's hire as supervisor, and were comfortable working with her. Although she was invited to accept a second term, she declined, leaving the profession to marry.

Frank Wells, another Buncombe County native and University of North Carolina graduate, succeeded her. Wells, who held a master's degree from Columbia and a doctorate from the University of Iowa, was a college mathematics teacher at the time of his appointment. In 1925 three new members, a majority, joined the board of education and, as a result of political infighting, Wells was replaced by another former college teacher, W. C. Murphy. The following year, Murphy left the superintendency, resigning to accept a position in Kentucky. The period from 1919 to 1926 was one of instability, limited superintendent autonomy, and political factionalism for the county schools. After Terrell's resignation, the system drifted. That ended in 1926, when Reynolds was asked once again to become Buncombe County's superintendent.

Reynold's return to the position marked the beginning of a sustained consolidation of power in central office administration. Reynolds now had four employees working directly with him in a central office: a secretary, a business manager, a bookkeeper, and an elementary school supervisor. Also working out of that office was the director of the adult literacy program. Reynolds added a high school supervisor before the economic reverses of the Depression slowed the pace of educational change. Only the positions of business manager and superintendent were occupied by males.

In 1933 Reynolds accepted the leadership of Biltmore College and the board brought back the previously deposed Frank Wells. Perhaps distressed at the ambitious agenda of the county board during a period of hard economic times, Wells left office abruptly in 1934 to accept a college position. He was replaced by T. C. Roberson, arguably the first man to view the superintendency as the culmination of a professional career. He served in that capacity for thirty-five years, becoming a regional mentor for men who followed in his footsteps in neighboring counties.

A Modern Mountaineer Superintendent

Thomas Crawford (T. C.) Roberson was the longest serving superintendent of the region's largest school district, Buncombe County. Because of his tenure, the location of the system he oversaw, his work with other area schools and school districts, and his position as a state leader, Roberson served as a model for what communities expected of their top educational leaders. He exemplified who they were and how they did their jobs.[18]

Born in 1901 in the town of Candler, located several miles to the southwest of Asheville in the community of Hominy Valley, he was descended from early settlers on both sides of the family. His roots ran deep, as did his loyalty. As his wife noted, he "lived his entire life in Buncombe County except for time spent in colleges elsewhere" (Roberson 1969, 1). Roberson's father farmed, but had also kept a subscription school during the winter.

Educated locally, Roberson's first collegiate experience was at Western Carolina Teachers College. He served briefly as principal of South Hominy School for a year. Continuing his education during the summers at teacher institutes, he eventually completed an undergraduate degree at George Peabody College in Nashville in 1927. Roberson also took administration graduate courses there and later at Columbia's Teachers College.

Completion of a degree at Peabody led to the principalship of Sandy Mush High School. He then went to French Broad High School as principal and, in 1932, returned to Peabody for advanced study. In 1933 he oversaw Flat Rock High School. The next year he started at Woodfin High, located to the north of Asheville. That December, after eight years of school experience in the county and five principalships, he was asked by the Buncombe County Board of Education to serve as interim superintendent. He was appointed to a regular two-year term by the board in May of 1935 and remained the district's superintendent until 1969.

European American, male, locally born, raised, and educated, Roberson epitomized the qualities that the region's school boards sought. They knew him and "his people," were familiar with his work, and believed his service in several schools ensured the goodwill of people throughout the district. His college career was safely predictable—an introduction at the local teacher's college, summer programs for educators at Asheville Normal and the university at Chapel Hill, and time in Nashville at Peabody, the training ground for many upwardly mobile Appalachian schoolmen. He was married, had two children, was an active churchman (Methodist), and engaged in a number of community civic projects. An ally of local businessmen, he served as a member of the Asheville Chamber of Commerce from 1955 until his retirement.

Roberson became superintendent during the Depression. His tenure included coping with hard economic times, a world war, the Korean conflict, the McCarthy period, the early part of the Cold War, an energetic period of educational centralization, and the beginning of desegregation. Miller (1965), summarizing Roberson's achievements, focused on growth, buildings, finance, and organization. Roberson led successful building drives, the consolidation of local tax districts, and the construction of six comprehensive high schools. Forty-five elementary schools were reduced to twenty-seven, each with new or improved facilities. School enrollment more than doubled during his time in office. He was a pioneer in regional accreditation. By the time he left the superintendency, all county schools met that standard. The district was poised in 1969 to move from the elementary-secondary (8–4) grade model to today's most commonly found organization scheme, 6–3–3.

The aspects of district supervision to which Roberson devoted the majority of his time were the recognized stuff of progress. There were more buildings and they got bigger. There were better ways to finance schooling and they became more predictable and systematic. The district established and operated a growing transportation system. It created a comprehensive, efficient cafeteria system. The central office increased in personnel and expanded in purpose. Modern educational administration was business gone to school. Roberson mastered its techniques, language, and priorities.

He became part of the budding network of educational leaders who helped shepherd the state's rural districts from local governance and community-based, multigrade schooling into a Southern variation of "one-best system." He was not simply the Buncombe County Schools organization man, but a state one as well. For instance, he was president of the state association's Division of Superintendents in 1942–43, a life member of the National Education Association as well as the state affiliate, a member of the American Association of School Administrators, and a member of the State Superintendent's Policy Board from 1962–1968. A regional leader, Roberson served as president of the North Carolina Western District for the state's education association in 1937–38 and of the region's Division of Superintendents from 1961–62. He oversaw state level system survey committees in Jackson, Haywood, Graham, McDowell, Polk, Transylvania, Yancey, and Mitchell Counties.

Roberson represents the convergence of local expectations and professional evolution. He embodied the characteristics of a trained practitioner. He had competent organizational skills enacted with a sense of firmness and moral rectitude in tune with the temper of his place and time. On the occasion of his retirement, friends and colleagues wrote memorials, eventually collected as part of that celebration. Complimentary, they were rarely warm.

Roberson was a "scrapper" for what he felt was right and "unusually shrewd" at surrounding himself with loyal, competent followers (Roberson 1969, 80). He was repeatedly lauded for his "good management," particularly in times when the money ran low (81). He had a "keen business sense" (103). A local commission member recounted how Roberson was able to get "more mileage from a dollar bill than any school administrator in the nation" (109). William Friday, influential president of the University of North Carolina, noted that he was "an extraordinarily adroit administrator" (91).

According to the superintendent of Macon County, he handled problems "with the grace of a fencer, the tenacity of a bulldog, and the strength of a gladiator" (82). He was a "'solid-as-a-rock' professional" (112). Roberson was "a man of strong professional convictions" and had "the courage to act on them" (84). Endowed with "rugged honesty" (98), he had been a fearless and aggressive advocate for education. Although placed in difficult circumstances, "he never lost his sense of humor" (99). He used "common sense" when tackling problems (103).

There is also an element of the democratic leader in Roberson. For example, he had a reputation for being accessible. "He was willing to listen to principals, teachers, and students" (99). "His office was always open to any who wanted to discuss even the smallest problem" (103). Yet, as one contributor recalls, "while he always courteously listened to his critics with an attentive ear, he persistently pursued undaunted and unafraid, the course he believed to be in the best interest and general welfare of the children and youth of Buncombe County." A former Buncombe County principal wrote that Roberson "welcomes advice given in the right spirit. He does not always take the advice, but makes his own decisions. He has great determination, which his critics (he has some) call stubbornness" (119). Like the kindly family leader in the 1950s television program *Father Knows Best,* Roberson reserved final decisions for himself. As if to confirm that judgment, an attendance counselor noted that "he was . . . stubborn at times, when the occasion demanded that he be so" (113).

Roberson was also a man of faith. He "made a great contribution to the religious . . . life of our county." He "contributed a moral leadership that is inestimable" (85). He had a "deep interest in the religious welfare of all the children" and "a fine Christian character" (89–90). "His faithfulness to his church," recalls his pastor, was "beyond the call of the ordinary." He coupled his desire to advance young people academically with a desire to advance them spiritually (105). He "lived his life clean and wholesome" (106).

Certain themes emerge from those memorials, in tone, in the achievements the authors cite, and in the words they elect to use. Roberson is courageous, energetic, and industrious. He gets things done, particularly things that one can touch and feel. Roberson builds—buildings, new classrooms, transportation systems, cafeterias, budgets, enrollment and attendance figures. He is a man of determination and conviction. He will listen to others, but he knows his own mind and it is that conviction upon which he acts. As a female instructional assistant concluded, Roberson had "withstood the storms which have blown about him as only a true mountaineer educator can." He moved the system forward "in spite of all opposing gusts," by his "steadfastness" (120).

The picture is one of a manly man leavened with the right dose of Protestant grace and democratic practice. Back in 1934, when the Buncombe County Board of Education was faced with an unanticipated superintendency vacancy and asked Roberson to accept an interim appointment, one of his predecessors, A. C. Reynolds, then head of Asheville-Biltmore College, noted that the system should be in the hands "of a strong young man" (30). Increasingly, it was to such young men that the school districts of Carolina's southern mountains were entrusted. Like Roberson, they were white, Anglo-Saxon, Protestant strivers—local boys made good, with college educations and deeply held traditional values that included a belief in helping rural children receive the benefits of a good education.

To Be a Superintendent

To be a mountain superintendent in the Southern Appalachians before the 1980s, candidates would do well to be:

1. male, although as we will note later that dynamic has changed over the past decade;
2. a manly man, by which we mean someone who administers with a sense of definitiveness, who is forceful in defense of his ideals, who knows his own mind, who is not afraid to share his opinions, and who is unafraid to act on them;
3. a native or, at least, someone from the region who is familiar with local customs, comfortable around mountaineers, from a rural community with an appreciation for the land;
4. a friend of businessmen, many of whom served on school boards, supported consolidation and a move toward comprehensive high schools, assisted with

literacy campaigns, and championed the idea that progress for country people meant making the countryside and its schools like the city;

5. at ease with professional colleagues, school-level administrators, and community patrons, almost all of whom were male, as well as able to work with subordinates who were almost all female; in other words, able to be a colleague with men and a supervisor with women;
6. practical, good with construction projects, able to work with local legislators, with a talent for completing visible, big projects;
7. frugal, parsimonious almost to a fault, able to stretch dollars, and emphasize efficiencies; someone with good business sense;
8. white, Protestant, married with children and a stay-at-home wife, an active churchgoer who lives a public life as a moral exemplar;
9. well connected politically, with sufficient sensitivity to changing political winds to make strategic shifts; and
10. increasing with specific education and experience in educational administration.

The Cover Story

The cover we chose for this book is a photograph taken of Qualla School, located in Jackson County. Built by Charlie Weels in the early 1920s, it shows a line-up of nineteen men and boys (perhaps, one lone woman) standing in front of a large, wooden, two-storied, graded school (Magers 1987). The time is winter; there is a light covering of snow on the ground and the roof. The building is not yet ready for occupancy. As physical plants go, Qualla School was about as fancy as it got in that part of the mountains. Located in a place that held money close, had few sources of county income, honored temperance in most things (including public spending), and was cautious about putting on airs, the building bespeaks the position that formal schooling had come to hold in the lives of local citizens. The majestic windows, the spaciousness of the top floors, discernible through a set of back windows, and the appointments by and above the door are unnecessary touches. Generally, schools in the uplands were austere. They were simple, utilitarian buildings of rough-hewn logs or clapboards enclosing a single room. Qualla School, by comparison, is an academic temple.

When we first looked at the photograph we imagined the men dwarfed by an ideal. A school this noble is a statement of promise, a pledge that learning will shine as brightly as the sun in the building's rooms. By their stance, the men in the photograph declare that they built this monument to their hopefulness. They are filled with the sense of accomplishment that motivated

Shelley's Ozymandias. Like the statue left to the sands of time in an Egyptian desert, Qualla School's promise shrank over time to human size. The school is gone, replaced by larger, less elegant buildings located outside this township. The men who gathered together on the grounds are probably all gone, too. But at that moment, they stood before a community's most visible statement of faith in tomorrow, community, and the next generation, looking directly at the camera. They asked not for a photograph that featured them, but one that showcased their work.

Qualla township residents believed in the value of education. They knew that women would probably make up the majority of teachers who worked inside the building, but its provision was a man's work. That is the context within which our informants were raised. Men took care of physical things—buildings, funding, resources. Only after they were gathered together and the construction done did women enter the picture. The boards on the ground suggest their time had not yet come. The size of the building, though, is too large for only the community's boys. Education is a dangerous enterprise. Introduce people to possibilities and nothing stays the same.

PART II

The Study

"People don't expect men to be good with particulars. People expect men to paint with a brush and somebody else to pick up the pieces and make sure everything is correct . . . People expect women to be good with the details and take care of the details themselves."

Female Participant

·4·

THE DISSEMBLING STUDY

Diana Pounder (2000) observed that much of the work on women's experiences in administration has drawn few comparisons to men's or has drawn comparisons to men's experiences a generation ago. She called for "more comparative studies designed to search for similarities and differences in the experiences of female and male administrators who are contemporaries of one another" (145). Heeding that advice, we compared current male and female senior educational leaders to determine the ways in which their experiences were congruent and the ways in which those experiences diverged.

We were also interested in the role of place, particularly as it intersected with gendered experiences. Other studies have examined setting in terms of advantages related to resources and size (Bell and Chase 1995; Tallerico and Burnstyn 1996; and Wolverton 1998). Because we suspected that factors other than gender per se might affect the acceptance of women as senior educational leaders, the ways they work, and the ways they describe their work, we decided to look at a sample in an understudied region that had a reputation for gender segregation and stereotyping. Race entered the study when the first African American superintendent was hired in the midst of our data collection. Our research questions became: "What role does geography play in the gendered and racial experiences of senior educational leaders in Southern Appalachia? How do these leaders socially construct their leadership roles?"

Methodology

We planned a multiyear study that had four phases. In phase one, we identified a potential sample of fifteen female senior educational leaders in the region.

Twelve women agreed to share their experiences en route to district-level administration positions. They were willing to discuss how gender contributed to and/or hindered both their professional journey and their leadership styles. In phase two, we developed a paired sample of twelve male senior-level educational leaders and asked them the same general questions we asked the females. In phase three, we solicited from our participants the names of three individuals who worked closely with them and were familiar with their leadership styles. We mailed surveys to forty subordinates, balancing our choices by gender, position, and school system. Thirty participants responded with their perceptions of issues related to senior-level leadership. In phase four, we looked at leadership from a community perspective using newspapers and school board members as informants. We mailed surveys to eighty-eight school board members; thirty responded with their perceptions of senior-level leadership. Phases one and two were completed in 2000–2003; phases three and four, in 2002–2003.

Phases One and Two

For phases one and two, we gathered autobiographical information from our twelve female administrators through a sociodemographic survey that included closed, forced-choice, and open-ended items and through focused one-on-one interviews. The interviews were conducted at a location designated by the person being interviewed (their offices except in one case when the participant elected to talk outside her office). The interviews were audiotaped, transcribed, and then coded. Interviews were semistructured, thereby ensuring a measure of consistency in the data collected, but allowing opportunities for exploring topics that arose during the course of conversation. We collected data from our male sample in the same way. One male participant met us away from his office for the interview.

Data analysis followed the constant comparative method described by Brunner (2000). Data were organized into broad taxonomies, coded, and analyzed for emerging themes; those themes were then related to other themes. (Glaser and Strauss 1967; Strauss 1987). Both of us independently reviewed the transcripts before we shared our reactions. Following data collection for the paired samples, we checked preliminary interpretations with male and female informants, providing them with transcript selections that we considered using. Participants had an opportunity to review our initial findings as well as quotations from their interviews and make revisions as well as additions. We incorporated their reactions and clarifications into the analysis that follows on the perceived roles of gender, race, and geography on professional life experiences of Southern Appalachian public school senior administrators.

Phases Three and Four

For phase three, we asked our male and female participants to identify three senior-level administrators in their system who worked with them. We collected sociodemographic data on these thirty individuals and disaggregated the data by gender. Using a Likert scale, participants responded to questions on the degree of importance they attached to certain qualities necessary for effective leadership in their systems. We calculated mean responses and standard deviations for this data. In addition, participants responded to three open-ended questions:

- What gets senior educational leaders in trouble in your district?
- What are the thorniest issues your district has had to contend with recently?
- Does gender matter in the role of a senior leader in your district?

These responses were grouped into common themes. Because both of us know the individuals who participated in our study professionally as well as many of their subordinates, most of whom were not part of the survey sample, we brought to the results of that survey a history of anecdotes and interactions. Although we did not use them in presenting our findings, they did frame the ways we considered our data. They were also useful in the collection of supporting data from print sources, such as local newspapers.

For phase four, we mailed a survey to all eighty-eight school board members in the districts of our participants. We collected sociodemographic data on the thirty individuals who responded and disaggregated the data by gender. They also responded, using a Likert scale, to items about the relative importance they attached to certain skills and attributes in choosing a senior educational leader for their district. We also asked them to rate items related to job performance. For these responses, we calculated means and standard deviations. We also asked this group to respond to five open-ended questions:

- What are the most important qualities you consider in searching for a superintendent?
- What three pieces of advice would you give to a new superintendent in your district?
- What three things would you advise a new superintendent not to do?
- As a citizen in your area, what kinds of things might cause a superintendent to get into trouble?
- What is the "thorniest" or most difficult issue your system has had to deal with since you have been on the board?

We conducted short telephone interviews with elected subordinates and three in-depth personal interviews with individuals we considered representative school board members. Their responses were grouped into common themes. We then disaggregated their responses in a variety of ways to determine if themes varied by gender, district, relative district size, native or nonnative status, and education. In addition, for this phase of the study, we reviewed newspaper articles concerning superintendent selection and district issues, board meeting minutes, school documents, and data provided by the North Carolina Department of Public Instruction as well as primary and secondary historical documents. To get a fix on Appalachia, we relied on local histories and memoirs as well as the rich literature on Appalachia in general. To understand Southern culture, we looked at comprehensive studies of the region, such as Cash's *The Mind of the South* (1941) and Woodward's *The Burden of Southern History* (1960), specialized studies related to gender (for example, Scott's *The Southern Lady*, 1970) as well as mass media explorations of Southern identity, such as King's *Southern Ladies and Gentlemen* (1993). We also reviewed fiction from the South as a whole (notably, but not exclusively, Faulkner and Welty) and Appalachia (Chappell, Morgan, and Smith), as well as published memoirs.

Our Participants

The Female Senior Educational Leaders

Ideally, we would have focused only on superintendents. However, we had to expand our sample to other female senior educational leaders because, when we began our study (2000–2001), there were only three sitting female superintendents in the region and one who had retired. The number then dropped to two when another retired in the summer of 2001. At the time of this writing (summer 2003) there are four. Three assistant/associate superintendents in our study were promoted to the superintendency in their home districts. A female, originally from South Carolina, was promoted by the system in which she worked as an assistant superintendent.[1] As we concluded our study, one of the associate superintendent participants was hired as superintendent of a mountain county outside the area of our sample. The pool from which we formed our sample included fifteen women who fit our criteria. Each of them held a central office line or staff position of authority that had one of the following titles: superintendent, assistant or associate superintendent, or director of curriculum and instruction.

Of these fifteen invited to participate, one did not respond to our initial inquiry letter. Another was scheduled for an interview, but called to cancel it and did not return our calls to reschedule. One had an extended illness, but participated in a series of informal conversations. We have formal interview and sociodemographic data on twelve. All are Caucasian. At the time of our data collection, they included three superintendents, four associate superintendents, four assistant superintendents, and one director of curriculum. The director of curriculum has since changed to a position of lead teacher. One of the superintendents and an associate superintendent have since retired. Two of the associate superintendents are now superintendents, one in and one out of the region.

Degrees

The women in our study have at least an EdS or educational specialist (sixth-year) degree and superintendency level licenses. Eight of the women hold a doctorate—until recently, a less than easy feat in our part of the state. Before 1996, there was no doctoral program of any kind available at the two public universities in the region, Western Carolina University (WCU) and the University of North Carolina at Asheville (UNCA). At that time, WCU began its first EdD program in educational leadership and, in May 2000, one of those eight women was in its first graduating class. Five of the other seven received their EdD from the University of North Carolina at Greensboro, which operated an off-campus doctoral program on the UNCA campus in the late 1980s and early 1990s. Most of the men and women who hold a doctorate in the southern mountains participated in that program, which taught three different cohorts during a period of approximately eight years. The women in our study received their doctoral degrees in 1987(1), 1988(1), 1989(1), and 1991(2). At about the same time that the UNCG program was phased out, the University of South Carolina (USC) began a satellite program near the state line and charged in-state tuition for North Carolina students who took advantage of it (a policy that has since ended). Two of the women hold PhDs from USC, receiving them in 1994 and 1997 respectively. One of the four women without a doctorate is currently in the last stages of her EdD at WCU.

Most of our female sample received their undergraduate and graduate (master's and specialist) degrees from WCU, with their years in various programs overlapping. Consequently, they are often well acquainted with each other as students as well as school leaders. That shared educational experience would also be true for the five graduates of the UNCG extension program. Only one woman was completely out of the regional education loop, a superintendent whose undergraduate work was at Wake Forest, and whose graduate work was in South Carolina at Converse College for a master's degree and USC for her doctoral degree. Undergraduate work was split between WCU and UNCA, with most women going to the former. Only one woman in our sample was born in another state and she attended undergraduate and graduate school outside the state before coming to the Southern Appalachians. She has, however, picked up master's and specialist degrees at WCU, thereby sharing classes with women in the sample. Only one other administrator completed her undergraduate work out of state, at the University of Tennessee.

Marital Status and Children

When we began our study, all twelve members of our sample were or had been married. One superintendent indicated she had only recently married; she did not know if she could have managed the level and extent of work that she had done previously if she had had to juggle both a personal and professional life. For her, those two lives merged into one for most of the time she spent in education. One superintendent was divorced at the time we began our study, but the divorce occurred prior to her being named superintendent. She recently married the former superintendent under whom she served as deputy. Four of the women have retired spouses. Several women mentioned how supportive their spouses had been, and continue to be, in helping to meet the needs of their family. Three of the women have no children. Four have one child and five have two children.

Career Paths

Career paths for these women represent both typical and atypical patterns. All had some administrative experience before moving into superintendencies. Their experiences varied. One superintendent followed the typical pattern of starting as a teacher, then moving into an assistant principalship, followed by a high school principalship, and then into a superintendency. Another was a teacher, an assistant principal, a curriculum supervisor, an assistant superintendent, and then a superintendent. A third superintendent was never a building-level administrator, but moved from bring a teacher and special education administrator into assistant and associate superintendencies before becoming superintendent. Five women never held a building-level administrator position. Another participant held only an assistant principalship and that for a very short time. Most of the women, when they moved into central office positions, did so in curriculum and instruction. On average these women spent a little over 12 years in the classroom as teachers (range of 4 to 22, with a mode and median of 13), and have averaged just less than 16 years in administration (range of 7 to 22 years, with a mode of 35 and median of 27.25). Six of the women are in their fifties; five are in their forties. One woman is over sixty. Most of them moved into their first administrative positions in their late thirties or early forties. The women have not been mobile and have lived in the counties where they have worked an average of 36.3 years (range of 12 to 53 years, with no mode and a median of 38). They have lived in North Carolina an average of 46 years (range of 21.5 to 62 with a mode and median of 50).

Career Locations

Seven of the women have spent their entire professional careers in the systems in which they were born, including three women who became superintendents. The mobility of the other women was limited. Two taught originally in the counties of their birth but moved eventually to the counties where they secured their first administrative positions. Only one woman was a geographic outsider. Although she has lived in the region for over twenty years, she still believes that some people consider her "from off." Only one insider taught out of the state and that was only for a brief time. For most of our female sample, professional work was done locally. They knew well the people in the communities in which they worked. They and their children grew up in the same neighborhoods, played and studied in the same schools, and attended the same churches as did the members of their school boards. For many, their extended families assisted them with their children.

Parents and Siblings

Four women had teachers for parents; both parents of one were educators. Generally, however, their parents were not college graduates. Two of their mothers did not finish high school (one got a GED) and two of their fathers did not finish high school. Most of their mothers were employed in clerical or sales jobs. Two stayed at home. One worked in a factory. Three held professional jobs working in educational or social service settings. Most of their fathers were self-employed or worked in construction. One was a miner or laborer, depending on job availability, and another worked in a mill. Three of the fathers were teachers.

None of the women was an only child and on average they had slightly more than two siblings (range of 1 to 4 with a mode of 1 and median of 2). Four women were firstborns and two were the youngest. Six were middle children. When asked to name the individual or individuals who most influenced them to decide on a career in education, they most often cited a parent or family member, followed by an influential teacher. Eleven never considered entering educational administration when they began their professional careers as teachers, but one knew she wanted to be a principal from the beginning; when she played school at home, she played the principal.

Comparison to the National Sample

Many of the characteristics of our sample resemble those of female school administrators in general. Women tend to move into central office positions, often associated with curriculum and instruction, rather than principalships as they move toward superintendencies. However, recent patterns for male and female superintendents show them spending more time in a central office positions than they once did; a significant number of them have been assistant or associate superintendents (Glass 2000). Female administrators have teaching careers that often extend beyond ten years (Schuster and Foote 1990; Morie and Wilson 1996). One indication that more women are moving into senior administrative positions is the recent extension of the average age of service as a teacher by sitting superintendents from five years to nearly seven (Glass 1992, 2000). Women tend to have advanced degrees and are likely to have doctorates (Boudreau 1994; Stouder 1998; Pavan et al. 1995). Their principalships are often at the elementary level (Edson 1995; Glass 2000). Women are likely to attain their positions within their home systems (Lea 1989; Crawford 1992). Most superintendents in the nation grew up in rural areas or small towns (Glass 2000).

In the United States, female superintendents tend to occupy districts of under 300 students or at least serve in small districts (Glass 1992, 2000). That is not true for the women in our sample, partially as a function of countywide school districting in the state. There are no systems in North Carolina that small. Only a few of the old incorporated city systems remain and they all contain well over 300 students. McCreight (1999) found that female superintendents tended to be more likely single, widowed, divorced, or part of a commuter marriage than men, something not evident in our sample. Obermeyer, in a 1996 study of California superintendents, found that most of them were white, in their late forties or midfifties, and married with children—all true for most of the women in our sample. The average age for superintendents is fifty-two, close to the ages that we have for the four female superintendents in our study, although they are a little older. Also, like the national trend, there are more female superintendents in the western mountains of North Carolina today than in 1992 (Glass 2000). In 1992, only 6 percent of all superintendents were women; by 2000 that number had climbed to 13.1 percent. In the southern mountains of North Carolina, females now constitute nearly 17 percent of the local membership of the superintendent council.

The Male Senior Educational Leaders

Of the fifteen male administrators we invited to participate, three did not reply. One said he would return our survey after we called to be certain he received it. Another indicated by phone he would give us the survey when we arrived for an interview but was not there at our scheduled time and did not return our phone calls. We have sociodemographic data on twelve administrators and eleven interviews. The men in our study represent eleven different school systems, ten county and one city school district. They include nine superintendents, one executive director for personnel, and two assistant superintendents. Since our study began, one superintendent retired in December 2002 and one accepted another superintendency within the state, but outside the region. Of the twelve members of the group, eleven are Caucasian and one is the first African American superintendent to be hired as a superintendent in Western North Carolina. His immediate predecessor was the first woman in our group to be a superintendent. She was also the first female to serve in that capacity in the past fifty years and the only female in the region to be superintendent in two different districts.

Degrees

All of the men in the study have at least an education specialist (sixth-year degree) and superintendency level licenses. Of the seven doctorates, two have PhDs, both from the University of South Carolina. The other doctorates, EdDs, come from East Tennessee State University, the University of North Carolina at Greensboro (UNCG), the University of Alabama, and Delta State University in Mississippi. The men received their degrees over a wide span of years: 1968, 1985, 1988, 1995, 1996, 1997, and 1999. Those administrators whose highest degree is an EdS received them in 1977, 1981, 1983, 1986, 2001. Unlike the women, they are far less likely to have spent time together in classes as students. However, also unlike the women, they are more likely to band together at meetings or to interact on a social level.

These men received their undergraduate and master's degrees from a variety of universities in North and South Carolina: Clemson, UNCG, Appalachian State, Furman, Winthrop, Pembroke, the University of Georgia, East Carolina University, and Western Carolina University. One man, a native of New York, completed his undergraduate and master's work there, his EdS at Western Carolina, and his licensure work at SUNY, Fordham, and Adams State. Another, a Mississippi native, completed undergraduate and master's work at Mississippi College and Delta State. Whereas the women were unlikely to stray from the region, the men were willing to seek their educational fortunes wherever those fortunes could be found.

Marital Status and Children

Of the twelve men, all are married. When we began our study, one was separated and subsequently divorced. He cited his residential move to a small rural district, a state requirement for his superintendency there, as a factor in the problems in his marriage. His wife was unhappy and missed her friends in the larger county system where he had worked. He remarried in the summer of 2002. The spouses of three of the men do not work. Of those who do, eight work in the education field. Eleven of the twelve men have children; six of them have children under the age of eighteen still living in the home.

Career Paths

Career paths of seven of the men follow what was once the classic upward mobility sequence of classroom to assistant principal to principal to central office. One participant in a small rural county moved straight from the classroom to the superintendency. Two worked in higher education at the assistant dean and dean levels. One superintendent retired as the state superintendent for public instruction in another state before assuming a superintendency in Western North Carolina. Seven had been high school principals, four worked as elementary principals, and seven had principal experience at the junior high or middle school level. One participant had Catholic school experience in another state and cited his religion as the reason a school board in Western North Carolina indicated he could not be hired as a superintendent. The men spent less time in the classroom than the women, an average of 6.7 years (range .5 to 20 years with a median and mode of 6). They averaged 20.6 years in administration (range of 6.5 to 33 with a mode of 19 and a median of 20.5) and 27.4 years in education (range of 13 to 39 years with a median 28.5 and mode of 29). One of the men (one of the youngest superintendents in the state and not from the region) is in his thirties, five are in their forties, five are in their fifties, and one is over sixty. With the exception of the younger male superintendent, both the male and female groups are roughly the same age and have spent roughly the same amount of time in public school careers. The men have held a greater variety of jobs, spent fewer years as teachers and more years as administrators, and today are more likely to hold senior positions. They are also more likely to have held superintendencies previously in another district. Two of the men have spent their entire professional careers in the counties where they were born, and another, though born in Ohio, has spent forty-four of his years in the county and his entire career there. Four have worked in education in other states: South Carolina, Georgia, Mississippi, and New York. One taught in Morocco before settling in North Carolina. One has worked in four different Western North Carolina counties. Unlike the women, the men have been more mobile in their careers, having averaged 15.7 years in the counties where they now work (range of 1 to 53 years, with a mode of 3 and a median of 3). They have collectively lived in North Carolina an average of 30.8 years (range of 2 to 53 with a median of 32.5).

Parents and Siblings

The parents of most of the men were not college graduates. The mother of the youngest member of the male group was a teacher with a B.S. degree. His father, who had some college experience, was a multistate regional vice-president for marketing. Seven of the mothers had high school diplomas and one completed her GED at age sixty-five. The other three mothers finished only sixth, tenth, and eleventh grades. Five were housewives, two were clerks, one was a cosmetologist, one a secretary, and one a factory worker. Of the fathers, one, a high school teacher and coach, completed an MA in education. Another, a chemical lab technician, completed one semester of college. Four finished high school, three eighth grade, one tenth, and one junior high. Other fathers' occupations included electrical contractor, industrial salesman, textiles and factory workers, farmer, and convenience store owner. It is difficult to detect significant economic differences in the socioeconomic status of the families from which the two groups came. Collectively, their educational, economic, and professional success sharply contrasts with that of their parents. Together these educators represent a successful, socially mobile group of strivers.

One of the twelve men is an only child. Five are firstborns. One is the youngest and the only male in a family of ten children. When asked to name the individuals or event that most influenced their going into education, most named a grade 7–12 teacher, coach, band director, parent, or college teacher. One said, "I just wanted to get out of Vietnam." Two mentioned jobs that involved some aspect of teaching as an influence.

Comparison to the National Sample

The characteristics of our male sample resemble those of male administrators in general. All but one has principalship experience. Most come to the superintendency or central office positions with experiences at a variety of grade levels. Nationally, three times more male superintendents than women district leaders have served as high school principals (Glass 2000). In our study, only one woman had been a high school principal, whereas six of the men held that position. Their average years in the classroom (6.7) are less than those of the women in our sample (12 years) and are consistent with the national average of 5 to 7 years (Glass 1992, 2000). Only two have spent their entire careers in the county of their birth. As in the national data, most of the men in our sample grew up in rural or small towns (Glass 2000). Eleven of them, the majority, consistent with the pattern in Obermeyer's 1996 sample of California superintendents, are white. Only one is African American. The men are close to the average age of fifty-two.

Like the women in our study, the men serve in what would be considered (from a national perspective) medium-sized school districts. However, their districts, with a few notable exceptions, are relatively small compared to systems throughout the state of North Carolina. Size is a function of countywide school districting in the state. Consolidation reforms throughout the twentieth century reduced the number of local, rural districts to a single countywide district. Only a few counties, for cultural or historical reasons, retain one or two special town district charters. There is only one city system in Carolina's southern mountains. It has, not so coincidentally, a history of hiring outsiders. It was the third district in the region to hire a woman and is now the first to hire an African American. This pattern reflects its regional reputation for a degree of progressivism that is somewhat out of step with the rest of the area. (For selected demographic comparisons of the male and female samples, see Appendix, Table 1.)

Other Central Office Educational Leaders

We wanted the perspective of those who worked in administrative positions in subordinate roles to our study participants. Thirty central office educational leaders in the region responded to our survey: sixteen males and fourteen females. All of the men are Caucasian. One of the women is an African American. A majority of the men (ten) have spent more than seventeen years in the district where they are currently working. One has been in the district only a year, three from two to five years, one from six to nine years, and one from ten to thirteen years. Of the females, most (eleven) have also spent more than seventeen years in the district, with one from two to five years and two from fourteen to seventeen years. Among the men, most (twelve) have lived in the community for more than seventeen years with one for only a year, two from two to five years, and one from six to nine years. Of the women, thirteen have lived in the community for over seventeen years and one from two to five years. Of the men, ten of the sixteen were born in Western North Carolina as well as six of the fourteen females. Among the men, four have doctorates, five have education specialist degrees, and seven have master's degrees. One of the females has a doctorate, four have education specialist degrees, seven have master's degrees, and two have bachelor's degrees.

School Board Members

In addition, we realized the community perspective was important to our understanding of how these leaders functioned in the region. Therefore, we surveyed eighty-eight board members and received returns from thirty. Each district had at least one board member survey returned. Twenty-three of the respondents are male and seven are female. Of the males, twenty-one are Caucasian, one is African American, and one is Native American. The seven females are all Caucasian. The males represent varying levels of experience on their district's school board. One has served more than seventeen years on the board, seven for one year or less, eight for two to five years, four for six to nine years, one for ten to thirteen years, and two for fourteen to seventeen years. The women have less experience with two having served between six and nine years, four from two to five years, and one less than one year. All of the men have lived more than seventeen years in the communities where they serve as board members, whereas among the women, only five have lived more than seventeen years in the community, one between fourteen and seventeen years and one from six to nine years. In terms of education, three males hold doctorates, three education specialist degrees, three master's degrees, four bachelor's degrees, three two-year college degrees, and six high school diplomas. One of the women has a master's degree, five have bachelor's degrees, and one has two years of college credit. Among the males, eighteen of the twenty-three were born in Western North Carolina, as were three of the females.

Conclusion

Glass (1992) considered the superintendency to be the most male-dominated leadership position in the country. Björk (1999) contended that the superintendency is still the most gender-stratified position in the United States. However, there has been an increase in females in the available labor pool and in the number of women in principalships, often a prerequisite to senior-level leadership (Sheldon and Munnich 1999; Coumbe 2001; Andrews and Grogan 2002). Logan (1998) found that "a convergence of school reform, supply and demand for administrators, and societal changes enhances opportunities for women to become school administrators" (1). We agree, but we see it happening slowly and not always for reasons that indicate an end to gender stereotyping.

The American South today is often considered, with good reason, the most gender-coded region in the country. The Appalachian Mountains are also known as a region with strict gender codes. The same type of exclusionary coding of occupations has historically applied to race. We synthesized our data to answer our research questions: "What role does geography play in the gendered and racial experiences of senior educational leaders in Southern Appalachia? How do these leaders socially construct their leadership roles?" Those findings follow in chapters 5, 6, 7, and 8.

·5·

TRANSFORMING BUBBA

Most of the men in our study were white males born and bred in the South and several in Southern Appalachia. Our African American participant was also born in the region. Like the women, they grew up amidst the myths and stereotypes of Southern men—the Southern gentleman, the good ol' boy, the Bubba—each with varying connotations. We found elements of all of these in the men to whom we talked. They warmly welcomed us into their offices. They shared the different roles they play to negotiate in the Western North Carolina region. Several of these men are Bubbas or brothers in the sense of comradeship that men understand better than women. Florence King (1993) in *Southern Ladies and Gentlemen* says that, over time, she came to see the good ol' boy as he sees himself: "the only man left in America who says words like 'honor' and 'pride' without smirking" (229). The men in our study spoke unabashedly of "honesty," "integrity," "ethics," and "courage."

Do Come In

A pattern emerged, especially with regard to dress and office décor, when we visited the offices of the men in our study. When we visited leaders in Asheville and surrounding larger county districts, the men appeared in what we might call the CEO look. They wore dark traditional suits and ties with Johnson and Murphy-style shoes, all in the middle of summer when school is not in session. One superintendent wore French cuffs and indicated he frequently does. Their offices were spacious with matching masculine dark woods and a few family pictures. Then we visited the men in smaller rural counties who wore their traditional Southern male uniform—golf shirt, khakis, and loafers.

Their offices were much smaller and not so very different from other offices in their building. One central office was in what had formerly been a small family house, now with a trailer attached. It was located on the campus of the district's three schools. Central offices in Western North Carolina are far from palatial. As one of the superintendents walked Anna to her car, he pointed out his large pickup truck in the parking lot and commented, "I could never get away with a Corvette here." These distinctions are not hard and fast, however. One participant in a more rural area greeted us in a Ralph Lauren shirt and a baseball cap—his dress an appropriate metaphor for rural districts in transition. The French-cuff superintendent dons his leather jacket when he rides his Harley-Davidson from school to school. He then parks, removes the leather coat, and enters the building in his CEO dress. He uses the motorcycle as a teaching tool. On sunny days when he reads to the children, he asks, "Would you like to own a motorcycle? To do that you have to be able to read to pass the driver's test."

Men on Harleys and Other Toys

In contrast to the women in our study who never seemed to have time to play, we encountered three spirited, fun-loving, male superintendents who make time in their schedules to ride Harley-Davidsons. Two work in rural areas and one in a large county district. We must admit, there is no better place than the winding mountain roads on the Blue Ridge Parkway to ride a motorcycle, to get away and relieve stress. Not only do these three ride individually but they also often ride together. Two of them have participated in a Vietnam veterans rally in Washington, D.C. Two went together cross-country to California for their own version of middle-age spring break, an example of what King (1993) calls the "Deliverance Syndrome" (59), that male desire to get away from it all ("it" often being women). Two men in the study collect and restore classic cars. Another, a skilled craftsman, crafted wood from his own logs and built a log cabin. All of them brightened as they described their hobbies.

The men seemed to be a more tightly knit group than the women. They talk frequently on the phone and carpool together to meetings. Now that more women are entering these roles, the women are invited to ride with them. "We love the ladies," one said. It is a long way to Raleigh, the state capital, and the ride is a good time for geographically distant senior leaders to come together. "You can talk to other superintendents that sit in the statewide meetings. They say it is completely different. They hardly ever get together for a meeting. . . . We are a real close-knit group." When the regional centers were dissolved, the one in this area was reestablished collaboratively. It continues to bring area superintendents together once a month as well as to design and develop collaborative staff development opportunities for teachers and administrators in the region. The casual conversation before and after such meetings is testimony to their professional and, in some cases, personal friendships. At state meetings they often cluster together and share tables at sessions.

Growing Up Rural

All of the men in our study, less one, were born in the South. All grew up in rural areas, even the participant who grew up in a northern state. The one African American superintendent in the region was born locally and came of age in a rural county. He left the region and then returned as superintendent in the area's one city system. Childhoods for these men were times of hunting, fishing, and outdoors. They played army, built forts, and participated in sports. The exception was the one northerner, who, as an only child, loved to read and finished the entire encyclopedia in elementary school.

A participant who grew up in rural Georgia remembered, "Never wore shoes. Didn't have to wear shoes to school." One said that as a little boy he was "as mean as a snake" and got many spankings. Competition seemed important to several. One man explained it this way, "See, my grandparents can't read or write, my mom and dad never graduated from high school, but they had an incredible work ethic that all three of us kids developed. We had jobs, we played sports, we were active in school activities." On a similar note, another said, "School meant a lot to me. It meant a lot to my family. My parents were not educated."

These men experienced college in different ways. One said he went "to get out of Vietnam." Another dropped out and joined the Marine Corps where he found his focus. He then married and said, "I came back highly motivated primarily because being married to a smart woman, I didn't want to embarrass myself. . . . I had a lot to prove because my parents and her parents were disappointed because we got married. She was nineteen and I was twenty." Another said that college was not a time for fun because he had to work to send himself to school. However, college years for several of these men were pleasurable and playful. One said, "I enjoyed the social aspect of being with people. I was from a small town, a very small community, a very small high school. It was a big thing for me to go to Western Carolina University. . . . Basically, I had never been anywhere in my life." Some found distractions: "Chasing women. I enjoyed photography. I worked a lot and played golf." Another admitted to "partying too much" and getting placed on academic probation. When one described his days at the University of Georgia, he said, "We chased girls and partied is what we did." Another who had been raised in a "very religious home and went to a very Baptist school" described rebelling by drinking and carousing. He then discovered that to be able to debate with his professors, he had to study so he would know what he was talking about.

Unlike our white participants, the African American in our study described growing up as a series of "firsts."

> I knew I had to be a good student. I knew that the expectation was whatever I decided to be a part of, that was fine, but I had to do my best. That is what led me to be the first minority Eagle Scout in the troop that I joined. That is what led me to make the only minority on the baseball team and I played ball until high school. I was in a lot of settings in which I was the first and only minority in that setting.

Always on stage because of his race, he was less able to participate in some of the typical coming-of-age activities of his colleagues.

Career Choices: Ending Up Here

The journey into education for the men in our study was unlike that of the women. Only four knew early on that they wanted to teach. One heard Elvis Pressley, knew that he loved music, and decided to be a band director. Two were inspired by tenth-grade teachers. One initially thought "I was going to be a teacher and coach baseball for thirty years in the same place." Others chose a less direct route to professional education. One started college as a business major, but was steered by his pastor into education. Another man wanted badly to be a highway patrolman, but during National Guard summer camp he turned a bulldozer over and sustained very serious injuries. "The Highway Patrol didn't want me as damaged goods. So here I was with a degree in driving that you couldn't do a thing with." He then moved into teaching reading and math for the Job Corps and eventually into education as a career. Another man concluded that he fell into education. It was not a planned venture.

> I've told this tale many times and it's true. I was at Western Carolina University as a junior. A friend said, "I've got to go down to the meeting." And I said, "What meeting?" He said, "Student teaching." I said, "What's student teaching?" He said, "I'm going to be a teacher.". . . And I said, "Do you get college credit?" He said, "Yes." I said, "I'm going to go with you.". . . So here I am.

Once in the profession they progressed to an interest in administration, some directly and some by more circuitous routes.

Moving into administration was a goal early on for most participants in the study. One knew that was his eventual objective from the time he did his student teaching. Another one made the decision at a point he called his "midlife crisis." One flipped a coin between going into a master of school administration program and a master of secondary social studies. One just decided to get certified and "fell into the superintendency" straight from the classroom. Another knew from the very beginning that he would move into administration and spent only a semester in the classroom. His life was methodical: "In fact, in my safety deposit box right now is an envelope where one day sitting in an airport, I wrote my entire life's goals . . . and there has been only one change. That is I don't want to be a state superintendent any more."

Once in education, some of the men considered leaving. One was very frustrated in an assistant principalship because all he did was discipline and he wanted to learn how to be a principal. He took the exam to be a mail carrier. By the time a postal job was available, he had moved to another school as an assistant principal to a principal who mentored him. "I went from doing the parking lot stuff to being a part of the program." Another man during his time as a junior high principal described himself as "tired, discouraged and questioning . . . whether I wanted to stay in it." A friend offered him a job at a higher salary to work as shift supervisor at a mill. He visited the mill and decided he didn't really care about "those machines." One administrator who considered leaving admitted it was for more money. He said he had more reasons to leave when he was a teacher than when he was an administrator. "My fourth year in education was probably the toughest. . . . And I don't know why, but we had a new principal that year and the school went down and I was tired of a job I was pigeon-holed in." He then started graduate school and did some reflecting. What kept him in education was the competitiveness in coaching and teaching his players to be good sports. "I was proud of the fact that we never had ejections or technicals and I felt that it was a life experience for them. I also worked in yards on the side to make more money and supplement my income for about ten years. Until I got this job!" he added. One man actually left to work for an oil company. He came back and was then recruited to work with an educational consulting company that trained teachers. He also worked in higher education, but discovered he wanted to move back into K–12. Six of the men never considered leaving, but one observed, "I have not considered leaving the profession. I have been disappointed and I have been worn down. And when those situations have happened, I have gathered strength by and through an ability to persevere."

Moving On Up

When we asked the men if they encountered any obstacles on their way up to a position of senior leadership, not surprisingly, none of their responses related to gender. One had to deal with certification issues and he mentioned learning "the political climate you have to go through for various positions." One mentioned that the only reason he got one job was that there were three Republicans on the board. A couple of men never encountered any obstacles, and in some cases, never had to apply for the jobs for which they were hired. One observed, "I was the only person in the district who was certified." One, who moved from another state, said he had to spend time finding a senior leadership position that was a good fit.

Two of the men spoke of age as an issue. The African American in the study encountered only one obstacle and said, "I don't believe it had as much to do with my ethnicity as it did my age. It wasn't the committee. I won the committee." But the superintendent said to him, "You impressed the committee. You are a smart young man. Go back and get your doctorate and look me up in about five years." Another, the youngest member of our study, also dealt with age concerns but forged ahead:

> I probably had more frustration getting my first superintendency than my first principalship. Age and lack of experience I think had a lot to do with it. Most people would pretty much tell me that I would have to do a central office position as an assistant superintendent or associate superintendent to move up. And I had some people saying that you are at a 2A school; there is no way you will get a central office position in a big district because you are in a small district with a small high school. And I just didn't listen. I just kept going after it.

Persistence in pursuing jobs was a common characteristic.

Being Southern

The men in our study are all Southerners except one. They, like the women, are proud to be Southerners and feel Southerners are more gracious and friendly. They see being a Southerner as an advantage, at least in their current positions. "You see it, too, in Northern leaders who come south and try to be superintendents. If they don't change their directive style, they're going to alienate not only their staff, but they're gonna really alienate the community." Another thought that being a Southerner gave him the people skills he needed to do the job. One, born to a teenage mother, described being a Southern male as taking responsibility by working hard all the time and having little recreation. One simply said, "I think I am a lot nicer than some of those folks up north. I think there is this air of hospitality and this genuine desire to help people. And I don't know if that's from all of that front porch sitting or what." He spoke of having many "half-backs" in his county—"people who grew up and worked up north and then retired to Florida and didn't like it that much and came up here so they are halfway back home." Working with Floridians presented him with a challenge. He often heard, "'Well, in Florida this is how we did it. And since it worked in Florida it should work anywhere.' And that is when I want to say, 'Well, why the hell did you move here if it was so great down there?'" The African American in our study who has had the opportunity to move all over the country said, "being from the South, I find that we tend to be kinder, gentler, more socially correct. That we try to use a certain amount of tact and hospitality . . . but I do think the South is losing some of that. We are becoming just as rapid paced and indifferent about things as other places." None of the men indicated that their Southernness inhibited them in any way. The one participant from the North felt that not only did his lack of Southernness affect his career, but he was also disadvantaged by his religion. He was a Catholic working in the Bible Belt. Once, when he interviewed for a superintendency, he was told by board members that his religion would be a problem.

Mentors and Influences

Most of the men in the study cited their fathers and previous bosses as significant influences. Two mentioned females—a high school English teacher for one, and, for another, his teenage mother who earned her GED at age sixty-five. Others spoke with fondness and respect for their fathers, many of whom never went to college but inspired them. "A good work ethic" was a phrase they mentioned frequently. The participant who became a band director was inspired by two previous band directors from whom he learned organization and high expectations. Another, whose parents were divorced, also cited his band director as someone who was there for him when his father failed to show up one Christmas to see him after he had promised to do so. One spoke of a principal he worked for. This man asked his principal, "When will I know I am ready to be a principal?" His response was, "You will know when I tell you, when you start getting in my way and not being satisfied making assistant principal's decisions and start crowding me in my decisions." One day the principal called him in and said, "I want you to go look for a principalship because you are crowding me now and I think you are ready to go." Speaking of his father, one participant said his dad was consistent and fair, "You knew where the line was. . . . There wasn't any discussion." Going into his first assistant principalship, he explained, "Everything was either in the black pile or the white pile and I have to tell you that my life was miserable because I didn't know about the gray pile. It's a very real thing, isn't it?" Influences were not always people. For one man, the type of educator he became was profoundly affected by the death of his nine-year-old son, who was killed in a tragic accident.

Teaching: A Step to the Next Level

The men in our study did not spend much time talking about their teaching, primarily because, in the case of all but two, they spent very little time in the classroom before moving into administration. Most began to look toward the principal's office within a few years of entering the profession. One described his teaching as very structured, taking skills and breaking them into parts. One said he "went outside the boundaries" of the North Carolina Standard Course of Study. One who taught for a very short time said he thought that he was "naïve and intense, to a fault." "Focused, disciplined, well-organized" was another man's description of his teaching. One felt he was very "student-oriented." Another remembered his teaching and coaching days when some of the coaches in his school would not show up for class or leave early. One day they came to his door while he was teaching and said, "You're making us look bad." His response was, "I have been hired to teach and that is what I am here to do." He enjoyed using role-playing and what he called "application-focused instruction." Another said a former student had come to see him recently and said, "We had a lot of fun, but boy you were always getting after us." The study participant with twenty years teaching experience said he moved around a great deal, used cooperative learning, and employed many hands-on activities.

To Follow in My Footsteps

We asked the men in our study to reflect on qualities that had served them best as leaders. What advice would they give to someone who wanted to follow in their footsteps? Some advised knowing the region and how to relate to different people. "I feel like I can work with the CEO of the local industry or I can work with the farmer down the road." Another described the same quality, "I can get along with any kind. Whether it be somebody from lower socioeconomics without so much polish, as they would say around here. . . . I dress myself to the audience that I deal with. I think it makes them more comfortable." Another in a small rural county said, "If I have to go around and tell people I am the superintendent, I am not in charge of anything." One man felt his determination and "hard-headedness" had served him well. He advised those who aspire to the superintendency to be sure their family is supportive and to work under people in good systems, "because you will learn good work habits." Another said, "Remember the old adage—You can't hit a moving target. That means keep the discussion going, don't settle for the status quo, keep pushing your organization for continuous improvement." Enthusiasm was important for one man, "When people ask me, 'How in the world can you take this job?' I say, 'I love this job. I can't wait to get here.' My wife thinks I'm a little crazy." Most of the men also mentioned the importance of listening and of honesty.

Conclusion

These men respect the women who work for and with them. One of the men who has experience as an assessor for the National Association of Secondary Principals Leadership Assessment Center spoke of examining data from the program: "If you had a pot of men and a pot of women that had been trained the same and had the same experiences, you were likely to get a better person out of the female group." Perhaps the men in our study would agree with a famous male Southern writer: "We love women here, they give us hope, and above all, they give us grace" (Shuptrine and Dickey 1974, 49). Bubba is indeed in transition. And he welcomes the Appalachian Steel Magnolia whom we meet in chapter 6.

·6·

APPALACHIAN STEEL MAGNOLIAS

James Fox (2000) in his biography *Five Sisters: The Langhornes of Virginia* described a real live Southern belle, his aunt Irene. He maintained that "the Golden Age of the Belle lasted thirty years, from the end of the Civil War until the appearance of Irene" (22). Irene made her debut in White Sulfur Springs, then married Charles Gibson and became the Gibson Girl, another American icon. Fox says, "She turned the vanishing Southern Belle into a modern media fantasy" (22). There were actually very few Irenes, but the women in our study grew up with this powerful mythology about Southern womanhood as part of their culture. It combined with the strong influence of mountain values, themselves gendered, to set boundaries beyond which proper Southern ladies did not go.

Yet the women in our study came of age at a time when barriers were being questioned. By the time they reached their first administrative positions, there were opportunities for women to advance in almost every profession. They are members of Hillary Clinton's generation who found expectations for their behavior limiting and, ultimately, unacceptable. Clinton maintains in *Living History* (2003) that "it seemed people could perceive me only as one thing or the other—either a hardworking professional or a conscientious and caring hostess" (140). She found herself and her generation trapped by stereotypes: "We were living in an era in which some people still felt deep ambivalence about women in positions of public leadership and power. In this era of changing gender roles, I was American's Exhibit A" (141). Clinton initially encountered Southern ceilings as First Lady of Arkansas. Many Arkansans were not happy with her decision to retain her maiden name and remain Hillary Rodham. Feeling it was important to her husband's career, she took the Clinton name. Her decision reflects a conscious accommodation behavior, a choice made to fit within culturally prescribed expectations. She dissembled, concealing her preference because an alternative that did not compromise deeply held values suited the moment.

We maintain that the women in our study encountered Southern Appalachian ceilings, but they used the regional art of dissembling to break through them. They are strong women who read their Southern Appalachian settings and communities well. They knew when to push and when to back off. They understood timing and they knew which battles to choose.

Belles in Their Settings

Our visits to the offices of the women in our study allowed us to interview them (with the exception of one who met us out of her district) in their own settings. Southern women (how well we know) are frequently judged by their decorating skills, so it did not surprise us that the offices of the women were more personally revealing than the offices of the men. Most of their offices reflected their teaching days with memorabilia, including gifts from and artwork by students. The ambiance was decidedly feminine. Family pictures were plentiful. We also took note of the women's dress. For most, we observed what might be called the classic, conservative, Talbots, kind of Junior League alumnae look. (Although in this rural area, the Junior League exists only in the city of Asheville.) This very professional attire (almost all suits) was accented with classic, conservative jewelry and pumps. There were two women who pushed the classic look a little. One wore last year's popular Ralph Lauren black wool double-breasted pants suit and periwinkle blouse. The other wore a sassier pants suit with mules instead of pumps and her chic asymmetrical haircut blended perfectly. Fingernail care was conscious, but conservative with a few sculpted french manicures. If people doubted their femininity claims before entering their workspaces, they were disabused of any doubts by the look of the office and the appearance of its occupants.

Growing Up Southern and Appalachain

These women were both aware and proud of their Southernness. All were born and bred in the region. They spoke lady language. The importance of being perceived as and behaving like a lady was a consistent part of their responses on how growing up in the South influenced who they were as leaders. As one woman said, "I think it is a privilege to be a Southerner. And I think being a Southerner gives a certain graciousness that we are expected to demonstrate as leaders in the leadership position. I try to remember that I should try and act ladylike, not that I always do and not that I always hold my tongue." Another said that being called a lady was "a supreme compliment." One described Southerners like herself as people who "seem to be easier to talk to. Less judgmental maybe. More embracing." Another participant viewed Southerners as more caring and religious, "much more concerned." One woman said that being a Southerner makes her more "polite" and "makes me focus on relationships a lot more." She also noted that "something that we have dealt with over the years somewhat is race and I think there are some Southern traditions there." She described being very hurt when a group of Native Americans called her prejudiced and a white, privileged, racist. She said she had become more comfortable over the last ten years dealing with racial issues and talking about them more openly.

Being polite often meant refraining from discussing unpleasant things or being confrontational. Southern ladies refrain from making social messes. One woman brought up one of the more powerful messages women in the region hear:

> I think that Southern women are to a fault trying to take care of their menfolk and I was brought up to take care of the men in my family and I think I still have that side that I want to. I hopefully am more of a friend to my daughter and I take care of my son. You know, it is still that role-playing. . . . I think that Southern women . . . have always taken a strong role in the family and I think that has made Steel Magnolias.

She went on to describe Southern women as having worked side by side with men in the family while at the same time trying to take nurture them. Another participant referred to "this Southern lady cultural thing," but to her it connoted morals and values, consideration and family. This theme carried through in the newspaper account of her swearing-in ceremony when she became superintendent, where her "role model" and religious associate . . . opened with a prayer (Miller, 2003, p. 1). Another participant talked about deciding to raise her daughters to resist the pressure to be ladylike.

> Growing up in the South, females are brought up to believe they are supposed to be sweet and proper, subservient and nice . . . all those kinds of things. You are not supposed to be a risk-taker. In fact, as children, that is not a good quality to have. In fact I purposely looked at my children when they were little and thought what I would want my children to be. And I raised my children exactly the opposite of the way I was raised. I overdid it. I thought I wanted them to be opinionated and strong and assertive and unafraid. And I got all those things when they turned thirteen. Every one of them. So they about killed me. Now

> they are both strong women. And of course now they vote for Ralph Nader. Very liberal minded and free thinkers. But I wanted them to have a different upbringing from me.

She believes that they stretched the boundaries that she had already expanded, but pride in their rejection of cultural compliance is obvious.

Growing up in Southern Appalachia was a fond memory for most of these women. As one said, "I can't think of anything I didn't enjoy as a child. . . . I loved everything about being a kid." Most participants recalled episodes that involved their families and neighbors. They remembered playing with brothers, sisters, and cousins. One described a special grandmother who lived in her home, her love for her younger sister, and the babysitting service she established at the age of twelve. Another remembered her small town and the freedom to roam and play with relatives. "I probably had about twenty-six relatives of my mother's within less than a mile." Another recollected her first job was, as a child, selling eggs in the neighborhood. Others recalled the pleasures of life outdoors in a rural mountain setting—hiking, swimming, biking. Another thought that patterns set early in life established the tone of their lives later.

> When we came home from school, we had a little routine that we always followed. We always took off our good clothes, of course, and then we had so much time to play and then we came in to do homework and then if there were any chores to be done, we did them. So we were in a real good routine that I think taught us values and respect for each other and also a good work ethic.

Childhood for these women was a time of love and family. It served them well as a foundation for later life. One woman described herself as a tomboy. "I still am a great deal. . . . I played baseball with the Boy Scouts. . . . I just enjoyed doing all kinds of sports." One of the superintendents we interviewed came from a very poor family where there were no books. She would memorize the books she read at school and then play teacher with her brothers and sisters, "reading" from memory. After school, she rarely saw anyone outside her family.

Little Time for Play

Life in college for most of the participants was a time of "seriousness of purpose." Three of the women married while they were attending college. Another woman, when asked what she enjoyed in college, cited her methods classes and working in a clothing store. She did, however, remember Florida and spring break. Sorority life was fun for one woman. Two participants acknowledged that coming from a close-knit, small community to a college environment presented challenges. One considered the college experience "very broadening." Another spoke of her lack of preparation for meeting the academic expectations of a university and struggling with its academic demands while working as a waitress. Seeking the security of her community, she noted, "I came home on the weekends, probably pretty frequently." Another played the organ for her church while in college. One participant, who described her mother as overprotective, found her freedom in college life. "I loved to go out and party and dance," she said. "I loved to dance. Just a free spirit." She added,

> That is another thing about being raised in the rural mountains. There are different expectations for girls here than anywhere else. Very different. . . . What serves you well as an adult does not serve you well as a child. And the bad part is that everybody remembers every little indiscretion you ever had if you stay in the same community.

One woman who rarely left the area of her birth described being exposed for the first time to different races and nationalities and having her first black friend.

Career Options

For many Southern women, adulthood options were marriage, teaching, and nursing. The women in this study entered education either knowing without a doubt they wanted to go into education or, as one said, never really thinking about a career. "I sort of evolved into that." "I didn't really decide on it as much as it just happened." One indicated that her only options were nursing and teaching and she "knew I was certainly not leaning toward nursing." For another woman who described herself as "pretty wide-eyed," her mother and guidance counselor decided she would be a teacher and completed her applications for a prospective teacher scholarship because she had no money. A mother was a powerful influence in the decision of another participant in the study who said, "My mother told me I had to be a teacher. You will not leave college without a teaching certificate. Period. She was a teacher." Another became a teacher because her husband was in the service and "in my way of thinking . . . hey, if I would just switch over to education then wherever he was, I could go and be a teacher."

Others entered knowing from a young age they were destined to teach. One woman whose parents were both teachers actually was discouraged by her mother, who wanted her to pursue music. "However," she said, "I just had a passion when I was a child." Her cousins recalled her setting them on the sidewalk and "holding school on the steps while I talked." Another remembered setting up her dolls and playing school. For one participant, "that was the only career that I had ever thought about. . . . You have your summers off and everything, and that was when I got married. I have been completely happy." One woman who also knew from an early age that she wanted to be a teacher described the playing school experience, although she confessed to actually playing principal. Of those women we interviewed, she was the only one who knew before she ever started teaching that she wanted to go into administration.

Except for the playing-principal participant, the women in the study never considered administration when they began their careers. One said, "I thought I would get certified in supervision. There were some women supervisors, but no women principals. Where I was, it was real rural and not progressive." Indeed, several of the women entered administration through the "you can be a supervisor at central office route." They bypassed the principalship. Three of the superintendents we interviewed have never been principals. One of these women felt that her extensive K–12 teaching experience validated her as an administrator, even though she had not served as a principal. She felt, however, that having not been a principal was an issue with some male colleagues who had been, especially the high school principals. One woman who did become a principal had never planned to enter education and changed her major several times before taking a foundations of education course and finding it intriguing. "It was never my desire to become an administrator," she said. " I certainly never wanted to be a principal and wondered why anybody would want that job, and as it turned out that job brought me the most joy out of all the jobs that I had."

Inspiration

Family, experiences, and other educators influenced the types of educators these women became. The administrator who attended a private Catholic school all her life (rare in this area) spoke of the positive influence of the nuns. One nun in particular, who knew of her love of math, told her, "Don't just work with numbers. You need to work with people." One participant recalled her second-grade teacher who said, "You can do anything if you can read." Another woman, who once again reminded us that who she became seemed to be very different from the women her mother was, said that she loved children for as long as she can remember and believed that love led her into special education. Yet another woman found herself inspired by her mother's creative teaching and by her grandmother, who was one of the first graduates of a normal school in the area. She added, "My dad died when I was fifteen, so I grew up in a house with my grandmother, my mother, and my sister. Very strong women. And that was the influence."

A vivid recollection for a woman whose mother discouraged her from teaching was the way the local political climate affected her mother's experience. Because of politics, her mother was unable to get a job in her home county. After finding a job in a neighboring county, "there was a time in her career when a candidate for sheriff came and asked her for money and she had to donate there right out of her classroom. . . . There was lots of pressure and very little money . . . and I think she thought I could do better for myself than teaching." Another participant cited her male high school principal as a strong influence on the type of educator she became. Noting his knowing every child's name and what they wanted to do with their lives, she added, "He was such a good role model to follow. And he is a local person." High school English teachers had a strong influence on one woman. Two others observed that fellow teachers and professional workshops probably shaped the educators they became.

Always a Teacher

The women in our study filled pages of transcriptions discussing their teaching days. These were women who went above and beyond. Commenting on how their colleagues described them as teachers, the words they used most commonly were *organized, dedicated,* and *going the extra mile.* One participant, who does not have children of her own, spoke of taking children home with her or picking them up and taking them to ballgames. Others used words like *passionate* and *caring, working hard, spending hours on lesson plans, doing far more than expected.* One observed, "I guess everybody did talk about me being dedicated and going the extra mile. You know, staying for extracurricular activities. It never occurred to me that you didn't do those things." One woman noted that even as a teacher she felt nudged into leadership roles by her teacher colleagues.

> Well, I think they did look to me more than I was comfortable with as a leader and often I felt the strain of that because they also turned to me to take leadership roles and I didn't feel like . . . I didn't want to be perceived as being pushy or taking over . . . and I often found myself in a state of flux, but I did find that they did often ask me to do things and came to me to initiate changes in the school or whatever and it wasn't a comfortable role for me as a teacher. It was very comfortable once I got the authority to do it.

Another woman felt her colleagues thought of her as child-centered and "a good team player."

Study participants provided rich descriptions of how they taught. One described her first day in a rural high school math and science class:

> I overheard a student say, "Look, she could work that problem on the board without copying it from the back of the book," and I turned around and I said, "What did you say?" And so they repeated it and I said, "Oh, yes" and then I thought, Oh my where am I? They must really need me here.

Another recalled her reaction to hearing another teacher say, "Just wait until you get that kid in your room, it is going to be heck to pay." She added, " I was more determined than ever that that child was going to succeed or at least that the child was going to feel good about himself in my room." One woman focused on the fact that as a mother, she knew what she wanted for her own children in the classroom and worked to

> treat them as you would your own children and I always tried to do that. I will never forget a little girl who came in and would not take her overcoat off on the warmest day. This was in the wintertime of course. But to get her coat off was a real challenge. And I knew she was probably being sexually and physically abused in her home because of other information I had and it was just so hard. So hard and I think of those stories. I remember the most those kids who . . . it was out of my hands, how to help her. I had to make others aware but there wasn't a lot I could do to change her home environment. So those were the tough ones you remember the most.

These women told many stories that revealed empathy for their students and a desire to do good work, to be of service.

One woman who taught math recalled from her own experience that she learned the multiplication tables, but never really used them. So one day when Rubik's cubes first came out, she bought some and used them in class to teach multiplication. She added, "I think that convinced me forever how important it is to have an understanding for students to get out of the abstract and into the concrete." Another woman spoke of her holding the same expectations for all students even in the days of tracking. She also described the experience of using powerful literature to connect to student experiences. One day, her students were reading aloud the story of a child who has a handicapped brother who embarrasses him. This woman used the story to think about the idea that we all have experiences in our families that may embarrass us. In this very emotional story, the boy dies. Our participant described what happened when she started reading the story aloud and began to choke up.

> So I was reading a part, and I choked up. And you know I had not done that so far but I stopped and said, somebody else read. And this football player who was sitting in front of me . . . started reading. And he read about two paragraphs and he said somebody else read. . . . By the end of the story, I was crying, the football player was crying and almost everybody in there was crying. Then the children started telling stories about their own brothers and sisters in special education. That was a good class.

Many of the women related anecdotes about teachable moments, indicating an awareness of teaching and learning as a creative process. It represented a puzzle to which there were answers that they could, often intuitively, find. Connections to students are important to these women. For one woman, the way she taught was not unlike the way she leads. Teaching a combination second-, third-, and fourth-grade class, she said, "My children had opportunity to give input, develop centers around the children's interests, and they had the opportunity for choice in my classroom."

Of the women we interviewed, one actually left the profession and went into business. Her reasons had a great deal to do with place. She had come back to teach in the high school from which she graduated, had her sister in a class, and children she had played with on her street as her students. "It was very difficult to draw the line," she said. "I struggled constantly between being distant in the classroom from people who were real close to me, but in a small community there is a problem. So it was not what I anticipated." She left and worked as an office manager for ten years. A superintendent recruited her to come back as a media coordinator. His argument was, "Your children need you to be at home during the summer." One woman considered leaving, but her husband convinced her that the business world might not be so attractive after all. He said, "I think you are going to find the business world quite different from education and I think you are going to find that it is going to be much more difficult for a woman, and it may not be what you really want it to be." She interviewed a couple of times, then changed her mind, realizing she would miss the relationships with students. Another woman was discouraged by her student-teaching experience at the age of nineteen. With no supportive mentoring and no enjoyment for what she was doing, this woman started her family. She considered going into the business world. "Only after I was told by a lot of people at that time fairly point blank, we don't hire women for management positions" did she reconsider teaching, this time at the elementary level. Here she found her niche.

On Hitting the Ceilings

Our interviews with the women in this study took an interesting turn. When we asked the question concerning any obstacles they faced moving into administration, a couple either said they had no obstacles or spoke guardedly about them, even though we knew some of the problems they had faced from other sources. These women, for the most part, had encountered barriers in their administrative careers. One woman who was very open about the problems she met wanted to "meet us out of town to discuss it." Our sense was that these administrators had spent many years and much hard work finally proving themselves and wanted to risk nothing to jeopardize it. And, too, they had been socialized not to raise unpleasantries in polite company.

One woman spoke of finally getting into a senior-level position when she earned her doctorate. All the men had theirs, so the superintendent said she must. Another woman described the challenge of being accepted after moving into a particular position. There was the problem of "having credibility in terms of knowing what I was doing. Being able to manage it, the school system . . . I have had some tough personnel issues, I mean really tough. And it is a miracle that I have survived a couple of them." She added that she prevailed because the law was on her side and because some faculty and parents knew what needed to be done.

Two women spoke of having been fortunate and invited to apply for positions, but one said that the superintendent who gave her such opportunities discouraged her from applying for a superintendency. She spoke of the "closed thinking" in the district and said, "I believe that if I had applied that being a woman would have hurt me." Another spoke of having been a principal and having the other principals' support to move into a senior-level position as easing her move up the ladder.

One woman from a small rural county attributed the long time it took to break into administration to four things: she was a female, the community remembered her as a child, she had children at home at the time, and she wasn't geographically mobile. This participant applied for thirteen or fourteen jobs before ever getting an assistant principalship. She described paying her dues by doing things like paddling children because the principal said "it would look better and I was so small. Nobody is going to say anything to a small woman about a paddling." She did all the scheduling for the school and never received credit and the assistant principalships she applied for were always given to someone else. Even when she obtained an advanced degree and was certified, a noncertified person was hired over her. When she asked why, she was told "Because of the physical demands of the job, it should go to a man." When she went higher up to ask the same question, she was told, "If you want to be an administrator, go back to the elementary school and get some experience teaching elementary school and you might be a principal someday." Her goal of being an administrator at the junior or senior high level looked impossible.

Seeking the advice of a mentor, she knew she could sue and probably win. He advised her that though she would win, she would also lose and probably die an assistant principal. He advised her to find some other way to get into administration and in the meantime not to be bitter or vengeful. "He gave me wonderful advice," she said. She found a way by becoming the local teachers' association representative and successfully leading an effort to overturn a board policy that was unfair to teachers. She became a presence to be reckoned with. Suddenly, an assistant principalship position opened at the level she wanted and she took it. She is now the superintendent in that district.

Another woman's first attempt to move into administration was disheartening. She had won many teaching awards, but a male got the position. She was told that everyone wanted their children in her classroom. She added, "They didn't realize what a slap in the face that was because I had worked so hard. I had much higher credentials than the person that got the supervisory position. But I said, I am not going to let that hold me back . . . the time is not right." She was glad she handled her disappointment in that manner because when she did finally secure an administrative position, the man who did not get the job became very upset. "I saw what happened to him," she said.

Taking This Same Journey

Participants in the study know themselves well, well enough to know how they function as leaders and what advice they would give to those who want to follow in their footsteps. One woman described herself as a strong "feeling type" and spoke of being warned by her husband: "You are so friendly and outgoing that I wish you would be very careful because I am afraid that somebody will mistake that and you might make somebody think something that you don't mean." She said she tried being more businesslike, but ended up telling her husband, "They're just going to have to take me for who I am." Another spoke of the value she had found in listening. "Once you let people in," she said, "you really do need to hear them and I think most of the time you can diffuse a lot of people's frustration and anger." She also advised aspiring administrators to really know themselves.

One woman spoke of the importance of lifelong learning and being flexible. "There are always other ways to do things," she said, "and you have to be open because this situation may demand an approach different from what you know or what you are comfortable with." Another participant emphasized knowledge and openness. Her version of flexibility was being on call twenty-four hours a day. "That is my job," she said "I have a beeper. If a parent calls and they can't come during their work time or whatever, I mean, I don't hesitate to give them my number at home because I feel like that is my job. And I know it's hard to wait twenty-four hours for someone to call you back, too."

Two women spoke how being organized and involving others had served them well. But they also warned of the hazards of the job. "It gets harder and harder," one said. "The time demands and the stress levels. . . . I think you have to weigh out, can I do that and balance everything else with the stress factors that are involved and with the emotional demands children place on you if you are really in tune with your job. I do think we need more women administrators." The other woman spoke of hard work and sacrifice:

> I have raised two children. But I have neglected them more than I should have. We all have. We had to. And I look back and think I should have done this. I should have done that. I went to the athletic banquet last night and thought, I never went to my children's. And I could beat myself up for it a lot. But really be sure you want to make the sacrifices and I still believe that women sacrifice more than men.

Balancing work demands and family responsibilities entered into conversations with women in ways they did not with our male participants. While one woman emphasized the importance of being " task-oriented and tenacious," another with many years experience spoke intensely of the need to be passionate. "Really be passionate about what you do and realize you do nothing alone," she said.

Conclusion

Most of the women in our study qualify as patient, astute, and intuitive observers. They are active participants in the counties in which they live and work. Though they may have encountered Southern Appalachian ceilings, they found different, sometimes long, routes to climbing administrative ladders. They believe in the importance of that place. Being Southerners, Appalachian natives, and females helped determine the shape and contours of their careers. In their often quiet, gentle, yet tenacious ways, they have become recognized as effective district-level leaders.

·7·

ROLE-PLAYING

Leadership is highly personal. The ways we lead result from who we are as individuals, our past experiences and observations of leaders, our education, mentors, people and ideas that inspire us, and we would argue, where and whom we are leading. We asked our participants to describe themselves and elaborate on the various roles they play as leaders. Comments by their central office subordinates and school board members added to those descriptions. Together, they helped us develop a picture of how senior educational leaders in the region construct their roles.

Men: Leadership as Life on the Edge

Our conversations with male participants gave us the sense that they approach leadership with a spirit of adventure. One man said it this way, "I live on the edge." Unlike the women, the men were not expected to practice gender deference. There were no inherent gender contradictions in their roles. Though they enjoyed the edginess, they spoke of tempering their styles with common sense. They used words like *pushing, moving, trying new and different things,* and *taking on a challenge*. A couple of them spoke of the focus on vision, "the visioning thing," as one called it. Another defined his mission as "keeping the main thing the main thing." One participant enthusiastically spoke of coming into a small rural county and turning the technology around. He gave PalmPilots to his administrators. "I had two principals who were adamant against using it who are my poster children now in terms of wanting to use it." One man volunteered that his leadership style had changed 180 degrees from his behavior earlier in his career. He had once been very autocratic; he now focuses on team leadership. Another described himself as providing the framework and letting people do their jobs. One man's leadership style centers on the participatory use of systems thinking. Another saw himself as taking the goals and objectives set by the board and facilitating their implementation. He accomplishes this by placing people where they can be successful. In the same spirit, one man saw himself as "an empathetic leader who is very client oriented, who sought to empower those around him." Even authoritative men were becoming team players, an indication that mountain leadership no longer requires a control-driven disposition.

Important Work: People and the Buildings That House Them

The men's responses to questions about the important work they do centered on students, personnel, and building projects. Several mentioned providing effective teachers who can provide quality instruction in the best facilities available. One man said, "If there is a good teacher and a better teacher, I want the better teacher." One emphasized the importance of hiring good principals. "Take a school of thirty superior National Board Certified teachers, put them in a school with a sorry principal, and you're not going to have a good school. And I'll take thirty mediocre teachers, give me a dynamic principal, and I'll have a good school." Concerning resources, one participant mentioned having to play "catch up" in his district. A school recently opened was the first new facility in his district in over forty years. Ensuring that students attend school only in safe and orderly environments was also important. Building a sidewalk for Pre-K children to walk to their busses was an example of another man's sense of important tasks. Facility construction was doing something good for children. One man mentioned the importance of fostering pride in the organization, "because you can accept less money and fewer resources if you've got a tremendous amount of pride in your organization." Another described the important task of "setting the agenda—the instructional mission agenda—and making sure we don't deviate from the agenda." "Stay on task" is a slogan that resonates with these leaders.

Accomplishments: Brick and Mortar Filled with Successful Kids

For the men, their accomplishments were related to work they considered important. Among the actions they mentioned were a successful middle school building project, the institution of an academic banquet, hiring good people, turning schools around, and saving an at-risk student. They defined their successes in terms of products and outcomes. For one male superintendent, the accomplishment of which he was most proud was the infusion of technology into the administrative and instructional work of the district. The facilities were important to several participants, often because years of neglect had rendered them unattractive, unsafe, or inadequate. One man said, "We're about 80 percent through with the completion of a bus garage. The garage we have is a one-bay rock building that was built in the 30s and we can't even get a bus in." Another spoke with pride of implementing the middle school concept in his district, while another cited the renovation of a middle school. He was also proud of revising a board policy manual that hadn't been touched in years. One superintendent spoke about the grants he and his team had been able to bring in. All of our participants talked about accomplishments in terms of what they would do for children. There was a decided emphasis on improving conditions for the sake of the young people in their districts.

Frustrations

Senior leaders expressed great frustration with things that stray from or disrupt their focus on children. Special interest groups, for example, appear to have another agenda. One man made this observation,

> The special interest groups have and continue to frustrate me . . . prayer, the pagans, the Christians, all these different groups haven't helped educators . . . abortion, gay rights, all the different things that are social issues now. People use the school as their springboard to promote their issue and I resent it.

Social issues also concerned another superintendent.

> We are the savior[s] of society . . . sexually transmitted diseases . . . substance abuse . . . Hepatitis B vaccine. . . . Doctors deal with medicine. Ministers deal with religion and soul saving. Accountants deal with taxes. Lawyers deal with legal matters. We deal with everything. . . . And it is very frustrating that the public still doesn't understand that the teaching learning process, that desire to learn must be instilled, nurtured, built up, celebrated, and there are so many children out there that it is not happening for. . . . I found the greatest fallacy is that they think we can do this job with the resources that we are given and in the time frame we are given to do it.

Another man was frustrated by reluctance to change or try new things, by what he described as "little pockets of resistance at different schools and people not rallying around what we need to accomplish. . . . There's always a little network of negativism . . . that bothers me because I feel like I am leaking oil."

One man described a similar frustration with the slow pace of change in his very conservative district. Resistance was also the concern of another man but in the form of "a number of retirees in the county who do not want to spend any money on education and are trying to nickel and dime us to death." Keeping parents interested and involved remained a challenge, as did working with State Department of Public Instruction bureaucrats in Raleigh.

Several men spoke of their frustrations with school boards, most of which resulted from a failure of some board members to understand their role. In anticipation of this problem, one superintendent actually had written into his contract that he, not the board, would run the district. Another had to "train his board." He said, "For personnel recommendations, the board had been used to the superintendent bringing them three names and the board then made the selection. I told them I wouldn't do that from day one." He explained that it was his role to recommend and their role to approve. "There were a lot of angry tempers but once we went through it a couple of times and the board saw it was working, then we could go on." Personnel issues with board members were a frustration for another man. The chairman asked his board to give the superintendent a salary increase and succeeded. "But he was salting the mine. A few months later, he asked me about moving his daughter into the central office. Well, I didn't do that. I had twenty-eight years going on [retirement]. If he had known me, he wouldn't have asked me that. Of course, I said no and it just went south from there." The board member told the newspapers that the superintendent got an illegal supplement (the raise he himself had proposed.) The controversy was sufficiently contentious that the board member was defeated in the next election.

For another, the actual board meetings were frustrating. He spoke of all the work that went in to trying to get board members to agree on an issue and then having "one little incident" cause it to fall apart. The tendency to micromanage on the part of some boards seems to be a continuing problem. We were made aware during our study of one county where a board member walked into the superintendent's office before a board meeting and told him that when a name for a principalship in the district was presented to the board at the next meeting, it had better be a certain person. In another county the board chair insisted on personally signing the checks for all system employees.

The Significance of Place

The men in our study are both insiders and outsiders and they differ in their feelings about the significance of place. These men represent those born and reared in Western North Carolina, those born in the South but not in the area, and a participant who moved south from a northern state. One of the participants in the study serves as superintendent in a county next door to the county of his birth. When he meets people in his district, if he is asked, "Are you from off?" he is quick to explain his connection with relatives in the county. He knows from the question that for that particular person, geography is important. One participant spoke of the power that comes with working in a place that is a good fit professionally. "I heard another superintendent say, 'You know when I was in such and such, I did all these things and they wouldn't pay a bit of attention. I went to a different district and did the same thing and they loved it. It's working.' You have got to analyze your environment to see what does that place identify with?"

Western North Carolina politics weighed heavily in the experience of one district leader who said, "I was the first Republican superintendent in the county in twenty-five years." He took on the powerbrokers. "I guess I challenged the board in trying to initiate sound business practices using the audit, for example, and bidding things off." He even challenged the rental of an unneeded building from a local legislator. "That was the death of me." He lost his job in that district. Another participant had to battle his board to bid banking and copying services. The board finally came around when he proved he had saved the district money. Another participant who moved into the region from a neighboring Southern state spoke of the impact of place on curriculum:

> Western North Carolina is very different than . . . the Charlotte Metro Area. There are curriculum decisions here I would make that I wouldn't make in the metro area. I would be much more involved with pushing . . . more liberal issues like respect for different cultures, different sexual preferences, you know, understanding and diversity. . . . Here I am very leery of most of those things. I tend to reflect the community in which I work and I know this community is very conservative. Also, I know in the debate issues I have to be extremely careful because many people in Western North Carolina would make up their mind about things but their reason and logic would go out the window. So you have to be careful how far you push people here.

A native of the area spoke of hiring a very strong principal who grew up in a northern state. He said the principal's one weakness was "being able to relate to these mountain people and you can't . . . be straightforward with them sometimes. You got to just walk on eggshells and get what you want to say across, but you got to know how to do that."

Another district leader described what it takes to be a superintendent in his small Southern Appalachian district.

> You have to be a good listener. You have to be close to your public. I drive a pickup truck. It wouldn't do for me to drive a Corvette to work. I would rather drive a pickup anyway. When I leave here, I wear blue jeans and t-shirts. . . . I have talked to people in this office about not wearing their jobs on their sleeves and I really believe that is the way to go. You will never see a name plate on my desk. I don't do business cards.

A participant who moved into the area from another part of North Carolina characterized some of his behavior as conscious self-editing.

> Sometimes when I want to talk about an issue or maybe somebody in the local government, that is a point of frustration to me. I really have to be careful because they have extended family working for me. . . . Probably the best piece of advice that was given to me before I took this job was that, whether they are your enemy or working with you, they are both camping at the same store. But if you tell one something different from the other, it's going to come back and bite you in the rear end. And they aren't going to trust you anymore. And trust is a big issue up here.

Still another man who moved from downstate to the uplands said that he is often told that he is "not from around here and let us tell you how it is." He added, "I'm not easily influenced by special interest groups and told the local TV station, 'I am not the social director for the county. If you want to talk about education, fine. I don't have time to talk about witches and Halloween parties. Good day.'"

Several men noted the advantages of working in Southern Appalachia. One observed, "I think there is a closer family unit here and when kids are displaced, there is usually an extended family within the area that can pick up the slack. That is not how it was in the Piedmont." One man noted the proud and resourceful nature of people in the area. Another participant spoke of the advantage of the small size of his community and district. He knows every parent and every child. However, there are disadvantages that concern him, "We just don't have employment for kids. We preach education and we say you've got to get an education to get a good job, but where is the job? You have to go somewhere else to find a job. We are a very poor county economically."

The remoteness of some counties is a disadvantage in recruiting and retaining superintendents who are not local residents. When one participant moved from a high school principalship in the largest school district in the region to a small, rural superintendency, his marriage suffered.

> One situation that has affected me directly is that I have been married for twenty-six years and my wife and I are now separated. I think one contributing

> factor would be maybe where we are living now. We used to live in another county and all of my wife's friends were there and I was gone a lot and that didn't work. So I think that in choosing to go to a rural system both parties in a relationship need to be willing to make sacrifices in it or there can be a significant negative impact on the relationship.

When his separation occurred, he told the board and that he was prepared to resign if the situation was a problem for the district. Instead, the board told him to be quiet, renewed his contract, gave him a pay raise, and said they appreciated his not bailing out on them. "I was pleased with that," he said. "I was very emotional about it, too. It was the only thing positive that had happened to me in six months." He has since happily remarried.

Only one participant in the study did not see the Southern Appalachian region as unique. "People are pretty much the same everywhere. They want to be happy. They want to be secure in their job. They want to be safe. And they want their kids to do better than they did."

On the Subject of Women Leaders

When asked about differences between men and women leaders, the males in our study were divided. Some did not see any difference. One felt the perception of a difference is changing. "It's about what people bring to the table—what skills they come to the job with. Some women are more caring and nurturing and I have worked with women who would cut your heart out." Five of the male participants felt men and women do lead differently. One said that women are more meticulous. Another volunteered that he had been reading a book on what women want men to know about women. He observed, "Sometimes women react differently to women in leadership roles. I think sometimes women think 'She's sold out to the other side. . . . She's become one of the good old boys.'" "Men," he thought, "are able to compartmentalize things a lot better. They don't take things as personally as a woman in a leadership role because quite often to women relationships are everything." Another man felt that males get to the point quicker. "I can say to a man, 'Meet with that sucker and get it fixed today.' If I say that to a woman, she reacts differently." "Men are probably quicker to pull the trigger than women," observed one man. "I think the good Lord has given them [women] more patience. To be a momma, you've got to be a patient woman."

Two men approached the question differently. One said that men and women do not lead differently but if something is coming from a female, rather than a male, it is perceived differently by some males. He recalled a woman who had supervised him who "put a spin on her leadership style that only a female could because it was sort of a 'mom thing.'" He mentioned another woman who was perceived as "very hard core, very inflexible, very tough. Had she been a man, she would have been perceived as very thorough, very focused, and very committed. I won't even mention some of the words used about her outside the office." The youngest member of our study (age thirty-six) had yet a different perspective. "I don't think it is so much gender as generational. . . . I find that in my interaction with those closer to my age, the gender doesn't matter."

Two of the men described the ceilings they encountered when they tried to hire women leaders. One hired the first female administrator in his county on a split vote of the board. "It was not without a fight." Another faced criticism as a high school principal where he had one female assistant principal and hired another. "The public in general thinks you need two big strapping men to go in there and kind of take charge. Well I disagree. I think it is important to have someone who can meet the job description. . . . That was the best decision I ever made in my life."

The Men in General

We found the men in our study to be a dedicated, likeable group, committed to providing sound educational opportunities, often with far fewer resources than counties downstate. As the region grows and more "outsiders" move in, they attempt to bring people together. In a more rural area in one of the districts in the Western Region, an affluent member of the community called his child's principal to demand that his daughter not be in a certain class where she would have to sit next to a biracial child. The principal explained he could not do that. Soon after, the principal received a call from a board member suggesting that he should comply with the parent's request. He then asked the principal when his contract was coming up for renewal. The principal, despite the not-so-veiled threat to his job, stood firm. The superintendent supported him. Loyalty, a mountain virtue, is also a professional one—particularly in educational causes that necessitate challenging parochial perspectives.

Women: Leading with Style

The women in our study showed a perceptive awareness of how their leadership styles evolved. A couple of them described moving from a telling to a participative style. A word they used frequently was "listening." One woman focused on her belief in consensus building, describing a meeting with the principals she supervises. She talked about how she worked with them to decide what kind of students should qualify for the district assessment center. Another woman described herself as "very hands-on":

> My personnel director says I remember everything. If somebody is going to do something, I will come back and say "What did you find when you did that?" and "How did you do that?" and some people don't like that. The group that we have as a team now, they just know that I am going to ask, "What did you find out on that?" You feel in a small place that you can never get that balance, but I am very hands-on. I want to know budgets month to month. I want to know everything I can about accountability standards. I want to know how many kids are ones and twos.[1]

Some women described their leading as setting parameters. "Your job is to set parameters and to interpret information in a way that is easy for them to do their job. All that information they don't need. They don't want it and they don't need it. You don't just turn them loose and say, do whatever you want to." She saw herself as a very direct person when working with subordinates. "If I have something to say to somebody I bring them in and close the door and I say it as directly as I can. Sometimes it is 'Do you remember when you did this?' and 'Yes,' and I say don't do that anymore." Holding her tongue was not a problem in such situations.

One experienced senior leader described getting feedback from those who worked for her that indicated that her standards were so high that they were not sure they could meet them. She said that ten years ago she probably did not give enough positive feedback and learned "that I needed to really pay attention to that and let people know that I appreciate what they are doing." In describing how others see them as leaders, one female superintendent summed it up:

> I think you would get two different reports on that . . . she works hard . . . cares for children . . . professional . . . well organized . . . well prepared . . . goal oriented. And it may be different now than it was ten years ago. You know I have been involved in this school system through a merger, through a lot of serious personnel issues. After I got to be superintendent, I changed six principals out of six in two or three years, and you don't do those things without some people feeling like, in a small community especially, that you are a tyrant, a bitch. . . . I hate to use that word, but you know what I am saying.

Since that time, this leader has pulled together a team that has been well accepted in the community.

One woman observed that people would say she was fair, impartial. Another felt others would speak of her interpersonal skills and love of involving others in decisions. One traced what others would say about her leadership back to her teaching days when she took a job as one of two white teachers in an all-black school. "Those were the two most wonderful years of my life." She was awarded tenure after two years and as the black high school was closing, she was asked to go with the black students to the white high school because she had developed close relationships with them and could ease their transition. She felt her leadership skills in helping with the merger were honored and recognized.

Important Work: A Place for All Children

The women in this study feel the work they do is important. For some of them, what is most important centers around their job descriptions or specific responsibilities. One cited the process of strategic planning, goal setting, establishing higher expectations, and fostering the premise that every child can learn. As one said, "That there is a place for all children in a school . . . we are there to serve all children." Another felt that her work with staff development was most important "because that is the most direct line that I have to the children." One participant named making sure that the "right, correct, appropriate developmental curriculum is being taught in all of our preschool through 12 [classrooms]. I feel totally responsible for that." For one woman, the most important thing she does presents a challenge:

> The most important thing, which I struggle to do, is to be in schools on a daily basis. But when you are in curriculum and instruction and you don't know what teachers are doing and you don't know what kids are learning, you don't know what principals are thinking and if you don't know the problems out there, then it is very hard to be on top of things and to offer solutions to help be a problem solver if you don't know what is going on.

These participants talked at some length about teaching and learning, their own instructional experiences when they were in classrooms and their roles as administrators who try to establish environments conducive to that process.

Others in the study focused on more intangible elements of leadership. Whereas the men built the house and set the table with the right people, the women seemed to focus on facilitating interactions and relationships among those people. One woman described her responsibility as a role model: "I think the example I set is most important rather than what I say or what I do.

It is what they see me do and what they perceive that I do whether I am doing it or not, it is the perception of me." Another described her work with principals:

> I feel like the principals are just kind of out there by themselves and I think having been a principal and you just have . . . you don't ever forget that relationship. . . . I think they have a lonely job and that they really need to be able to share problems and questions with others, and so, I really try to work with them.

Another administrator emphasized her role as a listener:

> Being a good listener is tremendously important. People call all the time to the superintendent to complain. That is the only reason anybody ever calls. And a lot of times all they really want is somebody to listen to them and sympathize and I would genuinely sympathize. Even when I have to say "No, I am sorry your child has to be long-term suspended" and I tell them I am sorry, I am legitimately sorry. I understand that you are having a bad time and I know that he is a good kid but the worst thing we can do for kids is to let them believe the rules do not apply to them.

Our female participants spoke of developing caring relationships, using skills that they acquired even before they went into education.

Not I but We

When asked about their proudest accomplishment, most of the women deflected credit from themselves to others. One woman said, "I feel really like it has been the effort of some really, really good people working very hard from the board down. Getting a strong administrative staff in place, and I certainly can't take credit for anybody who is elected to the board." Many used the word "we" in describing accomplishments. One woman recalled her experience working with a team to implement an extended day and year-round school program as well as working successfully in the middle of a difficult city-county merger. Another felt most proud of her experience as a role model: "I think the influence I have had on individual principals that have come back to me and said, 'You have been my role model. I have tried to lead like I have seen you lead.'" Another participant spoke of helping to maintain a focus on children in the midst of accountability pressures. One described working with a strong team to move her county into the top ten in the state in terms of academic achievement. Student success was the focus of another woman's proudest accomplishments—developing a comprehensive remediation program and personalized educational plans for children not performing at grade level. Another shared her development of an effective school pilot program that was later used by the state as "just the sort of a thing I did at my kitchen table one night so that people would not be crazy." She also cited the effective teacher training she helped developed for new faculty in her county and her hands-on role in delivering the program. For another administrator, her district's self-development program and effective communications among forty schools were things to be proud of.

In the Interest of Children

The women in this study feel deeply responsible for the students in their care. Their greatest frustrations center on those things that impede that care. One woman recalled a board of education in a previous system where she worked that was "very, very narrow minded." After presenting test results to the board, she was accused of manipulating the data to suit her purposes. This question of her integrity she described as "the biggest frustration that I have ever had." Another mentioned the North Carolina Department of Public Instruction. A polite Southern belle and very professional woman, she began with "This is no offense by any means" and then described different interpretations of policy emanating from different offices as well as heavy and meaningless paperwork demands for principals. Three women cited the lack of time as their greatest frustration. "I am a perfectionist and there is no time at all. It gets very frustrating for me. Whatever I do, I want to do it the best. And it is just not possible." Another added, "I don't have time to do everything I want and need to do with my family."

The pluses and minuses of "coming back to where you grew up" was one woman's greatest frustration. She described it this way,

> It is very rewarding to commit your life in working with children in a place that you have strong commitments and ties to, so that part, all that goes with that, is very rewarding. However, when you deal sometimes with personnel issues or you deal with student discipline issues and you have known the families involved for many years and you know the kids and you know sometimes they will never speak to you again for as long as they live . . . that and working with the county commissioners have been the most difficult.

Two women were most frustrated by working to narrow the racial achievement gap in their systems. One noted, "It is like eating an elephant. It's like how soon are you going to get that elephant eaten? It is a long-time problem created and the solution is not going to happen probably in my lifetime and that is frustrating me because I like to see results." The other woman, describing the same challenge said, "Never a day goes by that that is not foremost in my mind."

This Is My Home

Most of the women in our study find themselves in leadership roles in areas where they have lived all their lives. Though they have faced hardships along the way, they are there either by choice or because their children tied them there. On being asked about the advantages and disadvantages of being from the region, one woman noted, "I think it is a wash. . . . Initially, like I said, it was hard getting in [administration], but I have had wonderful success and luck and lots of opportunities to lead in really good jobs. But this is home, and I have done well, why leave?" She shared with us one of several Southern ceiling examples we heard.

> Several years ago we had some street preachers. . . . Eventually it got on national TV and Sally Jesse Raphael and all those other stories. And he would bring his children. What would happen is that he would put his children out to preaching on the school campus. The children were not attending class and shouting "whoremongers" and were suspended. He would never shake my hand because he said I was sinning against God because I was in a position of authority over men. And you still have to sort of play a fine line. I have to play it less now than I have in the past. But just not being too aggressive. It is not acceptable for women to be too aggressive.

Another woman secured her first teaching job because her uncle was on the local board of education. She had not completed her certification because her grandmother had been ill and needed attention. Having been initially turned down for the position, her family connection helped secure it. Another felt firmly that being from the region provided her with essential knowledge about the community and the people. Still another believed that being from the region provided an additional trust factor that worked in her favor. "I think it would be hard to get a job in another district without those relationships and I doubt I would get one." Another participant agreed with that sentiment, but did not necessarily feel that being from the region was essential.

Two women saw their rural mountain roots as an asset in leading others. "One thing about mountaineers . . ." she said, "is that we can be very stubborn. We can be very outspoken. We can be very proud of our background." She described one of her first experiences entering her husband's work-related social circle. Initially feeling uncomfortable in those social situations, she worked to grow beyond her discomfort. That experience helped her understand the feelings of parents who are intimidated in the presence of educators. "And I think that unless you have experienced some of those things in your own life, it is hard to have empathy. So I have been grateful for that." The other said being a native is an asset because she knows the importance of understanding local people. "I think it would be hard for somebody from New York City to come in and try to fit in. It's just a different world. Our values are different." She also thought that she would not have been hired as superintendent had she not been from the area.

Place: It Matters

All of the women in our study acknowledged the significance of the Southern Appalachian setting on their roles as leaders. One woman vividly recalled that when she was first hired as a principal, a female principal was unheard of. "I guess the saving grace for me was that I had been there for those eight years and I have good relationships with the community and the parents and everything and having seniors, I began having their children come back very quickly." She described learning that she "had to go the extra mile" to show people she was doing a good job. "It was not the superintendent or board of education that I was proving it to. I just wanted the community to see that I could do that." She recalled the superintendent being approached by a female in the community who said a woman should not be in an administrative position because she could not keep order. Years later, after she moved to another administrative post, the parent confessed what she had done. "I really didn't think a woman could come in and do the things that needed to be done and you certainly proved me wrong." Another woman cited the Scotch-Irish background of many people in the area, attributing it to gender segregation. "I think that a lot of that culture has to do with men, males being the leaders, and breadwinners, and I think there is a little bit of that still hanging in there." For another woman in a large school district, leadership positions for women are not a problem. She credits a previous male superintendent who was bold enough to hire a female high school principal. "That had never been the case before," she said. "And once that door was opened, women were able to seek more jobs. And women I really do believe have to do double the work and work twice as hard to get to a certain level. Once you get to that level, I think that people see that women can do it."

Other participants noted additional concerns about some communities in Southern Appalachia. One, concerned about cultural barriers on aspiration, talked about the

> very pervasive attitude of some parents . . . that they didn't value education. In fact, they were very suspicious of people who were educated and their message, their Southern message to their kids, sometimes is "Don't you get so high and mighty. Don't go out there and get above your raisings. I didn't finish high school and look how well I have done."

Another spoke of her frustration with the lack of resources for some of the children in her district. Because of the per capita wealth of retirees drawn to the beauty of the mountains, the district qualifies for very little additional assistance. Many children would go unserved without creative efforts, such as a full-day program for four-year-olds. Another woman described her efforts with the local arts council to expose children in the district to opportunities they might never experience.

Geography was seen as a potential political liability to one woman. "I think where we live we are disadvantaged from Raleigh, the state capital, because we are closer to some others than our own. So we have to rely on Atlanta, Chattanooga, and other states for a lot of things. We don't even get a North Carolina television network out here." However, she believes, "We have deep roots that make us strong people. There is something about the strength that runs in our blood and in the mountain culture." She also praised the work ethic in her community, noting that the Ohio School System studied her school district's effectiveness and concluded that the difference in the systems was the strength of the local work ethic.

Painting with a Big Brush vs. Picking Up the Details

Female study participants all agreed that, all things considered, women and men lead differently. As one noted, "People don't expect men to be good with particulars. People expect men to paint with a brush and somebody else to pick up the pieces and make sure everything is correct. . . . People expect women to be good with the details and take care of the details themselves." Though she described herself as good with details, she added,

> In my childhood days, I wanted to go out and hang out with the boys. I have spent most of my days with men. My two assistants are men. Before I was superintendent, everybody I worked with was a male. I travel with men. I like to go out and still have a good time. So it may be different for other women and, of course, I have been divorced for quite a while. So I am probably natured more like a man than a woman. But I think they lead differently in many ways.[2]

Several participants observed that women have to work harder. In her previous role as assistant superintendent, one participant said that a look at the district flow chart showed her duties increasing twofold, while those of others did not. She also thought that in her days as principal, she was different from her male counterparts in her belief in her school. She described the day the superintendent introduced her to a group of realtors and said, "This lady is going to tell you that she has the best school and if you don't believe her, you will surely know it by the time you have finished talking to her."

Some participants described females as more nurturing, tactful, sensitive, and inclusive. One contrasted the leadership styles of men and women by describing men as tending "to be more lone rangers. You know, they will do it but it is not for the same reason. They tend to just dive into battle and shoot more from the hip." She added also that some men "in their true and different way, they create a dependency."

The Women in General

Like the men in our study, the women to whom we talked willingly shared their time and observations with us. They are geographic insiders who share many of the same experiences growing up in Southern Appalachia. These administrators, while reluctant to discuss gender, acknowledge in other questions that they sometimes worked harder than their male colleagues and that they occasionally encountered community perceptions that worked to their disadvantage when they sought higher-status positions. Forthright at times, they also were adept at deflecting questions to which they did not want to respond (those initial inquiries about barriers). They were not timid about touting the good things in their school systems. Like their male counterparts, they have a keen appreciation for the setting in which they work and the people who populate it.

Similarities

The men and women in our study socially construct their roles in similar ways. Their rural backgrounds contribute to a strong work ethic. It also appears that their family backgrounds add to this work ethic as well. Their most important early influences tend to be family members. We had no conversation that did not provide us with anecdotes that emphasized the importance of kinship. In addition, families continue to play a significant role in their lives.

Collectively, they bring to administration an abiding belief in the importance of education in getting ahead. Education, they believe, is the way out of poverty, an engine for upward mobility. In some cases, that belief began when they were children and their parents, many of whom did not have much formal education, instilled in them the importance of doing well in school. Their success is also testimony to the rewards that come from education. All of them sought advanced degrees and most of them have college credits beyond anything they would need to qualify for either a principal's or superintendent's license. Men are more likely to hide their book learning than women, but have never been reluctant to secure what was necessary for career advancement.

The emphasis of their work is on children, doing something to benefit or uplift young people. Those who are native to the region use such language extensively. There is no reluctance to talk about their role as a service worker. Some administrators working in their home county noted that they wanted to give something back to their community. In focusing on children, our participants are aware of the unique attributes of the communities in which they work, although there are some subtle shades of difference. The women, for instance, are more likely to cite frustration with parents who do not want their children to "get above their raisin's."

Both women and men acknowledge that politics in their districts is an often fractious, personal enterprise. It is ubiquitous, something that they cannot escape and that plays a larger role in their professional lives than it might in other parts of the state. Political memories run deep and boards occasionally transgress their roles as policymakers by attempting to become implementers too. Neither group talked at length about local politics, their silence sometimes more telling than the anecdotes that they chose to share. There is a collective awareness of the peculiar politics of communities within communities. They recognize the need to establish some degree of insiderness to attain and hold positions like the superintendency.

Both men and women know that appearances matter (pickup trucks, conservative but feminine dress for the women) but they pay attention to different things. For instance, the women set up their offices to reflect their positions as wives and mothers or as caregivers with an interest in children. Most educational leaders who are natives to the region, male and female, believe that it is important to be perceived as a part of the community, as a regular person. In addition, there is a sensitivity to histories of personnel decisions based on patronage, a particular problem in the smaller, more rural systems, and a collective desire to move beyond that era.

Both the men and the women confront problems rather than wait for them to go away. They acknowledge the need to bid services rather than rely on patronage, to close the door, and to talk to people directly. They do not hesitate to address issues when they arise. However, there is also a sensitivity to "what won't work here" and how to talk to the "locals." They are also aware that some subjects, aspects of diversity and alternative lifestyles, are not yet ready for prime time in the mountains.

Differences

Although there are many similarities between the men and women, there are notable differences. While both have a strong work ethic, they actualize it differently. Women are often more conscious of details. They appear less willing to delegate some things. Women were more likely to mention the problem of time, particularly as it relates to finding sufficient time to be with their children and to meet other family obligations.

The men in our study were more playful, less serious (in a healthy way). They were more likely to have been rebellious and less focused in their early college experiences. They were less likely to identify themselves as intellectuals (at least publicly).[3] Even the women are at pains to avoid being perceived as simply an egghead. Their behaviors usually reflected gender stereotypes. No woman, for example, rode a Harley-Davidson. Few men decorated their offices with care and attention to detail. Men dressed down in rural districts when school was not in session; women did not. Men took charge of situations; women were more circumspect. Only one female in the study self-identified as "one of the guys."

The female participants are less geographically mobile, more likely to have deep roots in the region and system in which they work, and more likely to move into administration through the encouragement of someone local, rather than specifically seeking such a position. They express more concerns about family. One woman did not have children. "My life has been my work. I could have never put the time into it if I had had children. I can't even begin to comprehend it." Another woman said that she could not physically have children and that though she and her husband decided to adopt, "I started back to school and we haven't adopted yet."

Supportive husbands were keys to the survival of four women. One participant, after describing her nightmarish schedule, said that she and her husband have a dinner date every Thursday night. Another, who had been divorced, said that her parents had helped with her children and indicated that her former husband "was never a help. Never." Many females relied on extended family for childcare and support, an advantage of staying close to home.

The women are more likely to speak of inclusiveness and process, whereas the men speak more of delegation and product. The men are more likely to describe their job in terms of challenge and adventure. These differences are possibly reflective of their leadership styles as well as gender expectations in the region. Women are more likely to speak about teaching and learning from a classroom perspective, which is partially a function of their longer experiences in the classroom. When they talk of teaching, they have more to say about it and offer personal examples of creativity and success in the classroom. Their affinity to classrooms influences what they emphasize when they are in supervisory roles. It also influences the central office position to which they most often gravitate (curriculum and instruction).

The language of most of the women is more likely to be formal and deferential, more attuned to what people expect from them as women. They are adept at holding their tongues, taking care of men, and apologizing for certain language. In addition, they know that they are being closely watched and are more likely to play by the rules and adhere to expectations than the men. Our one African American participant, although male, was also very cognizant of being observed and judged in ways that were more akin to the scrutiny that some women experienced.

Observing the Leaders

What do others say about senior educational leaders in the region? To answer that question, we asked central office administrators and school board members. From their perspectives, what contributed to success in the region? What resulted in leadership disasters? Were the perceptions of our sample of senior leaders similar to those of people who worked for and with them? To the people who hired them?

Central Office Staff Observations

We asked central office personnel to consider the relative importance of several factors in the performance of a senior educational leader. Of the thirty responses to our survey, 40 percent of the central office respondents (mean response 3.43) rated being from the area as important, while 77 percent (mean = 2.6) considered being familiar with the area important.[4] Being a Southerner was important to 43 percent (mean = 3.43), and 87 percent (mean = 1.80) considered certification in educational administration important, with the same percentage acknowledging the importance of knowledge of curriculum and instruction. Business management skills and facilities knowledge were important to 93 percent (mean = 1.93) and 94 percent (mean = 2.00), respectively. Ninety-seven percent (mean = 1.73) of respondents rated school-community relations skills as important with 100 percent (mean = 2.47) rating educational research knowledge important. Teaching experience was valued as important by 90 percent (mean = 2.2) and principal experience by 76 percent (mean = 2.3). The item with the greatest number of responses marked "vital" (a rating of one) was certification in educational administration (57 percent), followed by knowledge of curriculum and instruction and school community relations skills, both 47 percent. (See Appendix, Tables 2 and 3.)

We also asked these central office staff members to tell us what gets senior educational leaders in trouble in their districts. Half of the open-ended responses dealt in some way with a failure to understand and communicate with the community. They phrased this concern as " lack of understanding of the community," "insensitivity to customers and stakeholders," "not appeasing special populations," "not understanding the values, customs, etc. of the local people," "school community relations," "underestimating the time needed to explain one's views and vision," "haste," "lack of understanding of school district issues and the failure to respond to the ever-changing expectations of parents and community," and "not being sensitive to local political, social, environmental, economic, and religious issues." Other responses dealt with decision making, micromanagement, and communication issues within and among members of administrative teams.

In another attempt to tease out the antithesis of effective leadership, we asked subordinates to tell us the thorniest problems facing their systems. They clustered in three groups: community relations, personnel, and academic performance. Community issues dealt with pressure to continue high performance, cooperation in dealing with Native American concerns, the economy and declining student enrollment, inclement weather conflicts such as child care, "moving from old ways to new ways," "C-H-A-N-G-E," and "Prayer at the Pole." Personnel matters involving coaches, band directors, embezzlement, and sexual misconduct all received mentions. The minority achievement gap and implications of No Child Left Behind legislation were generating concern in several districts as well as special education student issues.

Because gender was the original focus of our study, we asked them if they thought that it was a factor in leadership choices or performance. Twenty-two respondents said no. Other responses raised questions. One participant said she didn't think gender mattered, "but we have never had a female superintendent." Another indicated that "it may [matter] to the school board which has only one female. We have only one female senior leader." One man said that it does not matter unless the leader makes it an issue. "Some female administrators wear their pro-female gender bias on their sleeve. This makes it difficult to ignore." For a female participant, there was some doubt: "Hard to say. We have gone from a woman superintendent to a five-man leadership team. It does matter with pay. The top eight positions with regard to salary are men." Another participant acknowledged the role of the community in the issue. "Some community members see various positions being more appropriate for males or females."

In spite of the relatively low rating given to matters related to place on the forced-choice portion of the survey, it was belied somewhat by the unsolicited responses on the open-ended section relative to issues that got local leaders in trouble. Although most respondents did not see gender as an issue, a vocal minority contributed comments that suggested it was a barrier in some locations and with some populations. Female respondents were more likely to mention it as an issue than were males. Scattered comments alluded to parochialism and a reluctance to change. Religion received several mentions, including both a generic issue and a specific reference to "rally around the pole" prayer sessions. Many of the frustrations and issues that would elicit negative reactions could be found in almost every school district. They involved test scores, accountability systems, personnel, and communication.

Of the knowledge and skills considered important in performing effectively as a district leader, subordinates ranked school/community relations higher than any other category. It was followed by having the appropriate credentials, which includes the requisite education necessary to qualify for state licensure. That means that central office workers want their leaders to be adept people persons and familiar with the range of topics covered in a formal preparation program. Third on the list was knowledge of curriculum and instruction, and the fourth item, business management skills. We suspect the elevated stature of the former is a direct result of the state's emphasis on student achievement and the likelihood of senior leaders to have expertise in the business aspects of running a school district.

The least important attributes for a senior leader are related to geography. While that is probably an accurate measure of its value relative to the specifics of job performance, working with the people in the region and being a skilled communicator suggest that leaders must be able to take their message convincingly to the community. Again, looking at some of the open-ended comments that stress the uniqueness of local residents and the districts in which certain respondents worked, it appears that it remains an issue in some counties (the more remote, the more likely it is to be a concern) and not in others.

Other items receiving relatively low ratings include knowledge of educational research and specific experience as either a teacher or a principal. It was more important to have experience as a teacher than as a principal, but not vital or even very important to around a third of the respondents. Assuming that administrators learn about what works and what does not work from a professional research base, it is notable that the former is considered neither vital or very important by nearly half of central office subordinates. In a similar way, we suspect that most of us want our physicians to be familiar with medical research. Either someone else is monitoring that part of the educational house or the usefulness of the current knowledge base is less than obvious. It might be interesting to consider the relative worth of experience and scholarship in effective districtwide leadership. Given that several superintendents in the region have not been principals and are performing well might be one reason that such a background is considered relatively unimportant.

School Board Observations

For a community perspective, we asked board members their perceptions of the importance of certain factors when selecting a senior educational leader. Fifty-seven percent of respondents in the school board survey rated being from the area important (mean response = 3.23). A larger percentage (63 percent) thought being familiar with the area important, while being from the South was important to only 54 percent (mean = 3.47). Certification in educational administration is important for 85 percent (mean = 1.89) despite North Carolina's decision to drop that requirement for the superintendency. Just as important (85 percent) is the candidate's knowledge of curriculum and instruction (mean = 1.92). All of our respondents (100 percent) consider business management (mean = 1.79) important, while 93 percent (mean = 2.46) believing that facilities knowledge is important. Ninety-nine percent rate school-community relations as important (mean = 1.67). Knowledge of educational research is important for 78 percent of the participants (mean = 2.89). Seven percent thought a candidate did not necessarily have to have teaching experience and 26 percent felt that a successful candidate could forego being a principal. (See Appendix, Tables 4 and 5.)

It is interesting that one of the highest percentages in the vital category is certification in educational administration (46 percent). Board members in Western North Carolina appear unlikely to hire a superintendent outside the education profession. Their emphasis on teaching and principal experience confirms this as well. The importance of principalship experience could serve as a barrier for some women who, according to our study, often bypass the principalship for central office positions. Respondents seem evenly divided on the importance of being from the region and the South. We attribute that indifference to increased outside hiring practices. Again, disaggregating the data by county suggests that the more populous the county, the less likely it is to consider geography a disadvantage.

Like central office staff, board members believe that school/community-relations skills are the most important skill a district leader can have. Also like subordinates, board members rank knowledge of curriculum and instruction and business management skills only slightly lower, but they reverse the order. They think more highly of the business side of the role, whereas the central office is more concerned about teaching and learning. The difference reflects the work each group does with system leaders. Boards are more involved with budgets and buildings; support staff members are more involved with classrooms and accountability.

Board members identified many of the same problematic issues that were mentioned by central office respondents. Their responses to a thorniest issue open-ended item clustered around students, curriculum, personnel, and budgets. Student issues included expulsions, suicides, child molestation, student attendance, redistricting, and special needs students. Instructional concerns included sex education and the implications of No Child Left Behind. Personnel matters ranged from a teacher assistant charged with molesting several children and theft in the finance department to more mundane problems like coaching decisions. Budget issues weighed heavily on the minds of several board members. A charter school lawsuit in which the school sued the district for funds, transportation funding, getting money from county commissioners, and condemnation procedures to obtain land for a new elementary school were typical of the responses we received.

One district's thorniest issue dealt with a high school mascot for female sports, the squaw, deemed derogatory by a local Native American tribe. Tempers flared as locals and alumni of the school protested the proposal to change the mascot. Board members felt intense pressure on both sides. The district resolved the issue by changing the mascot name to warriors (like the males) and removing stereotypical murals from walls. More attention was also given to the infusion of Native American literature into the curriculum. Teachers also received additional staff development in the area.

We interviewed several school board members, looking for people with several years of board experience who had worked with more than one superintendent. Board members, when asked directly on the survey about the importance of being from the South or the mountains, minimized the value of place. Yet they, like some respondents on the surveys, were almost universally inclined to emphasize getting to know the community was one of the most important things a superintendent should do. As one board member said in an interview, "It's okay for them not to be from here if they understand the culture." In the mountains of Western North Carolina, part of this understanding includes regional weather protocols. "The culture is when it snows, the first drop of snow that falls, you send the kids home. That's the way it is." A previous superintendent in her district (who was not a native) decided to have school anyway. Within one hour, his decision was broadcast via the prayer chain, a communication tool used not just for prayer, and by the sheriff's dispatcher. "The churches are the big communication tool for anything and to be successful with anything you have got to be in with the churches." The superintendent never recovered from this mistake. When it happened, this board member told the superintendent, "You need to start working on your resume."

Another board member who has lived in his county for twelve years also contributed examples of the need to understand the community. He described a former superintendent, not a native, who supported a minority view on the board to consolidate the district's high schools into one central high school. The board member admitted, "I was one of the minority members who saw the educational and economic value, but I ignored the social implications in the community opposition."

He thought the superintendent should have ended the discussion, "but the board had to step in and do so." "We lost a lot of ground in overall school improvement." One year later, a referendum on a five-cent property tax increase to improve the existing high schools was voted down five to one. The people had lost their trust of the board and administration. For the community, small schools were valued over large ones. Neighborhood schools were seen as places where their children could receive more attention and their athletic programs would be protected. The traditional place of schools in the community, according to the board member, "was too powerful a bond to break."

Board members were also specific about what aspects of their communities that superintendents need to know.

> We're in the Bible Belt. Churches play an active role. Church groups can help you getting money in. They are very political. Also, the Masonic and Eastern Star organizations. A lot of those people are retired teachers. The North Carolina Retired Teachers Association is strong, savvy, and educated. They have a lot of influence. Everybody in the county is related. Superintendents must remember, there is no such thing as a closed executive session.

Another board member pointed out that people are reluctant to spend much money on tax increases. He spoke of the importance of athletics and added, "Don't mess with high school football."

We also asked board members about what specific actions superintendents should avoid doing. What things upset mountain boards? All mentioned not getting information or being "out of the loop." One noted that board members liked to have an opportunity to give advice. She recalled advising one board member to be careful of another board member. The superintendent initially rejected her advice, but later let her know she was right.

Board members are not reluctant to share political advice. One noted that in her county, people voted party lines in state and federal elections, but crossed those lines at the local level. She cautioned, "Don't go to any political meetings. That will be used against you. A wise superintendent will say, 'Who can we work with?'" Another board member advocated one type of political action: "They [superintendents] have to make the needs of the school system known to local, state, and regional politicians and be a spokesperson for our schools in terms of local and state funding as well as become involved in statewide educational issues that have an impact on the schools." He cited the example of the recent federal cutbacks in vocational education. He added, however, that superintendents should not play a partisan role. He described the political history of his county as one of generations of school boards influencing positions in the system based on party politics. "When I started in the district twelve years ago, I had Democratic party leaders calling me. The person who sat to my left at school board meetings pointed out to me a person on the front row from the Republican party who was watching her." He described personnel decisions that were made based on promises and favors. "Things are changing now," he says, partially due to more outsiders moving in. However, "the political power remains with the natives even though the electorate may be more cosmopolitan." He described that local power in his community as being primarily matriarchal.

On the subject of local leaders and whether they lead differently, one board member observed that local leaders have to deal with favors: "If you have lived here a lifetime, if this is the only place you ever worked, you don't have that bigger perspective." She herself left the county for several years, and upon returning, was "shocked at how little had changed." Another board member observed that the current superintendent in his system was a native, but that he felt she had the integrity to resist the personal favor issue. His district had gone outside to hire a superintendent in the past because his predecessor was perceived to be partisan, alienating certain groups and favoring others. The thinking of the board in going outside was that such a hire would "lead to a perception of an unbiased individual leading the schools that would diffuse the division occurring in the system." He added that the current superintendent was hired solely on her merits, but by having a great deal of local support, she made it "an easy call."

On the matter of gender, some board members were more candid than local educators. A female board member said, "It's still a man's world here in the county and in Western North Carolina." Women leaders

> have to be twice as smart and they have to know when to play the game—to not let them [men] know they're twice as smart. To be an administrator and advance in the school system, all you have to do is be a P.E. teacher if you're a man. If you are a woman, you have to have preferably your six-year degree and you have to be sharp and you have to be able to do everything.

Another board member, a male, noted that the most recent male superintendent started out "gangbusters," with a detailed outline of goals and plans for the district. This board member observed that the female started out more slowly and tentatively, but had made some courageous personnel decisions and established herself as a strong leader.

In one of the larger districts in our study, a popular retirement area, we spoke with a female board member, the mother of three students in the system. Her original role in the system was as an active parent who helped lead the opposition in a recent failed bond referendum. Her concern was a lack of trust in the board to spend the money appropriately. She then ran for the board herself and described the board on which she now serves as largely professional. She added, "We may disagree, but in the end we reach consensus and work together as a team." She had nothing but praise for the current superintendent who has tackled some tough issues in his tenure. She now believes a bond referendum could pass successfully.

Board perspectives differ in subtle but important aspects from the perspectives of the professional educators in their system. They are more concerned with what were once the classic issues of superintendents: the buildings, the money, personnel, and public conflicts. These matters get the most public scrutiny and the most press attention; they are the agenda items that are most likely to lose a board member votes in the next election. Board members are slightly more inclined to see the advantages that ensue from being a native but, like central office staff, consider other attributes and skills more important in the selection of candidates. However, like subordinates, they stress the importance of knowing the territory, the local nuances about how school systems work in the region. Don't, for example, tangle with football. Don't decide to keep children in school when a flurry falls in the highest part of the county. Don't go to political meetings. Although they rank experience as a teacher and a principal (important, but neither vital nor very important), they have an even lower opinion of educational research. Board members are more direct about some issues, lacking the need, perhaps, to retain a modicum of professional reserve. For a comparison of board members' responses to those of the educators in their systems, see Appendix, Table 6.

Summary

There is a limited edginess in these leaders; after all, this is a conservative region. They are, in spite of that natural conservatism, successful. Their students perform extremely well on state assessments. Their systems rank high on the annual report cards. With few exceptions, those outcomes occur in low-wealth and/or low-supplemental-tax systems. The current accountability climate with its narrow focus on test scores also limits edginess. District leaders in the region generally work within expectations. The exceptions are likely to be found in systems that are more open, have higher populations of outsiders, or are led by outsiders.

All districts in the system have been successful on state tests. Of the 156 schools in the counties we studied, only 15 did not make expected growth on the 2002–2003 state assessments (See Appendix, Table 2.) The city system and two of the larger districts made significant improvement toward lowering the achievement gap. No Child Left Behind is, however, forcing a reconsideration of this improvement as schools that do well on state tests may not meet adequate yearly progress for all demographic subgroups.

There has been less inclination on the part of many of these leaders to move to another system once one becomes a superintendent, even though the pay in Western North Carolina is far less that it is elsewhere in the state. That is changing, however, as more geographic outsiders become superintendents. A history of staying in one school district has served many of these leaders and their systems well in some respects. They retain the comfort of stability, working with known entities, dealing with few surprises, and knowing the territory. Not moving, however, serves them less well in other ways. It diminishes the potential for innovation and revitalization, and makes more likely the perpetuation of localized "best" systems.

Depending on the county, boards intervene in personnel issues more frequently than elsewhere in the state and board members, especially in the smaller, more rural systems, are likely to know and be related to school people. It is difficult to ignore those connections in making decisions. In some counties there is a long and troubled history of patronage, political affiliation prerequisites for employment, and partisanship. In one county, the board handles approval votes separately for outside candidates. In two counties, superintendents left because of pending board elections. In one county, the superintendent was able to rise to the position straight out of the classroom. Such districts require politically adroit leadership to secure and maintain positions.

Leading in the Future?

Leading in these systems is likely to become more problematic in the near future for several reasons. First, unfunded mandates will place increased pressure on underfunded small school systems. The Bush administration nearly succeeded in deleting Federal Impact Aid from the budget and will likely try again.[5] The loss of supplementary state funds for small school districts is a distinct possibility. There will be intense pressure on districts to make "adequate yearly progress." Under the No Child Left Behind legislation, parents will have the option to change their children's schools if they do not perform. Systems will have to provide transportation to alternative sites, a severe handicap in some counties with limited options often far apart. In addition, the geographic necessity of continuing some K–12 union schools in the face of demands for comprehensive high school programs will necessitate finding ways to deliver programs to remote areas in a fiscally responsible manner. Union school staffing needs simply do not fit state staffing formulas. Nor do they readily meet new teacher certification requirements in No Child Left Behind. Added to potential financial strains is the region's persistent resistance to local taxation manifested in the reluctance of natives to raise taxes and the reluctance of second homeowners and retirees to worry about schools where they have no children. Although North Carolina's funding system is highly centralized, county differences stem from property taxes. It is not a mountain eccentricity that teachers have among the lowest salaries in the state. They have those salaries not because of performance, but because they work in districts that either lack the tax base or the willingness to raise taxes to secure supplemental money for public schools.

Looming teaching shortages, particularly in certain disciplines, combined with rigid certification requirements, have the potential for wrecking havoc in remote mountain districts. Union or K–12 schools and middle schools, especially, are already struggling with certification requirements. Advanced math and science teachers are in short supply. Salary inequities exist. Few districts are able to provide the local money necessary to compete with wealthier districts for licensed teachers in special areas. Districts will continue to deal with the challenges of an increasing presence of Hispanic students and demands for more ESL (English as a Second Language) teachers. The introduction of significant numbers of racial or ethnic minority children in some counties is a new issue. Though significant gains in the black-white achievement gap have been made in the city system and two larger county systems, the pressure remains to close it entirely. Escalating accountability stakes will result in increasing competition with charter schools. Many mountain counties already have one and a few counties have more than one.

Other issues will compound the challenges that system superintendents face. As more outsiders move into the region, there will be increased insider/outsider electorate friction over who should run schools and who should sit on boards. Successful candidates will have to contend with the issue of the disconnect between jobs and education. Well-educated mountaineers have difficulty finding local jobs. Doing public education well in the mountains makes more likely the departure of the region's most talented young people. Also likely to continue are debates about what schools should teach (sex education, for example, remains an assured way to raise a ruckus) and how they should teach it (whole language or phonics?).

There is an increasing frustration with outsider micromanagement. It arrives routinely, in simultaneous and sometimes contradictory fashion, from Raleigh and Washington, D.C. Educational decisions once reserved for local communities and their professional educators are being made somewhere else by noneducators. Yet districts will be asked to do more with less in the immediate future. They will be asked to do it in the glare of mass media and in the midst of occasional derision from their critics. And they will be asked to do it in ways that satisfy a bevy of special interest groups whose objectives clash.

The senior educational leaders in Western North Carolina to whom we talked are dutiful people who take their work very seriously. They know their community's rules and how play by them. They also know which ones they can safely transgress and which they cannot. They meet (and usually exceed) expectations for their performance. They are service oriented and often idealistic. Their stories evince an ethic of care about their fellow human beings and they exhibit a high degree of empathy. They have become insiders, whether by birth or adoption. Trouble begins when that insiderness begins to lose its luster.

·8·

CARPETBAGGERS

Being "From Off"

Western North Carolina locals often refer to an individual who is not a native of the region as being "from off." Both of us, even though we have Southern roots, are "not from around here." On a consistent basis, we hear that people did (do) things differently here. There was (is) no county like (the name varied depending on who was talking to us). An outsider can live here for most of her life and still not be considered a local. Anna's husband was born and raised in Jersey City, New Jersey. He moved to Florida to do his doctoral work and came to this region thirty-four years ago as a professor. He is still considered a Yankee and knows it. It is a Southernism to consider one's place of birth home, even if a person left there at the age of one. Many people in the region still believe that outsiders, because they are from away, will never understand the region or its people. In that quintessential Southern novel, Faulkner's *Absalom! Absalom!* (1936), Quentin Compson attempts to explain his home to a Northern friend, Shreve McCaslin. Finally, in exasperation, he declares, "You can't understand it. You would have to be born there" (297). Appalachians also feel a need to explain themselves. Mindful of common stereotypes that portray them as isolated, ignorant, naïve, violent, or foolish hillbillies, mountaineers have generated a paradoxical publishing history. On one hand, visitors find books on uplands cuisine and colloquialisms in visitor centers. They come with moonshine recipes and instructions on how to talk redneck. On the other, scholarly tomes challenge facile and erroneous assumptions about the place (Billings, Norman, and Ledford 1999; Cunningham 1989; Shapiro 1978; Whisnant 1983; and Williamson 1995). One result of generations of do-gooders, economic exploiters, and tourists is a weariness of people "from off."

Insiders and Outsiders

Southern Appalachian communities are powerful places. Anthony Cohen (1985) defines the community as a "sense of things either generally or with respect to specific and significant interests" made by its members. It is a perspective that "may differ from one made elsewhere" (16). "People construct community symbolically, making it a resource and repository of meaning, and a referent of their identity" (118).

In a few of the small rural counties in our study, there remains an insider advantage. It grants easier access to positions of power than being from off. Schoolwork is sometimes one of the most stable and lucrative occupations available, and administrators are among the most highly paid residents. They hold desirable and desired positions. Local competition for them is sometimes fierce, partisan, and political.

Geographic insiderness remains an important variable in local elections. Candidates will establish their geographic credentials before declaring political affiliations, although knowing the local community from which a person comes is usually a clue to his or her party. True, geographic insiderness is less an issue today than a generation ago. More people "from off" have become permanent residents. Demographic and economic shifts alter allegiances. Education broadens perspectives. But your familial and place roots still count for something, particularly in the more remote counties in our sample. Female administrators still occasionally hear from local residents that "women don't do those jobs." Someone's accent, religion, or manner may qualify him for carpetbagger status. Northerners are still suspect. Bumper stickers decrying Florida invasions, while not common, are in sufficient number that we see them weekly. Newspaper letters from local residents routinely wonder why outsiders want to change things. "If you liked it so much back there, why did you come here?" Conversations with local superintendents about important tools for prospective administrators always lead to communication skills and having an understanding of the district in which one works.

Northerners were (are) automatically carpetbaggers. We found, however, that outsiderness is a moving target. What was a carpetbagger yesterday might today be considered sufficiently inside to be welcomed as a seminative. An individual demonstrates respect for place, people, and regional tastes. Someone once considered local can become a carpetbagger. Going outside the region was commonplace and necessary for generations. Coming back—on vacations, for family reunions, and important holidays—meant that the region stuck. There is always the danger, however, of committing the Thomas Wolfe sin of becoming distant or different. "You were from here, but went away" refers to more than geographic distance. It means leaving the mindscapes as well as the landscapes. Sometimes you cannot go home again.

One regional superintendent left Appalachia and established a successful career in another part of the state. When she returned to become the head of the county district in which she grew up, she found herself accused of "getting above her raisings." In spite of geographic credentials, her time away diminished her insiderness. Another woman in our study, not a native of the region, challenged her district's salary system. A central office director, she wondered why more recent appointees were paid more and given higher status titles. Not content with in-house inquiries, she eventually took her concerns to the school board. They sided with the local superintendent and she decided to leave that position. She failed to play the game, exhibit appropriate deference, and wait. As a result, her career stalled. Another woman in our study, when confronted with what she believed was a pattern of gender discrimination, thought seriously about filing a formal grievance. She deferred action after being advised that she would win the grievance but lose any opportunity for administrative advancement in that system and, probably, in the region as a whole.

In another county, in the 1990s, two superintendents from "off" were hired in succession. The first, a female, never achieved insider status in spite of being from a neighboring county. An active administrator, she was passionate about quality instruction. However, she alienated some of the professional and local community, who considered her pushy. Her successor, also not born in the district, had already achieved insider status when he was hired. He had been one of the county's high school principals, was a former coach, and had mastered the countenance and manner of a good ol' boy. He looked remarkably like another "from off" superintendent, two hires back. That person was, like the woman, from a neighboring county. He was, like her successor, a tall, former coach. "Being from off" can be a function of a combination of variables. Where one is born, where one has lived, where one's professional career has been, what one has done in that career, and how one behaves in a particular role combine to determine whether a critical mass of insiderness has been achieved. Take the last two superintendents in that district. Both had been high school principals and neither had been born in the county. Differences included gender, demeanor, leadership style, immediate past employment location, and formal education (the woman had a doctorate and the man did not). Being male, being somewhat country, and being attuned to the community (he had, after all, worked there) enhanced the insider credentials of one leader. Not being those things diminished the insiderness claims of the other, who also had the outsider liability of being female.

Derailment

Career derailment is a somewhat innocuous term for an interruption in an individual's upward mobility. Some occupations are more susceptible to derailment, voluntary or involuntary, than are others. The superintendency is one of the more vulnerable professions. In North Carolina, district leaders are appointed by school boards and granted, typically, a two-year or four-year contract, renewable at any point. Their senior central office staff also works on contract and at the pleasure of the board. But boards themselves are subject to change. Elected usually for four-year staggered terms, they are open to educational firestorms whipped up by aggrieved individuals or special interests. Hired by one board, a superintendent can shortly be working for another. "Losing the board," even the prospect of that occurrence, is a common factor in voluntary decisions to derail or seek other employment. Lost boards sometimes precipitate derailing decisions by ordering superintendents to behave in ways contrary to their professional or personal values (hiring a favored local teacher candidate over a more qualified outsider, scrapping a sex education program that includes a unit on birth control). They are inclined to nonrenewal decisions if their views and those of the sitting superintendent differ significantly. In some cases, they buy out contracts of individuals whose performances they find objectionable.

Leslie and Velser (1996) define derailment as leaving the organization nonvoluntarily, through resignation, firing, or retiring early. A derailed leader may plateau because his or her personal characteristics and skills are a poor match for the perceived demands of a particular job. They note that derailment does not necessarily mean the end of a career. Often leaders go into other organizations and are successful. One reason for superintendent mobility is system climbing to bigger and more prestigious positions. Another reason is the absence of good fit between the local district embodied in the school board and a particular leader. What appears to be, or actually was, a good fit with one board may sour after an election.

McCall and Lombardo (1983) studied senior executives in three U.S. industrial organizations. They found derailment was commonly the result of insensitivity to others, failure to delegate, failure to build a team, performance problems, and being overly dependent on a single mentor. In school settings, that list would include being dependent on a particular board. Administrators who were successful in climbing the corporate ladder had diverse career experiences, managed stress well, worked well with all types of people, used poise and grace to handle mistakes, and focused on problem solving.

Morrison et al. (1987) replicated the McCall and Lombardo study, but focused on women. Females who derailed had early career success and were highly intelligent. Factors in their derailment included performance problems, being overly ambitious, not adapting to a boss or culture, an inability to be strategic or lead their subordinates, poor image with the board or community, and problems with relationships. In their summary of similar derailment research, Leslie and Velser (1996) note that successful leaders wanted to succeed, had help from the top, could manage their subordinates, took career risks, had a good track record of achievements, and could be "tough, decisive, and demanding" (2). Derailed men apparently did not suffer image problems nor did they have difficulty "being tough."

Lombardo and McCauley (1988) looked at 355 ratings of male and female subordinate managers by their supervisors. They identified six derailment factors: strategic differences with management, trouble with molding a staff, difficulty making strategic transitions, lack of follow-through, overdependence, and interpersonal relationship problems. Leslie and Velser (1996) concluded that "interpersonal skills and the ability to adapt" are "critical factors . . . and not the specific features of the environment (the norms, values, and ways of being) that one is asked to adapt to" (35). Accommodation abilities and finding good fits are crucial administrator skills.

The turnover rate of superintendents has been the subject of numerous studies (note, for example, Brubaker and Shelton 1995; Brubaker and Coble 1995, 1997; and Hood 1996). Brubaker and Coble used the six Lombardo and McCauley factors to look at district leadership derailment. In descending order of frequency, educators derail because of "(a) strategic differences with management, (b) problems with interpersonal relationships, (c) making strategic transitions, (d) difficulty in molding a staff, (e) lack of follow-through, and (f) overdependence" (21). They attribute some derailments to the tendency of local school boards to micromanage. Board members sometimes transgress their boundaries, moving from the domain of policymaking to implementation. In their discussion of difficulty in molding a staff, Brubaker and Coble (1995) cite the example of a superintendent who encountered rampant nepotism in a large rural system. Unable to alter the culture of the board and unwilling to participate in an unethical practice, that person lasted only two years. In 1995 Burgess presented the case of a female superintendent who spent twenty-three months and sixteen applications in search of a position. In interviews, she encountered questions about whether a woman could delegate and follow-up effectively, check roads for bad weather and make school closing decisions, and inspect a roof problem. What, she was asked, would her husband do?

Derailment studies confirm what our participants already know. The most important skill a leader can have is the ability to work with and through people, to form relationships, and to listen. If a candidate is not a people person, then he or she should not apply. A prospective leader must be able to adapt, to accommodate to the local culture, or risk being perceived as outside it. Precisely what that culture is matters less than whether one can recognize and adapt to it. The ability to read an environment, then, is important. So, too, is a deep self-knowledge, because that becomes the basis of determining whether there is a sufficiently close fit between a candidate and a setting. If a prospective leader is from off, then the question of whether one can live in a particular setting is really an inquiry into the ability to fit in. The best candidate overall is not necessarily the best candidate for a particular place.

Cultural Tourists

Marginalized populations are outside the mainstream. They occupy space at its social and cultural borders. In the United States, the identity of people at the margins changes. Roger Williams was put outside his community in New England for having the wrong beliefs. Baptists were executed for the crime of maintaining their religious convictions in the wrong place. Being Irish in antebellum Boston was sufficient to put a person beyond the pale. Before the election of John Kennedy, Catholics were considered suspect candidates for the presidency. Native Americans were physically removed from white society. Heretics and sinners were at one time buried outside cemetery walls to signify their lack of insider status. Ostracism is a community's most powerful sanction. Although America's margins fluctuate, throughout most of its history certain groups have been consistently stigmatized. Race and gender were factors that divided populations into insiders and outsiders. Majority race males are normative insiders. Minority race males and females of any race were varying degrees of outsider.

When desegregation came to the South, it was black students who generally had to move. The costs of transition, a side of the ledger sheet only recently explored in academic literature, were high. Applebome (1997), looking at the closing of Williston High School in coastal North Carolina, concludes that the black alumni now sound much like 1960s white segregationists. One former student noted that "the closing of Williston High School contributed to further disruption of the lives of hundreds of teachers, students and citizens within the community." "We lost the bond between school, parents, and teachers. We lost the ability to love and live together in the way to which we were accustomed . . . it still hurts" (213). Another student claimed that she and her friends "went from our own land to being tourists in someone else's. It never did come together, and . . . it's on the verge of falling apart altogether now" (214).

Until desegregation, Stephens-Lee was Asheville's African American high school. Its faculty, students, and parents formed close bonds. "Sure, we had hand-me-down band uniforms and textbooks, and that was hard. What no one could take away from us, however, was our pride. We were proud to attend Stephens-Lee and we weren't afraid to let everyone know. We were a true community back then" (quoted in Hammond 2000, 129). A music teacher at a former Transylvania County African American school wonders "if integration really bettered the quality of education for children. At Rosenwald they knew they had friends, instructors willing to give anything" (quoted in Reed 2000, 110). Vanessa Siddle Walker (1996) and David Cecelski (1994) have documented similar feelings for lost black schools, focusing on the strengths of the community found within those institutions and their loss with desegregation.

At a Public Policy Institute forum on diversity held in Cullowhee, North Carolina, in 2000, several African Americans students from Asheville's only high school captured the frustration of being marginalized. "It's just the way they look at us. I can tell by how they look at us." "When my mom and I moved here, we were looking for a church and we didn't know about churches at all. We ended up in this white church and when we walked in, they just stared at us. Finally, one of them came over and asked if we were lost or something." "Like when we went to Washington with this other high school. They didn't have any blacks at their school. They were all white. And our school has a lot of blacks in it. So, when we got together they didn't know what to do with us." "Yeah, they saw us and they thought drugs and guns and gangs. We don't have any more of that, not any more than they would." "Now I came from Madison County to Asheville and there were no blacks in my school there. I went to a school in the [Buncombe] county system first and there were only four blacks there. Two of them go to my school now." "They don't know. I mean, they are ignorant because they haven't any black people. How are they supposed to know?" "You know there are differences. Like in church, I went to a white church and all they did was sit there and be quiet. Now in my church people are falling out and raising their voices and moving. Not like that white church. I guess we go where we feel comfortable" (quoted in Smith 2000, 28–29).

In the early 1970s, Ben Chavis claimed that desegregation destroyed black institutions (Applebome 1997, 227). Joseph Lowery of the Southern Christian Leadership Council concluded that desegregation meant not a "passage from all things wrong to all things right" but a journey "from all things black to all things white" (231). To be marginalized is to be a tourist in someone else's culture. The first outsider candidates for any leadership position must, to be successful, go from tourist to resident. They cannot lead a culture in which they remain a guest. Neither can they continue to lead when they turn their backs on that culture. The balance that leaders must find necessitates accommodation, perhaps, but not capitulation. "All things white" is more unsatisfactory a situation than all things white and black, but separate. As our participants note in their descriptions of frustrations, the pace of change is slow. As derailment examples from our sample indicate, the path to change is uneven and sometimes difficult to find.

Machiavelli's Second Admonition

Machiavelli's (1515) prince is not the model we recommend to today's educational leaders. He proposes some clearly inappropriate means to attain dubious ends. However, he has advice that our leaders in Washington and state capitals might consider before embarking on certain legislated or executive-mandated adventures. For example, Machiavelli argues that it is far easier to stay in power if one maintains a society's "old way of life" and refrains from altering "their customs" (6). Anyone who has sought, in dramatic fashion, to change how things are done in an organization knows the difficulty of that task. "It is worth noting," he tells his prince, "that nothing is harder to manage, more risky in the undertaking, or more doubtful of success than to set up as the introducer of a new order" (17).[1]

Machiavelli urges his prince, when not engaged in making war (his primary role in life), to train his body and mind for that exercise. It was his second admonition about preparation for war that we fail to teach our prospective leaders. As we write this chapter, U.S. troops, having succeeded on the field of battle in record time, are finding that winning a peace is far more difficult than winning a war. In a contest for the minds and hearts of the Iraqi people, policymakers have discovered that American rhetoric plays less well in the Middle East than here. Certain actions (ensuring safe streets and a functioning economy, for example) sometimes trump talk of liberation. Machiavelli would blame the difficulties of securing peace on a lack of familiarity with the cultural territory.

Machiavelli's prince prepares himself through "a great deal of hunting, and thus harden[s] his body to strenuous exercise, meanwhile learning to read terrain" (41). We are not suggesting educators take up arms and march into a real forest. We do advocate becoming familiar with the nuances of a particular community, with learning to read the cultural landscape. From such study, a leader

> will see how the mountains rise, how the valleys open out, and how the plains lie; he will know about rivers and swamps—and to this study he should devote the greatest attention. What he learns will be doubly useful; first, he will become

> acquainted with his own land and understand better how to defend it; and then, because he knows his own country thoroughly, he can easily understand any other country that he is forced to look over for the first time. (41)

As for exercising his mind, Machiavelli recommends the reading of history, especially the lives of great men. (We suspect that there were a few great women around by that time, but not many of them were in his reading audience and fewer still were potential patrons. Ever pragmatic and stressing a muscular construction of leadership, Machiavelli probably saw nothing to be gained from that quarter.) Leaders who wish to be successful learn from past human triumphs, gleaning lessons that translate successfully to those site-specific mountains, valleys, rivers, and swamps of the present that they have learned to read so well. They also make the introduction of different people, learning the lessons of human nature played out in various ways in different places. Princes make war or prepare themselves for it. Administrators fight ignorance or prepare for that battle.

Successful system leaders engage in their administrative chores within particular boundaries. If they are wise in the ways of Machiavelli's prince, they monitor their settings continuously. They are abroad in the land, in schools, in community meetings, on Main Street. That context is more than the sociodemographic and economic statistics traditionally found on environmental scans or in strategic planning documents. It includes cultural norms and taboos, dominant and dominated (silenced) ideologies, and spoken and unspoken assumptions about how things are done here. It is the mind of place. Translated into educational organization terms, Machiavelli's second admonition commands leaders to act or to prepare themselves to act through the study of the milieu in which they work. As salesmen in Meredith Wilson's *The Music Man* remind us, they "gotta know the territory."

Situated Leadership

When we asked central office staff about trouble spots for district leaders, several responses focused on learning "the values, customs . . . of local people." Be sensitive to the community. Staff members warned against closing down lines of communication; keep stakeholders informed. They cautioned leaders to take care in cultivating teams and to avoid working outside them; move slowly and cautiously in responding to public questions or concerns. When leaders do respond, they should do so with candor. Administrators must earn respect and build trust; they are not conveyed automatically. Do not decide in haste. Understand the district and its issues. Avoid assumptions. Leaders should be sensitive to changing perceptions and expectations. Make accommodations, if necessary and possible. Know how shifts in politics, economics, and belief systems affect the schools.

Board members recited the same advice, only they were more direct. Know the background of events. "Become a part of the community." Avoid being political. "Build relationships in the system and the community." "Be available to everyone." A district leader should avoid becoming isolated. Get into the community, and get to know it. Beware of ivory towers. Be visible. "Do not come into the system with preconceived notions." "Get out and mix with the school family." Use the board's expertise on local customs. Leaders must "never talk down to locals." They should never alienate their boards. Carolina administrators must never get "on the bad side of the county commission." Effective leaders know the people to whom they are talking.

Board members were also more explicit about leader behaviors that clash with local norms. Be cautious "about socializing with school personnel." Keep appointments. Do not be "out of pocket." Refrain from drinking alcohol or at least ensure that the practice is not common knowledge. A leader should have a "stable private life" and be married. Keep promises. Watch the money and keep hands off the opposite sex. Leaders are role models, so they must avoid setting bad examples. The public pays the salaries of district leaders and expects good value for their money. Do not leave the office early on Fridays. Beware of "talking negatively about other community agencies." Do not say bad things about the previous superintendent. Local leaders must not "get involved with petitions." Administrators court trouble when they get "into conflict with the churches." If there is local staff that can do the job, do not go outside to hire someone. One board member listed the following as guaranteed troublemakers: "personal or private life issues, such as DWI [driving while intoxicated], extramarital affair, gambling habit." "Sex" can get you in trouble, one respondent wrote, as can "being lazy." Do not be arrogant.

Among the things leaders need to know are the locations of the district's "sacred cows." Several board members mentioned the role that high school athletics play in mountain communities, citing coaching assignments and changes as one of the thornier issues with which they work. A measure of the difficulty in positioning with regard to items that fall into this category is that both sides are likely to be loudly represented on the board and in the community. A large patron contingent wants district leaders to avoid involvement in athletic and coaching issues entirely. Another equally adamant group wants athletics to be kept in its appropriate place, subordinate to other educational priorities. District leaders, as one of them reminded us, deal with gray areas. To find one's way through the haze requires knowledge of which signposts to trust.

Much of that advice would work in any setting. Good leaders listen, circulate, observe, and refrain from making hasty decisions. Some of it is more place specific. For example, social drinking in moderation would not be a problem in many districts, even in North Carolina. One's private life is allowed to stay more private in one community than in another. However, both sets of behaviors occur somewhere. Generic is not a place on anyone's map. Success depends more often than not on an ability to navigate gray areas. They are defined by nuance and prone to vary from one geographic point to another.

Being from off has inherent, but not insurmountable, disadvantages. Part of the frustration that the Asheville students shared with us comes from not being known for who they are. To become an insider requires convincing people already there that you know and care about them. That does not necessarily mean agreeing with them about everything nor does it mean abandoning personal visions of what schools can and should do. It does mean learning to lead without recognizing or outdistancing, to return to the *Music Man* allusion, the band.

PART III

The Story

"We are the savior of society . . . sexually transmitted diseases . . . substance abuse . . . Hepatitis B . . . Doctors deal with medicine. Ministers deal with religion and soul saving. Accountants deal with taxes. Lawyers deal with legal matters. We deal with everything . . . And it is very frustrating that the public still doesn't understand that the teaching-learning process, that desire to learn must be instilled, nurtured, built up, celebrated, and there are so many children out there that is not happening for . . . I found the greatest fallacy is that they think we can do this job with the resources that we are given and in the time frame we are given to do it."

Male Participant

·9·

CEILINGS IN TRANSITION

At one point in the Appalachian rediscovery process, a writer, perhaps thinking of Edgar Rice Burroughs's 1924 trilogy of the mysterious country of Caspak, characterized the region as "the land that time forgot." Any casual visitor knows that designation no longer applies. Indeed, it probably never did. Roads, airwaves, wires, fast-food restaurants, and commercial chain stores ensure that mountaineers have opportunities not unlike those of lowlanders. They can and do travel abroad, watch the Atlanta Braves on television, visit Internet chat rooms, eat Whoppers, and shop at Wal-Mart. The news arrives in real time in the mountains as well as in Raleigh or Charlotte, read by accent-free and racially diverse reporters. The outside world is inescapable in twenty-first century America.

When we initiated our study, we thought in terms of a simple investigation into occupational segregation by gender. We encountered a far more complex and interwoven phenomenon. That traditional trinity of difference (gender, race, and class) did not neatly apply nor were these variables separable. Geography proved to be an important factor in making hiring decisions. Class was less an issue in the mountains than in piedmont or coastal plains counties. There was economic disparity among population subgroups, but it differed from patterns in other parts of the state. The region had a history of sustainable agriculture and only one truly urban area. Wealth came, most often and even today, from the lowlands in the wallets of seasonal or transient residents. Race, while a factor, was a minor one. There were proportionately fewer ethnic and racial minorities in the mountains than downstate. There were women.

A pattern of expanding access emerged over time. Geographic outsiders were welcomed first, then female insiders, and only then African American insiders. This chapter examines the ways we have chosen to explain the pace and nature of that change. It begins with a brief overview of occupational segregation, moves to a definition of a quality we call *insiderness*, and concludes with aspects of that quality that have proven useful in our efforts to understand what we found.

Occupational Segregation

Occupations that are associated either with males or females are considered gender segregated.[1] Men are architects and engineers; women are social workers. Men major in business; women in English. Men are physicians; women, nurses. Men direct operations departments in major corporations, while women head up personnel units. Males can dream of becoming president; women can aspire to be their personal or professional helpmate. There are First Ladies; there are no First Gentlemen. Males are chefs; females cook, mostly for home consumption. Men write great works of literature; women scribble romances. Men work in steel factories; women labor in textile mills. Men aspire to lucrative careers in professional football, while women hope for fleeting fame as an Olympic gymnast.

Even though occupational barriers have become more porous in recent years, job categorization by gender remains an easy game to play. In spite of the blurring of roles, particularly in the past two decades, a division of occupational pursuits persists. On one side are auto mechanics, telephone installers, brick masons, electricians, plumbers, butchers, groundskeepers, and truck drivers. On the other side are telephone operators, receptionists, bank tellers, dressmakers, child-care workers, beauticians, and homemakers. Within the ranks of teachers, men are more likely to be found in high schools than in elementary school classrooms. Men teach physics, chemistry, mathematics, and shop. Women teach English, business education, and home economics. In the school office, women are attendance counselors and men are principals. At the central office, women direct food services and exceptional children's programs, while men oversee facilities and school transportation. Men are superintendents and women supervise curriculum and instruction programs.

In spite of recent changes, a residue of segregation remains in almost all occupational arenas. Some of it is the result of lingering legal prohibitions. For example, women in our armed forces are still formally prohibited from the ranks of military fighting units, a prohibition that effectively excludes them from the military's top ranks. Legislated exclusion, however, is fast disappearing. Far more common is the persistence of segregation based on our perceptions of what is appropriate, of what meets our culturally shaped expectations for certain roles, of what is natural or normal. Local communities dictated, and to a certain degree continue to determine, position appropriateness. Local attitudes are nested within a national predisposition to believe that men, by historical precedent and an ideology grounded in a Judaic-Christian tradition, are destined to lead and women to follow. Men head states as well as families. Women obey and enable.

Gradually, over centuries, the public work available for women grew in number and type. Often, those increases were the result of a national parsimony. As the common school movement expanded, education reformers like Horace Mann touted the availability of cheap labor. Women could teach the children, particularly the younger ones. That work was a natural extension of their work at home. Moreover, they could and would teach for less money. They, mostly single women at first, were not the primary wage-earners in a family and something was accounted better than the nothing they usually got for work at home. Men would then be free to supervise their work. What resulted in the nineteenth and early twentieth centuries from that arrangement was a system of male supervision and women workers, Tyack's educational harem. Mistresses of one-room schools retained a measure of autonomy and power, but reforms associated with consolidation resulted in more complex institutions that minimized female management and maximized standardization. As Tyack (1974) observes, "hierarchical organization of schools and the male chauvinism of the larger society fit as hand to glove" (60). Occupational segregation was both the result of, and an impetus to, the bureaucratization of America's public education.

Although many scholars have documented the presence of female administrators at the turn of the last century, as public institutions modernized, becoming larger and graded, female leaders lost their positions to males. That pattern was not unlike what happened to black administrators throughout the South following racial desegregation. As dual school systems merged, African American principals filled subordinate positions like assistant principalships or left administration altogether. Their revised roles reflected the power of the majority to dictate the terms of enforced desegregation.

Different Spheres

The process of gendering specific responsibilities has long been a part of human experience. Some tasks are automatically gendered by biology. Women bear children. Men have more muscle mass, are stronger, and, consequently, are more likely to dominate roles in which size and strength make a crucial difference. Work was gendered because of its proximity to roles that were biologically defined. Women became the custodians of the children they birthed, taking care of the home, overseeing the preparation of meals, and supervising play. Men foraged beyond the home, providing meat for the table through their prowess as hunters in a literal sense in the early years of the species and in a metaphorical sense when they became the breadwinners by securing paying jobs outside the household. Men oversaw the cash crops. Women tended the family garden. Although some roles were less distinct in agrarian societies, they became more explicit, at least in the Western world, with the introduction of industrialization.

By the nineteenth century, for the advantaged classes, life was lived in two spheres. The private sphere, the domain of women, revolved around the home. Men continued to serve as its titular head, but their real work took place in the public sphere. There they struggled with their peers in a Darwinian tussle for limited resources. Even today some people in the Southern Appalachians refer to labor done off the homeplace as "public work." Public work, because it was gendered male, took precedence over work done in the home. Women were domestic scientists; men pursued the natural sciences. An indicator of relative importance is that omnipotent American value signifier, the dollar. The private sphere, where women's work was centered, generated no money (keeping one's own house was unpaid labor) or a miserly income (servant wages, often earned by females who were geographic, racial, or class outsiders, or pin money from selling or trading household products for which women were responsible, such as eggs). Public work resulted in wages, dividends, and profits.

Women, particularly the wives and daughters of wealthy or moderately wealthy white men, remained at home. Public life was too contentious, too physically and emotionally demanding, and/or too salacious for their tender presence. Conversely, poor white females, immigrants, and racial minorities were always part of public sphere work. They labored under the supervision of or for majority race men, routinely in poorly paid, demeaning, difficult, and dirty jobs. Their participation in public work failed to disrupt the collective illusion that genteel women were too delicate to be there or that immigrants and racial minorities were too intellectually limited and crass to be elsewhere.

In the nineteenth century, the idealized division of separate spheres and segregated lives started to come undone. That story has been told elsewhere (see, for instance, Douglas 1977; Kemp 1994; Kessler-Harris 1982; Smith-Rosenberg 1985; and Wolfe 1995) However, it is important to recall that pedestals, if only as romantic images, reigned in the South, owing in large measure to its cash crop-oriented agrarian economy, the persistence of slavery, and its demographic and cultural insularity. In the nineteenth century, in spite of the presence of "unruly women" (Bynum 1992), the myth of the frail Southern lady persisted (Scott 1970), aided by formal education in the antebellum period (Farnham 1994) and an ideology steeped in race and gender consciousness that endured beyond the Civil War (Wyatt-Brown 2001).

That Southern lady narrative was (had always been, is) a falsehood, albeit a convenient one for justifying the South's peculiar institution, race-based slavery, and its postwar corollary, race-based segregation. It was the persistence of that narrative, intricately associated with, and supportive of, prevailing racial attitudes that relegated African American men and women to prescribed roles in the Southern economy until late in the twentieth century.

Separate spheres did not crumble suddenly nor have they disappeared completely. Progressive legislation included employment prohibitions to protect women and children. They served as noble justifications for exclusion as well as noble attempts to control abuses of child labor. Perhaps laudatory in intent, they prohibited women, for example, from jobs that were considered too physically taxing or dangerous. Not coincidentally, they were positions that provided a viable income. Jim Crow laws encoded a social system of separation that ensured a pernicious economic separation, creating almost insurmountable barriers to upward mobility. Legislation in the second half of the twentieth century rescinded earlier statutes that were once considered social advances. The federal government, spurred by the Civil Rights and feminist movements, dismantled formal segregation laws. It encouraged affirmative action remedies to redress historical inequities. New economic realities, the marketplace's emphasis on efficiency, an increased access to education (a prerequisite for certain positions), historical circumstances, and an altered consciousness about what constituted social injustice contributed to the dissolution of different spheres and opened economic opportunities to previously disadvantaged groups.

Industrialization led to manufacturing enterprises knitted together by burgeoning bureaucracies and expansive transportation and communication networks. Paperwork proliferated and with it the need for inexpensive ways to produce and distribute business documents. Whereas the position of secretary had once been a starter position for aspiring males, it became a plateau job for women, who would work for a lower salary and did not object to making the coffee. Within a relatively brief span, the percentage of females doing office work ballooned. In 1870 only 2.6 percent of office employees were female; by 1910 almost 38 percent were.

Men also found business work attractive partially because it excluded "undesirables" from competition for jobs (Strom 1992, 65) but, by the 1930s, there were only certain types of office work to which they were drawn. Men had a two-to-one advantage in bookkeeping and cashier positions in 1900. As the positions became more routine and a less likely starting point for advancement, that advantage reversed. By 1930 there were almost two women for every male doing that work. By 1930, there were over one million female stenographers and typists, but only 66,000 men (Strom 1992, 49). Men continued to operate heavy machines, do union factory work, and manage. Numbers continued to diverge as certain positions became more strictly gendered. In office work, women, when they became supervisors, oversaw other women. They managed secretarial pools, but they did not supervise men.

The same dynamics that first excluded and then included women in particular positions applied to other minority groups. "The nineteenth century had implanted firm notions of men and women in the industrial world" (Strom 1992, 188). Native-born white men were skilled artisans. Native-born white women could, with protective supervision, engage in light factory work. Immigrants and African Americans did manual labor. That hierarchy in the South translated to white ownership of land and African American tenancy or sharecropping. In the twentieth century, it was readjusted to fit the requirements of new work. Poor, white women, for example, could work in textile manufacturing, employing poor, black women to clean their houses and do their laundry. Certain shop spaces and jobs were reserved for African Americans males; others for white men. Education limited opportunities disproportionately, as women were excluded from business schools and elite colleges and African Americans were, certainly in the South, often without access to any schooling beyond basic rudiments.

World Wars I and II took men from their civilian jobs in this country to fight in another. Because of their absence and, particularly in that second global conflict, because of the length of America's involvement and the need for intensive manufacture of the instruments of war, women assumed roles from which they had previously been excluded. Rosie learned that riveting was something she could do and that she derived pride and good money in doing it. When men returned from the war, two forces contributed to the formal dismantling of most occupational segregation. The G.I. Bill and a desire to help the country's veterans combined to send women packing from factories and white-collar jobs to early weddings. Their proper destiny was a June Cleaver life of raising children, making dinner, and vacuuming floors in high heels. African American soldiers, having sacrificed on a field of war in defense of freedom, refused to return to their semi-independent status before the conflict.[2]

Occupational Desegregation

One difficulty in challenging occupational segregation is the tendency to see it as an individual rather than a collective problem. Because one or two or a dozen people overcome barriers, then failure to do so is not a consequence of cultural or organizational bias, but resides within failed aspirants themselves.

Because an African American becomes a Supreme Court judge or the head of the Joint Chiefs of Staff, the failure of others to follow in his footsteps is a matter of relative merit and not racism. That a woman has been a Secretary of State or that several women are now in the U.S. Senate lets the nation off the sexist hook. Women lack training or ambition. They do not have the requisite desire or persistence. Their aspirations are low. The marginalized, once inside themselves, chided their colleagues who failed to make the trip. Eleanor Gilbert, who wrote *The Ambitious Woman in Business* in 1916, thought "opposition from some men is not an insurmountable obstacle to the able woman, trained and ambitious for executive responsibility" (quoted in Strom 1992, 351).

Legal desegregation, the process of formally breaking down separation, reached a crescendo in the 1960s and 1970s in the United States. Cultural desegregation is an ongoing process. We began to use a concept common to anthropologists to describe placement within a culture. One is either inside or outside, with advantages accruing to the former position and disadvantages tied to the latter condition. Insiderness meant the end, at least for that person or a group of people with certain features in common, of occupational segregation.

Insiderness

We began this study with a focus on gender and quickly realized that looking at only one dimension (gender) was inadequate in explaining candidacy issues. Accustomed to parsing differences in terms of race, class, and gender with an occasional nod to learning styles and abilities, our informants forced us to consider the inclusion of geography. None of those attributes (race, class, gender, or place) occur in isolation. A person is a combination of them. Possible permutations are almost endless when one considers that they can no longer be considered simple binaries. People are multiracial, multiethnic, and somewhere along a spectrum of gender dispositions and behaviors. They come from particular locales within regions, which are themselves nested within larger geographic entities. They possess a socioeconomic status derived from a combination of factors beyond a simple declaration of income or wealth. Mere money will not, in some places, grant a desired social standing. Family ties and education, even in the absence of money, will sometimes elevate a person's status.

Because several of our informants talked about outsiders and because both of us had encountered variations of the question "Are you from off?" we thought "insiderness" captured the concept of candidate viability. As long as applicants for a senior-level leadership position met current standards for inclusion, qualified as an insider, they were considered. Using insiderness, rather than a single attribute or set of attributes, gave us a construct that can generalize to populations anywhere. What is an insider to a nineteenth-century Southern Appalachian might not be an insider to a twentieth-century Midwesterner from Omaha, but the existence of insiderness is common to both places. Insiders are people who have an "in" with someone, who are "in the know" or in a position of privilege within a clique or an organization. It is a commonplace term. Widening access was a function of shifting definitions of who was considered an insider.

Think of insiderness as a box that contains a specific set of cultural definitions of what is and ought to be, of what constitutes "the natural" in a particular community. As long as a culture is isolated, the dimensions of that box shift almost imperceptibly. Things move, but like the air that whirls around us as we spin on our planetary axis, we are unaware of the journey. Geographic isolation in places like the Galapagos Islands results in distinctive flora and fauna. Geographic isolation has a similar effect on cultural truths. Once appearing quaintly frozen in time, the inhabitants of such places inevitably respond to external intrusions.

The Southern Appalachians were never as parochial as early travel writers made them appear to be. The mountains might be high and the hollows narrow, but they were always open. Educationally, the region was richly endowed with a robust, albeit uneven, set of institutions, even in the nineteenth century. It was neither a bastion of Elizabethan England nor as strange a land and peculiar a people as reporters suggested, nor was it as porous or heterogeneous as other parts of the state. It did, however, have a set of values and expectations that, taken together, constituted a culture that made it a distinctive place. Everyone inhabits a cultural box, be we mountain or lowland residents. Each one's boundaries divide insiders from outsiders, from the people "from off."

One can, for example, review the history of public schooling in the United States from the perspective of expanding definitions of student insiderness. Initially, at least in North Carolina, schools were places for local, white children who needed a modicum of reading, writing, and arithmetic to function as responsible citizens. Public colleges were for males. Women, destined to be wives and mothers, had little need for advanced education. There were no public secondary schools.

Over time, the years that one was expected to attend school increased. More students meant more teachers and more teachers meant that women could entertain aspirations for at least a normal school education. After the Civil War, the federal government required public-supported schools for African Americans. It eventually set up schools for Native Americans. In the twentieth century, the definition of *student* widened further, eventually encompassing all young people. Regardless of race, religion, ethnicity, gender, class, location, and/or disability, all North Carolina young people between the ages of seven and sixteen must go to school, and most children between five and twenty-one may attend. Whereas the state once directed women students to Greensboro, African Americans to a number of historically black institutions (such as North Carolina A&T and Winston-Salem State), and Native Americans to Pembroke, all of Carolina's public colleges are now open to any student who meets the academic criteria for admission.

The story of public schooling can be read as a history of revised definitions of insiderness. Today's inclusive definition was certainly not the image that the state's leaders had in mind in 1820 or even 1900. Expanded access did not translate automatically to equitable access. There are still inequities in educational opportunities. Some students, because of where they are born, attend a system whose local tax base supports a generous supplement to the state allocation. Others attending school in less economically fortunate districts are more likely to study inside inadequately maintained or underequipped facilities. Systems that pay teachers higher salaries routinely entice veteran educators from lower-paying counties. The state's public schools privilege certain types of knowledge in ways that advantage some people and disadvantage others. The general story is one of broadened insiderness, but the particular stories include persistent unfairness.

Insider Elasticity

Insiderness changes over time and varies in one of two directions. A revised definition can narrow the number of people who meet it or it can increase that number. Both Blount (1998) and Shakeshaft (1987) tell us that the number and proportion of female education leaders, both at the school and district levels, were greater at the beginning of the last century than they were in the 1950s and 1960s. Insiderness, the quality of meeting expectations for a particular role, contracted to maximize the exclusion of women by mid-century. In the 1980s, it began to expand again. Insiderness is elastic.

There was an explicable pattern to the insider elasticity of senior-level educational administration positions in the uplands. Initially, and in concert with national as well as local norms, insiders were Anglo-Saxon, Protestant males who were born and/or raised in the region or who qualified as "local boys." In some counties, a particular political party affiliation was also an expectation. In the nineteenth century, it helped to be a Confederate veteran. The first important attribute to become elastic was geography itself. A candidate could be "from off" if he (it was, with only two exceptions before the 1990s, still a he) demonstrated a sensitivity to the people in his district and an awareness of mountain culture. It also enhanced insider claims to have lived in and worked for a mountain system. Political party membership gradually became a less stringent prerequisite in those counties in which had mattered. All viable candidates still demonstrated a proclivity to tradition and a general conservatism, independent of formal affiliation.

The second category to be flexed was gender. A local woman could become an insider. None of the women who gained a superintendency in the region was a geographic outsider. Some nonlocal women work in other senior-level positions. The one female in our study who voluntarily derailed herself did so following a conflict with her superintendent about salary and status that eventually ended in a failed appeal to the local school board. Not only was she "from off," a condition that was not erasable even after decades of residence in the region, but also her decision to confront her superintendent directly and then appeal his decision contradicted the local ethic for resolving differences in house.

In 2002, the barrier of race was bridged, when an African American was hired as a superintendent of the region's city system.[3] He was born in a neighboring county, but compromised his geographic insiderness by doing most of his administrative work downstate, including his initial superintendency. Yet he never lost the insider claim to family from the region.

The likelihood of access for African Americans was, until recently, so slight that some potential administration candidates left the region entirely. A notable example is an African American woman of the same generation as the first two female superintendents in the region. Born in Transylvania County, she ended her career as an interim superintendent of a large, urban piedmont district. She did not stay in the mountains. In Southern Appalachia, there were, at the time she came of age, few professional opportunities, even for teachers. There were far fewer openings for administrators (Smith 1996).

In Southern Appalachia insider elasticity as it relates to access reflects the region's propensity for and pattern of inclusion. Local white insider males as system leaders were first joined by geographically outsider white males and only then by local white women. The first person of color to serve as a local superintendent was, predictably, male and a geographic insider. Our findings affirm the model of leadership succession described by Strober and Catanzarite (cited in King 1993). They considered the variables of gender and race, finding that white men were followed by black men or white women in access gains. Only then did the candidacy of a black female become feasible. "An economy operating within a patriarchal and racist culture allocates job opportunities (and all resources) first to white men and last to women of color" (1103).

Sue Paddock, in a 1981 study of gender and educational leadership, contends that "gender may be the most difficult career contingency." She concludes that once women gain access to such positions, "other attributes may no longer carry weight as a precondition for employment" (190). In the southern mountains, access to senior-level educational leadership positions was opened first to local white men; then to geographic outsider white men; followed by local white women; and, only then, local African American males. The next expansion of insider elasticity will likely be the inclusion of either white women from outside the region, black men from outside the region, or black women from the region, probably in that order.[4]

A schematic of insider elasticity in another geographic area will probably differ from the one we found in the Carolina mountains. Robeson County, for example, has a large population of Lumbee Indians, so access to leadership positions for them would be greater there than in a rural county where there are very few Native Americans or where the dominant tribe is Cherokee. Eastern counties have large African American populations. There, African American men might become superintendents before women of any race. Elasticity will also vary by position. A county might welcome a geographic outsider to a school superintendency, but not to the mayor's office. In other places, degree of localness is no longer nor has it ever been a particularly high barrier. In the North Carolina highlands, however, geography will probably continue to be an important marker and an ongoing consideration in the more remote counties. It no longer excludes someone with otherwise attractive credentials from candidacy, but it continues to provide local applicants with an advantage.

Insider elasticity describes definition change. It includes direction (expansion or contraction), intensity (degree of change), and speed (pace). It also suggests that change, at least for something like occupational access, is not so much a substitution as an addition. When geographic outsiders began to apply for and attain positions as superintendents, local districts did not cease to consider geographic insiders. When women were hired for leadership roles, there was not an abrupt exclusion of men from consideration for those positions.

By looking closely at where elasticity began to appear, we developed a list of factors that appear to contribute to its arrival. For example, early adapters of expanded access tended to be counties close to, or including within their borders, interstate highways. They were more immediately connected with other parts of North Carolina or surrounding states, providing safe and quick routes to urban centers like Atlanta. Taken together, those factors provided a profile of elasticity readiness.

Elasticity Readiness

Elasticity readiness describes the willingness of a community to alter cultural expectations. Elasticity readiness is somewhat like reading readiness. There are certain things that adults can do to help children become ready to read. They can introduce them to printed materials, like books or signs. They can read to them. They can teach them the alphabet. They can demonstrate that combinations of letters represent certain sounds. Even if educators treat students in the same way in school settings, they receive different levels of readiness preparation outside school. Moreover, children are different in terms of interest, disposition, ability, and experiences, ensuring that they have individual readiness points in spite of the commonality of formal readiness preparation they might have encountered. Although teachers know a good deal about an individual student and although they select readiness activities to fit individual needs, they do not expect all children to be ready to read on Tuesday, October 12, at 9 a.m., even if they are in the same class.

Knowing about the school districts in our sample and the degree to which elasticity readiness predictors are present does not ensure an ability to predict when, or even if, any one of them will hire an insider female or an outsider Hispanic superintendent, any more than knowing absolutely when Johnny will begin to read based on our knowledge of him and his schooling. However, it increases the chances of guessing correctly which systems are likely to expand their definitions of insiderness before others. It also provides a list of factors to encourage, provided expanded insider elasticity is a goal. The presence of certain sociodemographic and economic elements appears to be an important, but not necessarily sufficient, indicator of cultural change readiness.

In Southern Appalachia, counties were more likely to entertain an inclusive range of candidates for senior-level district positions if they possessed certain characteristics. Their economy was more diverse. They were wealthier and their population was larger. They were among the less geographically remote counties and they were home to a growing number of retirement communities and summer homes. Their population was, relative to the region, well educated and the county housed or had easy access to higher education options. They had a history of tourism that attracted out-of-state visitors who made the county a focal point for extended stays. They had a disproportionately higher number of African Americans than the region.

Features that appear to contribute to insiderness rigidity are often the opposite of those that appear to enhance elasticity. Counties with a succession of white male superintendents, few of whom have been outsiders, include Clay, Graham, Mitchell, Swain, and Yancey. They are geographically removed from Asheville, mountainous (Clay is a minor exception), with few roads and no interstate highways. They are less economically diverse, smaller both in size and population, and contain large tracts of land designated national forest or national park. With the exception of members of the Eastern Band of the Cherokee, those counties are demographically homogeneous. None of them has more than 1 percent of the population classified on the last census as African American.

In county rankings of economic prosperity indicators, they fall in the bottom quartile for the state, a function of geography, lack of manufacturing, and distance from transportation and communication centers. They have few banks. Unemployment tends to be high, with seasonal fluctuations based on tourism.

Politics in a few of those counties has been contentious, partisan, and personal. Rather than housing four-year colleges, they are home to the region's two operating folk schools, Campbell and Penland. Several of them housed missionary or settlement schools in the early and mid-twentieth century. Ethnographers find these counties attractive field sites (Hicks 1976; Beaver 1986). Natives and visitors have penned colorful descriptions of life there, sometimes emphasizing their remoteness and difference (Dargan 1925; Kephart 1913; Larimore 2002; Morgan and LeGette 1958; Morgan 2002; Sheppard 1915; Sloop 1953). They have no towns of any size.

Three additional reasons for elasticity rigidity in these counties are the relative stability of senior leadership in these school districts, the paucity of central office staff, and their potential unattractiveness to outsider candidates. In the past fifty years there have been only five superintendents in Clay County.[5] The current officeholder has been there since 1982. Modeal Walsh headed Graham County's schools from 1970 to 1984, to be followed by the local high school principal, Lowell Crisp. Swain County was led by T. L. Woodward for over a quarter of a century and, after a two-year term by Max Skidmore, was followed by a superintendent who oversaw the system for ten years. There has been relatively little turnover of superintendents in these counties, a trend that is true for the region as a whole, but less apparent in some early adopter counties. The opportunities to select an outsider have been few and far between. That lack of opportunity holds true for central office positions as well. These counties have small school systems. Of the sixteen systems that we studied, in terms of student population, they occupy ranks 10, 12, 14, 15, and 16. At the low end, Graham County has only 1,188 students and, in the tenth position, Yancey County has 2,483. They lack the resources to fund a large or even moderate number of central office staff. Individuals who hold those positions tend to stay in them, preferring to remain in the district rather than seeking their professional fortunes elsewhere. Although that trend is changing somewhat (there is more movement among school administrators in the region now than there was twenty years ago), it still means that opportunities for outsider hires occur infrequently.

Finally, the ability to attract geographic outsiders and/or minority candidates rests in part on what a place can offer. The region is far from the geographic and educational policy center of the state. It has few resources or has chosen to keep tax rates low, thereby limiting the availability of funds to supplement state salary schedules. There are fewer support people to assist in central office work. Until recently, there was no doctoral program in educational administration and, consequently, limited opportunities to add to one's academic credentials. Spouses have fewer opportunities for employment. Gaining access to certain types of cultural experiences (opera, symphonies, art galleries) necessitates going at least to Asheville, not an easy prospect in winter from any of these counties and a several hour drive from some of them. Candidates with opportunities in downstate districts that can offer more amenities and higher salaries are likely to go there rather than come to the mountains. It is possible, then, to appear low on an elasticity readiness scale, yet be open to hiring an outsider. When a position opens, few applicants from outside the region find it sufficiently attractive to apply.

The presence of difference contributes to its acceptance. Geographic isolation and conditions that flow therefrom (low levels of economic diversity, few manufacturing enterprises, limited transportation and communication options, distance from urban and political centers) help maintain the cultural status quo. Students in these counties do well in school, at least as measured by state accountability assessments. Education alone does not stretch insiderness.

Accommodation Behaviors and Dissembling

Educators wishing to advance to positions of power must establish their credentials as insiders. They have to possess or appear to possess those attributes, skills, and attitudes that a particular local population expects to find in school leaders. For most of the twentieth century, in the southern uplands that meant being a Protestant, white male, born and raised locally or in the neighboring mountains, whose politics reflected those of the majority of the citizens with the power to make superintendent decisions. Formal education became an important variable in the twentieth century as did, increasingly, a commitment to and experience in public education as a teacher and, more importantly, as a secondary school principal.

As twentieth-century school systems became centralized bureaucracies and as the position of superintendent was professionalized, expectations shifted from fairly visible attributes (race and gender) to demonstrable skills. School boards wanted candidates who both looked the role and who were competent managers of money, facilities, and people. Their expectations grew higher and, in response, candidates accommodated by gaining appropriate credentials and embodying desirable traits, such as a quiet authority, confidence, an ability to listen to people, and skill in working with local school boards.

Individuals who did not look or sound the part (they were not white, from the area, or they were female) had difficulty gaining access to roles for which they, because of who they were, challenged expectations. They were outside the boundaries of local norms and, consequently, considered abnormal. To compensate, they adopted accommodation behaviors. Unable to change the way they looked or where they had been born, they could and did alter their behaviors.

They did that by adopting accommodation behaviors, selecting from a repertoire of options the ones that were place and situation appropriate and that met local expectations sufficiently to be authentic. For social encounters to be effective, actors must meet audience expectations. "To *be* a given kind of person . . . is not merely to possess the required attributes, but also to sustain the standards of conduct and appearance that one's social grouping attaches thereto" (Goffman 1959, 75). To be a superintendent in a particular place a candidate must possess more than the requisite preparation and credentials, more than knowledge and skills. That individual must, both in conduct and appearance, be sufficiently congruent (sufficiently an insider) to be accepted as a superintendent.

Geographic outsiders, women, and people of color did not, initially, meet those criteria specifically because they were not locals, men, and white. Because they were unable (unwilling) to alter those conditions, they developed compensatory attributes that challenged, then expanded, local definitions of what was acceptable in particular roles. Over time and nationally, legislation removed legal barriers. Social movements and popular culture challenged others. Mass media, notably through television, came to isolated sections of Appalachia, carrying messages of acceptable difference. Local changes, such as demographic or economic shifts, contributed to elasticity and regional variations.

External changes demanded internal correspondence from prospective candidates or current leaders who hoped to retain their positions. They had to ensure that, as definitions changed, they presented themselves in ways that matched altered standards. For instance, insider men might become more sophisticated in appearance and language when conversing with newly arrived wealthy outsiders with urban expectations, but retain and use their truck for rural school visits.

Southern women and people of color are particularly adept at accommodation behaviors, in part because they have a long history of dissembling. They live in what is still a white man's nation. To create individual or group space unencumbered by the demands of white male privilege, they presented themselves in ways that duped their cultural (during slavery and Jim Crow, their legal) masters. Their selection of a particular presentation, a conscious choice among options, should not be dismissed as hypocrisy. We all, as Goffman reminds us, perform when we engage in a social encounter. Some people, simply in order to live, had (have) to become adept at selecting effective performances.

That Southern icon Scarlett O'Hara is a fictional example par excellence of deliberate selection. Her behaviors accommodated the changing conditions of Civil War Georgia, enabling her and some of the people for whom she was responsible to survive. Her initial forays into dissembling, playing the eyelash-batting Southern belle, were successful with almost all of the men in the area less two (Ashley Wilkes and Rhett Butler). They served as training for her later performances. A more recent, nonfiction example of accommodation and resistance, as well as the frustrations and opportunities inherent therein, can be found in Azar Nafisi's *Reading Lolita in Tehran* (2003). One of the strengths of that memoir is that Nafisi illustrates the interplay between changing cultural norms and individual responses in a number of different cultures through the literature that her Iranian book club reads, while examining the conflicts that occur following a conservative religious revolution in her own country.

It was the South that clung to traditional, agrarian patriarchy with fierce tenacity. So it should come as no surprise that in the South there is a cottage industry in advice to prospective belles. See, for example, such helpful tomes as Jill Browne's (2001) *God Save the Sweet Potato Queens*, Ronda Rich's (1999) *What Southern Women Know (That Every Woman Should): Timeless Secrets to Get Everything You Want in Love, Life, and Work*, Deborah Ford's (2003) *The Grits (Girls Raised in the South) Guide to Life*, and Maryln Schwartz's (2001) *A Southern Belle Primer or Why Princess Margaret Will Never Be a Kappa Kappa Gamma*. Nothing comparable exists for women in other regions.

Whereas twentieth-century belles can approach dissembling with a touch of humor and their nineteenth-century counterparts mastered the etiquette of finishing schools with perky earnestness, to Southern African Americans it was sometimes a grim and serious task. Blassingame (1979) explores the intricacies of putting on one type of performance before white people and another backstage with one's peers. African American fiction is replete with examples of public deference and resistance, of dissembling and refusing to dissemble. History is a record of disturbed performance expectations. Changing one's place on stage, a small decision, can lead to larger consequences. Rosa Parks, for example, merely refused to change her seat.

Women who were successful in putting their feet against administrative doorjambs knew how to arrange themselves (feminine, with attention to details) and behave (consciously deferential on the way up, with a side order of Steel Magnolias when required). Women who had difficulty had usually failed to dissemble sufficiently, stumbling most often on deferential blocks. Early, successful, male geographic outsiders mastered the conversation of pickups, God, family values, and football. If they could not, they did not win their insider credentials.

In 1974 Patricia Schmuck (1999) identified the "Who, Me?" woman as someone who becomes a person of authority, not because of an assertive search for such a role, but because she is asked to assume it. Her description fits perfectly the way in which the region's first female superintendent took office.

> For about a month we did not have a superintendent. Although I was greatly concerned whom we would have, I never once thought of applying for the position. . . . I did not know that I was being considered by the County Board. Not one of them had ever suggested it to me, I was in a remote section of the county visiting schools when the Board met and elected me over a large number of male applicants. I am sure I was the most surprised young lady in North Carolina when I read in the morning paper of my election as Superintendent of Schools of Buncombe County. (Quoted in Miller 1965, 128)

Elected in 1919, Terrell resigned two years later to marry. There was not another female in that position until Mrs. Lucy Jones, who ceased being the Haywood County superintendent in 1952.

Twenty-five years later, Schmuck posited that such women were no longer to be found. She had obviously not come to the Carolina mountains, where several of our informants talked about being pushed into leadership roles. We heard, in the background of a few conversations, a sense of "Who, me?" However, we do not believe that these women meant that they were not qualified for leadership or that they had not thought of it. Rather, we suspect that they were performing their Southern woman part with the measure of modesty expected.

Professional Socialization and Assimilation

The trick of dissembling is to retain a consciousness of the act, an awareness that a particular behavior is a selection from a repertoire of potential behavior choices. The omnipresent risk of dissembling is that accommodation can slip into assimilation, the cost of which is one's cultural independence. Choice evaporates when it becomes unconscious.

We found that none of our participants escaped some degree of assimilation. No one can. A degree of assimilation is not necessarily a damaging thing. Without a measure of assimilation, there would be no community; national coherence would be impossible. One example of assimilation in our study was the absence of gender talk by females.[6] In spite of evidence to the contrary, sometimes even in their own stories, most of our female informants did not consider discrimination a factor in their administrative careers. Given that culturally it is unseemly for women (and, at one time, African Americans) in the South to use discrimination talk and to confront conflict directly, their silence is understandable. Women are still expected to exhibit deference behaviors.

All administrators become socialized to their work in supervisory positions. Some students of the socialization process consider it a generic event (Wimpelberg 1988). Subtle socialization begins through recognition of the leadership qualities that are prized nationally and locally in various positions. It continues through experiences working for and with individuals who occupy the administrative positions to which one aspires, through formal education for administration credentials, and through the books one reads about leading.

For most of the twentieth-century professional socialization, at least in the Southern highlands, was toward a "manly man" image and leadership style. Women wishing to become part of that group had to develop performances congruent with manly men, while retaining their femininity and projecting an image that was not threatening to males. They had to be tough, decisive, nurturing, selfless, and deferential simultaneously. They enacted an administrative equivalent of dancing as well as Fred Astaire, only backwards and in high heels.[7] Florence King (1993) has written a fitting description of the challenges some of our informants encounter. "The cult of southern womanhood endowed her with at least five totally different images and asked her to be good enough to adopt them all. She is required to be frigid, passionate, sweet, bitchy, and scatterbrained—all at the same time" (37).

So, females are modest until it is no longer a conscious selection but part of who they are. Good ol' boy behavior becomes who a person is, rather than a performance selected for a particular occasion. Critical distance ceases. Superintendents wishing to retain their position lead in a particular way. They set specific educational goals, because that is what their audience, their school district, expects and because the cost of accommodation remains relatively low. It is, for instance, a style with which they feel comfortable, or the goals are reasonably congruent with their own. Over time, independent of what they once might have thought, that style and those aims cease to be selections from a range of options and become theirs entirely. Lost in that process is former preferences.

Accommodation becomes assimilation. Performances vary with the players, but the play is the same. It is in the transition from dissembling to assimilation that presents a danger to the individual and to the institution. The individual loses a measure of freedom and the institution misses an opportunity for change whose nature is more than cosmetic. Schools continue to present William Shakespeare's *King Lear*; only the individual actors' interpretations of their roles are modified. We mistake cosmetic for substantive change.

Power Migration

When insiderness becomes elastic, the likelihood of cultural change increases, at least temporarily, with the addition of new and different players. Because privileged people usually want to retain their privileges, they have a tendency to resist elasticity and, when it becomes inevitable, to alter the terms of engagement. When slavery ended and former slaves became not only citizens but citizens with the right to vote, the white Southern power structure established grandfather clauses and Jim Crow laws. When they were outlawed, Southerners implemented poll taxes and literacy requirements. Supporting the entire system was a network of intimidation, reinforced by public atrocities.

Intimidation does not, however, have to be crass, overt, or physically violent. Words and stories work as well and perhaps even better. Males who fail to meet certain public performance standards for, say, aggressiveness, are called sissies. Women who have not yet mastered proper femininity become, in kinder language, tomboys and, in more extreme cases, dykes. Ask a class of students to divide a sheet of paper and on one side list all the pejoratives they can remember for "male" and, on the other side, all of those they can remember for "female." The list for the latter is longer, meaner, and, if the class is linguistically talented, skewed toward an embarrassing sexual explicitness.

As we finish this book, the phrase "if you're not with us, you're against us" is being used as shorthand for national loyalty. Agree with the political status quo and be a patriot. Disagree and be a traitor. Someone is either in or out; there is no line to straddle. Behavior determines inclusion. The powerful (the ultimate insiders) define the behavior. Controlling the political conversation through controlling the language is another form of coercion.

If intimidation fails to maintain local power structures, power migrates. If women or other marginalized groups act in their self-interest or promote an agenda of social justice that challenges those people in authority, they minimize the power inherent in the positions to which they have access.[8]

Reposition real power. The presidency remains in the hands of white males, who are safely religious (only one Catholic so far), generally educated in elite institutions (but not particularly intellectual), decidedly masculine (it helps to be tall), and surrounded by people who look, act, and talk like them. Although there are more representatives from marginalized groups today in the federal government's executive branch than in the past, they tend to be well assimilated and remain outnumbered and in subordinate roles to "the man." We turn to the implications of such power shifts in our final chapter.

Summing Up

Chapters 4 through 8 outlined the dissembling study and our findings. This chapter presented what we believe to be the bigger story. It is the meaning we constructed from the data we reviewed. Viability as a candidate for senior-level positions as well as the ability to remain there once selected are dependent on maintaining a congruence between who one is and local expectations. Those expectations, taken together, determine insiderness, a necessary precondition to consideration for jobs like the superintendency.

Insiderness changes over time and from place to place. It is an elastic quality that is geographically dependent. Insider readiness indicates the likelihood that cultural expectations may change. It can be calculated by looking at factors like access to higher education, economic diversity, demographic fluidity, and transportation systems. Candidates can also enhance their insiderness by presenting accommodation behaviors that meet or approximate audience expectations. Individuals retain a degree of autonomy and an ability to influence expectation parameters.

However, autonomy can diminish. There are professional and cultural socialization forces at work that limit the consciousness necessary to deviate from expectations. Educators are socialized to appropriate or normal administrative and personal behaviors through practice, observation, education, and credentialing. Over time, accommodation behaviors can become assimilation. Assimilation results in cultural blinders and an end to choice. Assimilated insiders lack the critical distance necessary to change the status quo. They will deviate from local norms only after some external stimulus makes change necessary and even then they will attempt to domesticate the conditions indicating change.

None of that detracts from the fact that within expected norms excellent administration is possible. Kuhn distinguished between normal science and revolutionary science. Most of the time scientists operate in the world of the former condition. They do normal science, often very well, and make significant contributions to their field. They do not, however, win Nobel Prizes. Most of the time educators engage in normal, rather than revolutionary, practice. They do so in a field in which there are no prizes for divergent thought.

·10·

TRIPPING AT THE TIPPING POINT

Traditionally, students of leadership pay attention to tasks and people. A specific problem requires a particular administrative style, depending on what needs to be done and the resources available with which to do it. People lead situationally. If buildings are on fire, leaders do not convene committee meetings; they direct people to exits. If a new textbook needs to be adopted, leaders delegate the decision to districtwide committees that include teachers who will use it, parents whose children will read it, and board members who will have the responsibility of approving it and defending their decision to the public. Leadership style is task situated and influenced by the expertise and experience of the people whose participation is necessary for its completion.

We have emphasized throughout this book the importance of place, the significance of geographic location. The needs of students differ not only as a function of who they are, but where they are. What works well in one part of a state does not necessarily work well in another. What succeeds in the South might be less successful in the Midwest. What seems appropriate for Westerners can appear outrageous to a visitor from the Orient. Although distance is no longer the physical or social barrier that it once was, cultural communities were and remain place-bound. Even nomads travel within bounded space. As long as a local collective consciousness exists, leadership will be place-situated too.

In this chapter we consider whether schools will change in fundamental ways as a function of who leads them. Occupational segregation in school and district leadership positions, as we have known it, will end within a generation. The numbers are already turning with regard to the principalship and they are in place to change at the highest district levels. It will be replaced with another form of segregation, one with unintended, negative consequences. Scholars have claimed for decades that the promotion of marginalized people to educational leadership positions will alter, in fundamental and positive ways, the nature of schools and schooling. Although their presence is likely to emphasize collaboration and enhance working conditions, it probably will not challenge the current organizational structure or mission. The push toward educational standards is really a push for standardized education, a homogenization of schooling that threatens the distinctiveness of local communities and is unlikely to be in either the best interests of the nation's children or the nation. It is not coincidental that the current hyperrationalization of public education is happening at precisely the same time as minorities gain access to district leadership positions.

By the Numbers

Complaints about the number of women and minorities in administrative positions have been a staple of gender scholarship (Jones and Montenegro 1982; Bell and Chase 1993; Hammer and Rohr 1994; Joy 1998; Mertz 1991; Shakeshaft 1989; Yeakey, Johnston, and Adkison 1986). Recently, critics have moved from a focus on numbers and percentages to arguments about proportion as a function of the percentage of women in teaching (Riehl and Byrd 1997). The reason for the change is simple. The numbers and percentages have increased dramatically, beginning slowly in the 1970s and accelerating in the 1980s. Today, women are either a majority of the administrators nationally in school-based leadership positions or coming close to being one. They have yet to achieve the same gains in the highest central office positions, but even there access increases are sizeable and likely to continue.

Forsythe and Smith (2001) found that in Missouri the "relative percentage of females-to-males was increasing . . . for all school types." Doud and Keller, authors of *The K–8 Principal in 1998*, note that the most significant difference between 1988 and 1998 was the percentage of females in the principalship (Harmel 1999). In a review of gender and the superintendency in the state of Washington, Wolverton (1999) writes that "when women do 'men's' work, they do it disproportionately in less desirable locations, with expanded responsibilities, with fewer support staff, and for lower pay." She acknowledges that there are more women doing that work, at least on the initial rungs of the administrative ladder. Although only 14 percent of the state's superintendents are female, women comprise 52 percent of central office administrators, 35 percent of assistant superintendents, 28 percent of secondary school principals, 37 percent of secondary school assistant principals, 51 percent of elementary principals, and 52 percent of elementary assistant principals. In Florida, in

1989, 45.3 percent of the public school administrative staff was female. Thirteen years later, 57 percent were (Florida Department of Education 2003). According to Mertz (2003), in 1972 women were in the majority in only one administrative position, elementary school principal (54 percent). By 2002, they were in the majority in five of the nine categories Mertz studied and within ten percentage points in three others.[1]

According to the National Center for Educational Statistics (2000a), the percentage of public school principals nationwide that were women was 24.6 in 1987–88 and 43.7 in 1999–2000. Percentages for minorities are also increasing. In 1987–88, 13.4 percent headed schools; eleven years later 17.8 percent did. The figures are even more dramatic when only new principals are considered. In 1987–88 the percentage of new principals who were females was 40.6 and in 1999–2000 it was 53.9. For minorities, the percentages were 15.6 and 20.5 respectively.

The picture is the same in North Carolina (Department of Public Instruction 2002). In 2001 women held 52 percent of principalships and 58 percent of assistant principalships. Minorities held 23.19 percent of principalships and 26.6 percent of assistant principalships. Graduates from preparation programs in 2000–2001 included 62.6 percent women and 26.7 percent minorities. In 1997–98, a peak year for female and minority graduates from Carolina educational administration programs, they earned over 77 percent of the degrees. Fifty years ago, in 1953, only Dare County Schools had a female superintendent (Public Schools of North Carolina 1952–2003). For over thirty years there were never more than two women in superintendencies in any one year and often there were none. Things began to change in the 1980s, with three female superintendents in 1987 and six by 1989. In 2001 there were seventeen. At last count (fall of 2003), seven of the fifteen districts we studied had, since 1992, employed a female or African American superintendent. In 2002, when an eighth system reduced its search to two candidates, one of them was a woman. In a ninth district their assistant superintendent, a female, was selected to head another system in the northern mountains of the state.

In the near future, at least, the women are coming, and with them representatives of other, but not all, minorities.[2] Given the numbers of previously marginalized populations in springboard roles like secondary school principalships and associate superintendencies, as well as changes in preparation program demographics, their presence in increasingly proportional numbers seems inevitable. Rather than focusing on whether inclusion will happen, we should begin to consider what inclusion in the current educational milieu would mean.

Tipping Point

According to Malcolm Gladwell (2000), the concept of tipping was commonly used to describe the beginning of epidemics. A tipping point is that moment when a disease becomes contagious, expanding in a seeming uncontrolled and uncontrollable fashion. In *The Tipping Point: How Little Things Make a Big Difference*, Gladwell is interested in social, rather than medical, epidemics. He applies the concept to cultural changes, such as the spread of adolescent smoking, fashion fads, neighborhood crime rates, or the sudden appearance of an unlikely best seller. It is also a construct that can be applied to segregated employment (M. King 1993).

Tips are like Kuhn's paradigm shifts, writ small. Things on one side of a point are unlike those on the other. "We reframe the way we think about the world" (Gladwell, 257). Gladwell identifies three tipping agents: Charismatic or connected people are powerful messengers for change; an idea or product is made so compelling or seductive that it sticks; and something about the context within which a message is delivered alters our perception, and we see it anew or for the first time.

Initially, school superintendencies were reserved for white men. Access is expanding to include others. Given the demographic shifts underway in educational leadership positions, we believe that the profession will tip rather than reach equilibrium. Instead of being gender and race neutral, increasingly schools and then district administration positions will be considered women's work.[3] If history is any guide and that is what happens, unattractive consequences will follow.

The good news, according to some scholars, is that women lead differently and their leadership style is more appropriate for twenty-first century organizations.[4] Not so, write other researchers, who contend that evidence for a difference argument is weak and/or inconsequential.[5] Our sample provides evidence for both sides. There are differences in how men and women perceive what they do, and tangential evidence that they do some things differently. However, those disparities do not appear to alter in fundamental ways how educational organizations operate. Former outsiders in our study are cautious about deviating from accepted insider practice. The system leaders who have challenged their districts the most are outsiders, but the districts in which they have done the stretching all fall into the high elasticity readiness category. Although women and people of color will eventually outnumber white men in senior-level leadership positions, they will not necessarily make public education more responsive to individual and local community needs nor less vocationally oriented. They are likely to train "productive citizens for a global economy," with an emphasis on economic productivity (a currently popular public school mission statement). They are not in the business of educating in ways that develop curious, empathic, happy children. Although that may be their desired mission, the external constraints under which schools now operate make, one test at a time, that goal more difficult to attain.[6] They are likely to make schooling a more pleasant and participatory process. Their skills and dispositions appear well suited to guide school districts on a more serene trip to the same place.

Throughout the last century, the employment of racial and gender outsiders in the United States has haltingly moved toward a more equitable share of executive positions in the worlds of business and the professions. The reasons for widening access vary, often are initiated by federal mandates or court decisions, are unevenly welcomed by practitioners, and occur at different speeds in different arenas. There are more women and minorities studying law, medicine, and dentistry today than at the turn of the last century. Although not increasing as rapidly in rate, they are more likely today than a generation ago to be candidates for engineering and architecture degrees. Access continues to move in a positive direction in spite of ideological backlashes and legislative backsliding.

Females have made strides in the latter half of the last century. Today more women than men graduate from colleges. They earn more graduate degrees. They delay marriage and enter the labor market with aspirations that routinely fail to stop outside the executive office door or, for educators, in a classroom. They are poised to reach the highest levels of management. According to one consultant, "If you look at the ranks of any corporation below the top twenty people, you'll find that fifty percent of the next group of managers are women" (quoted in Towery 1998, 137).

Does that mean that at some point in the near future we will look up to discover that the senior leaders in our nation's school districts are female in proportion to their numbers in the teaching ranks? People of color proportional to their number in the P–12 student population? Based on what we have seen in North Carolina and read about trends elsewhere, it appears likely. The pace of change is discouragingly slow for prospective candidates and their champions, but it is persistent. However, there remains another possibility. We may look up and find that they are all that are there. Once women and/or minorities attain a tipping point number, will white men scramble to exit the profession? Rather than reaching equilibrium, will system-level leadership become, like K–12 teaching, primarily women's work or the work of marginalized males? Will it be something that "real" men (majority race men) do not do?

The conclusions we drew from the shifts we saw were not the sort to warm feminist hearts. The process is, admittedly, incomplete. The past does not have to be a prologue to the present, yet it provided us with the only case studies available of public work that tipped.

Lessons from the Past

We looked closely at a small sample of women's work as it changed over time. The occupations at which we looked were chosen because of the extent to which they became occupationally segregated. We also sought examples from different types of work and we wanted jobs that gender-segregated at different times. Our examples are taken primarily from early work in textile mills, department store clerking, office work, nursing, and education, with occasional illustrations from other fields. They mostly concern majority race women, but the consequences that follow their labor history reflect that of other minorities or marginalized groups.

Historically, when a sex-segregated or race-segregated occupation tipped from male to female or from white to black, four things changed: the position declined in status, at least to white males and, relative to comparable roles in which men were the majority, to the general population; it lost autonomy, and became standardized, routine, and narrowly bounded with strict role descriptions; practitioners were often subject to strict supervision; and salaries stagnated or declined relative to comparable positions occupied by white men. Finally, once tipped, always tipped. After a job became women's work, it was difficult to attract men back into it. When positions become associated almost exclusively with one race or gender, they remain so until something happens to disturb the status quo. Women taught and men led schools. In the nineteenth and early twentieth centuries, white women worked in textile plants and black women in domestic service.

Most early nineteenth-century labor performed by women was linked to household work, in their own homes, in their homes for someone else, or in other houses as domestics. Other than schools, a steadily growing option for educated women throughout that century, textile mills were the largest provider of public employment (Dublin 1979). Like later public work, the mills were, paradoxically, both circumscribed and emancipatory. Young women could attain a modicum of independence from their families, earn their own money, live in communal settings that were more commodious than those they had left, enter into a social circle of like-minded individuals, and access a variety of educational opportunities (Eisler 1977; Marchalonis 1989). In exchange for those opportunities, they exercised little control over their wages (which were kept relatively low), were supervised by men, and could not move into managerial positions (Dublin 1979). They entered a Dickensian world that was less like Oliver Twist's and more like that in the opening paragraph of *A Tale of Two Cities*. It was, simultaneously, the best and the worst of times.

The mid-nineteenth-century shoe industry, another venue that women entered early, continued patterns established at Lowell. Women and men did different work. Gender segregation reflected value attribution; men's work was worth more than jobs done by women. Consequently, men earned more than women. Opportunities for advancement, either to other areas within the shoe industry or into management, were not available to females. Moreover, the benefits of communal life in mill villages like Lowell disappeared as even single workingwomen were likely to live in the bosoms of their families, contributing money to a collective pot, rather than living independently or with friends. Dublin (1994) concludes that their work and wages "were reintegrated . . . [to] a patriarchal family wage economy." The "window of opportunity" for independence that opened slightly at Lowell swiftly closed, setting the stage for female economic dependence for the majority of the twentieth century (257).

In the late nineteenth century, the business world grew exponentially. In the United States certain kinds of office work gender-tipped with the Industrial Revolution. As demand for employees increased and the supply of educated men willing to do certain tasks declined, business managers turned, initially with reluctance and then with enthusiasm to women. Males in clerical positions worried, with good reason, that the presence of so many females would compromise their status and pay. By the twentieth century, "real salaries began to decline as jobs were rationalized and women entered the office in large numbers" (Strom 1992, 8). Labor divided along gender and race lines, giving men access to managerial roles, consigning women to support positions and, in white-operated enterprises, at least in the South for much of the twentieth century, excluding people of color from white- or pink-collar jobs entirely. Not only was the kind of work one did segregated but also a vertical segregation was introduced into modern bureaucracies. Majority race men were free to scale occupational heights, but marginalized employees could not. Women and minority race men rarely complained about those divisions. The jobs that were open to them were often the best alternative available. Southern teachers, for instance, frequently earned less than office workers and labored in less attractive settings. Life in an urban factory with a regular paycheck was usually an improvement over sharecropping.

In the early twentieth century, department stores, like modern offices, were new institutions. Shopkeeping was public work. Most early stores were small and operated by men.[7] When an enterprise grew to a size that required more than one person, proprietors, after exhausting family options, hired male clerks. Department stores, unlike the village general store, were far larger than previous retail enterprises had been and consciously designed to attract female customers. They became female counterparts to men's clubs (Benson 1986). Because these stores needed many clerks, wanted to check costs by placing a ceiling on wages, valued "control, predictability, and efficiency," and desired women with genteel dispositions as customers, females were attractive candidates for sales positions. Department store hierarchies paralleled those found in modern businesses. Men supervised, women served, and racial minorities swept. Males had options for advancement and earned more money in comparable positions.

At first few women did public work in the professions. They were routinely excluded from institutions such as medical schools or law offices, which provided prerequisite training. Moreover, in the nineteenth century, professions were not yet as organized as they are today nor had they attained the status that came later. Among those quasi-professional roles that were open to women, nursing and education were the two in which they found the greatest welcome.

Nursing, once a male profession when practiced outside the home, tipped early. By 1930, 98 percent of nurses were female. Nursing has transitioned from what was basically domestic service in the nineteenth century to a highly skilled profession, but nurses continue to work under the supervision of physicians, most of whom are men (Kemp 1994). In spite of an expansion of opportunities for nurses (supervisor, nurse practitioner, university teaching positions) and energetic recruitment efforts aimed at men, the profession in 1991 was 94.8 percent female and in 2000 was 94.6 percent female. Once women's work, forever more women's work. Nurses have never attained a status commensurate with the importance of the work they do, and continue to draw a relatively low salary, when compared with that of other jobs that require the same degree of preparation and responsibility.[8]

America's initial teaching corps was male. Eighteenth- and early nineteenth-century men taught during slack seasons on the farm, as a preliminary step before moving into another field, or, less often, as a career. When Horace Mann's idea for common schools took root, it necessitated a substantial increase in the number of teachers. To afford them, policymakers turned to literate, unemployed women. As educational requirements increased, autonomy declined and wages stagnated, conditions tolerable to females with few options, but less attractive to males who were already stigmatized in some communities for doing women's work. By the nineteenth century, men were leaving the field in droves. By 1900 most American teachers were women (Kemp 1994; Strober 1984).

Working men advocated keeping women in segregated roles for a number of reasons. They worried about a reduction in their wages, lowered status, increased supervision, lessened independence, and altered work conditions, including the deskilling of craft or artisan work. To encourage the ladies to stay home, men complained, staged protests, supported restrictive legislation, conducted work stoppages, and kept women out of unions or minimized their roles therein (Greenwald 1990). Given economic trends subsequent to female entry, men had good reasons to be concerned.

Salaries

Dublin (1979) found that even in the early days of textile manufacturing, when women began to enter the factory work force, wages for women were not only lower than those for men, but were also flattened. For men, salaries became indicators of worth, a comparative scale of the value of what they did. Wages became one way of defining who they were, not merely compensation for the work they performed. Women were considered less valuable than men and, consequently, were inexpensive labor. Greenwald (1990) concluded that the most often cited reason for male opposition to the entry of women in the labor force was that their presence lowered wages for everyone. No field that tipped male to female paid women more than the men.

Accountability and Efficiency

During industrialization "the reification of both efficiency and accountability . . . became a critical part of the search for order" (Strom 1992, 20). Taylorism emphasized the manliness of a rational, by-the-numbers approach to problem solving, stressing the role of science in lieu of emotionalism in decision making. Scott and Haynes (1921, cited in Strom), in their aptly named *Science in Working with Men*, claimed that their advice differed from that offered by advocates of the Social Gospel and utopians. They dismissed their methods as inept and effeminate. Indeed, throughout the nineteenth and twentieth centuries, as paid and unpaid work was linked to the weaker sex, it was criticized as ineffective and even dangerous (Douglas 1977). America was a John Wayne kind of place, where manly men held sway. Billy Sunday, a 1920s evangelist, characterized Jesus as "the greatest scrapper that ever lived." He was "no dough-faced, lick-spittle proposition" (quoted in Hofstadter 1966, 116).

Janiewski (1991) emphasizes that when Southern white women and children entered public work in textile mills, manufacturers justified their employment by asserting that they would work in safe environments at jobs suited to their abilities under the "protection and care" of male supervisors (82–83). What was true for women in one work environment was generally true in others. Women, for their own well-being, were closely supervised in almost every role they filled.

Females gravitated to jobs associated with caregiving. Even there, their work was judged as less valuable. Health professions gradually divided by type and value into actual caregivers (nurses, dental technicians specializing in cleaning teeth, and dieticians), who were likely to be women, and diagnosticians (physicians, surgeons, and dentists), who were likely to be men (Kemp 1994). Even within specific fields, there were distinctions. For example, when women became physicians, their areas of practice were afforded less status than those practiced by men. Females were more likely to care for children or to enter family practice; males practiced surgery or entered esoteric specialties.

Women were librarians; men, head librarians. Women were secretaries in offices; men, secretaries in the president's Cabinet. Women were telephone operators and, once services were consolidated, closely supervised. Men were telegraph operators and worked independently. In education, the more a position was linked to caregiving (elementary school teaching, counseling, or social work), the more likely it was to be gendered female. The more a position was linked to management (principal, superintendent, or coach), the more likely it was that it was gendered male.

Efficiency experts advocate breaking jobs into discrete undertakings and determining the most cost-efficient way to accomplish them. Whenever possible, they assign one individual to a specific task, thereby minimizing training costs and enhancing quality control. To motivate workers and to ensure that they are accountable, managers establish a set of rewards and sanctions based on productivity. As soon as a job is broken into distinct steps, supervisors design task hierarchies. Those assignments that are deemed more important, more dangerous, and more likely to require mechanical skills or a scientific orientation become men's work. They bring a higher status to the people who do them. Moving up a hierarchy was something men did (vertical segregation); women's work was relegated to bottom rungs or placed on a different, much shorter ladder. The higher up the ladder a worker climbed, the more autonomy he gained.

In K–12 public schools, district organization is as much a bureaucracy as are the organizational structures of modern businesses. It was common in the 1920s and 1930s to tout the ways in which business methods were part of school processes and procedures. Comparisons with factories were considered flattering. The CEO of a school system is the superintendent. Individuals in that role have the highest salaries; the least direct, daily supervision (the school board and, through them, the public); the most autonomy; and the greatest status.

Standardization and Routines (Rationalization)

Women's work in the Lowell mills provided scant opportunity for the acquisition of additional skills. Tasks were so much a matter of routine that jobs were virtually "interchangeable" (Dublin 1979, 192). Historically, women, unlike men, have persisted in particular jobs rather than explore other, potentially more lucrative options. That, too, became true of teachers by the twentieth century.

Changes in women's work paralleled changes in how jobs were constructed. As tasks were standardized, technical and repetitive work like typing became the province of females. Baking was once considered a skilled job. Early bakeries employed a disproportionate number of men. As commercial baking became routine, governed by mass-production processes—in other words, when it was deskilled—more women were hired. They were, after all, cheaper. Today bakers working production lines and part-time in grocery stores, positions requiring fewer skills and bringing fewer tangible benefits than custom baking, are filled by women. Dessert chefs are more often men (Steiger and Reskin 1990). Greenwald (1990) notes that the admission of women into machine shops to do welding and molding was accompanied by a "dilution of craft skills" (238). As often as possible, managers removed the human element from public work. There was no premium for creativity on a production line. Nor was there room for innovation in the classroom, for the likes of Superintendent Rigler, the Oregon educator from chapter 3 who knew at any moment what every teacher of a particular grade was teaching and from what book.

Throughout the twentieth century, most starkly perhaps for skilled artisans in the early part of that time period, industrialization degraded manual and factory work, segmenting and standardizing tasks in ways that made labor monotonous and that limited upward mobility. Even the professions, particularly those dominated by women (teaching and nursing, for example), came with policy manuals and required procedures. Teachers, for example, worked in one grade and/or in a specific school for an entire career. Superintendents, teacher supervisors, and later principals worked toward minimizing variability within grades and across schools. Curriculum guides came with pacing guides. Textbooks provided teachers with teaching scripts. Remember Rigler, with his centrally planned scope and sequence scheduled for every moment? We can laugh about that degree of compulsiveness yet, given the persistence of central (statewide, in some cases) textbook selections, common courses of study, detailed curriculum guides, approved supplementary materials guidelines, standardized testing programs, required test preparation regimens, and explicit exit criteria as well as teaching evaluation procedures and licensure exams, we now have more in common with educators like Rigler than not. Some systems in North Carolina have devised Rigler-style systems that require teachers to post their daily schedules and to teach prescribed skills in prescribed sequences within prescribed time blocks. If a central office administrator visits the classrooms, that person expects to see the teacher working on schedule, using approved strategies.

Manliness

Behind some of the anxiety about women and workplaces was a fear of feminization, of males becoming more woman-like and, as a consequence, less manly. Managers worried that the advent of female workers might corrupt work itself, particularly since women were known to be the weaker sex—less rational, more emotional, less able to face difficulties, more likely to avoid competition.

Harrington Emerson, writing in 1911, notes that "woman makes teepees, but men build . . . sky-scrapers" and "organization must replace intuition" (quoted in Strom 1992, 69). Samuel Haber (1964) concludes that efficiency was linked to effectiveness, hard work, discipline, and masculinity (ix). Early twentieth-century managers required "strength, assertiveness, and rationality," attributes in which, common wisdom held, men excelled and women fell short (Kemp 1994, 221).

Typical of admonitions to early twentieth-century women with aspirations is the 1903 observation of a *New England Farmer* contributor. "We respect, admire, and love a female woman. . . . But a male woman, who can bear! We cannot read of monster meetings, in which women perform the leading parts" (quoted in Juster 1979, 247). In the same year, a writer for *The Week's Progress* notes that men and women "are different in nature, in temperament, in function. . . . If man attempts women's function, he will prove himself but an inferior woman. If a woman attempts man's function she will prove herself but an inferior man." Nor should anyone attempt to intervene in that dynamic. It "is universal and perpetual" and, anticipating political popular slogans in the late twentieth century, "It underlies the family, which could not exist if this difference did not exist" (quoted in Juster 1979, 253). Sunday morning sermons ring with similar messages in some churches even today.

Early popular caricatures of teachers were not favorable. Washington Irving's Ichabod Crane was a cartoon, even before Walt Disney made him the subject of an animated short feature. Washington Irving (1819–20) describes him as "tall, but exceedingly lank, with narrow shoulders, long arms and legs, hands that dangled a mile out of his sleeves, feet that might have served for shovels." He had a small head, "flat at top, with large ears . . . and a long snipe nose" (1060–61). "The schoolmaster is generally a man of some importance in the female circle of a rural neighborhood." He was a gossip, music master, "esteemed by the women" and envied his access to them by local boys (1063). Enamored by Katrina Van Tassel, Crane is a stark contrast to his primary rival, Brom Van Brunt. Van Brunt was "a burly, roaring, roistering blade," famed throughout the countryside for "his feats of strength and hardihood." He was handsome, self-possessed, and mischievous with "a mingled air of fun and arrogance" (1069). A man's man, he succeeds in winning the maiden's hand and scaring poor Crane from the county.

In early (Eggleston's *The Hoosier Schoolmaster*, 1892) and late (Stuart's *The Thread That Runs So True*, 1949) depictions of heroic teachers, authors go out of their way to demonstrate the masculinity of their main characters. They stand up to bullies and win fights. They take risks, demonstrate cleverness, win the girls, and exhibit courage. Unlike books that feature female teachers from the same era (Julia Gordon's *My Country School Diary*, 1970, originally published in 1946), they emphasize physicality and minimize self-doubt and pedagogy. Popular culture perpetuates the Übermensch image of educators in films like *Stand and Deliver* and *Lean on Me*. Men in a suspect profession deflect implications that they are insufficiently masculine to pursue another profession by manifesting their manliness in very obvious ways, like using motorcycles and trucks.

Mixed Messages

Benson (1986) found, in her comprehensive review of the history of department stores and saleswomen, that differential access contained mixed messages. Retail work held attractions not found in other alternatives. Women got out of houses and relieved from household drudgeries to earn money in social settings. Early office and retail work provided higher salaries than some classroom teaching jobs. Even teaching offered a respite from the home, an opportunity to interact with like-minded adults, and the gratification of doing work well. For many (never all) women who elected or had to do public work, it was better than where they had been.

In spite of limited opportunities for advancement, there were some females who reached positions of authority. They symbolized the possibility that others might one day join them. As in the field of education, retail employment had niches for female managers, who tended to cluster in areas like personnel or who succeeded as specialized buyers.

There were occasions to demonstrate creativity and initiative. Like schools, which could not operate without a core of hardworking, underpaid teachers, department stores, hospitals, libraries, and offices relied on a similar complement of enterprising women. Although positional authority rested elsewhere, day-to-day authority within a confined sphere (the classroom or a particular store section) rested with frontline workers. Women and other marginalized populations carved out spaces in which they labored with a degree of dignity and satisfaction, even when closely supervised. Public work brought rewards from the beginning, even if it were not gender neutral in rewards and privileges.

Transitions

By the 1950s, economic dislocations as a result of World War II, the subsequent enrichment of human resources by the G.I. Bill, an economy stimulated by military spending, and Cold War rhetoric resulted in labor shortages in sectors that benefited minority wage earners. There were more jobs available, although they continued to be or became gender and race segregated.

By the 1960s, however, there was a growing affluent middle class whose daughters began to enter the marketplace in professional jobs. The Civil Rights and feminist movements led to antidiscrimination legislation and affirmative action programs. Kessler-Harris (1982) found that women raised in the 1950s and college-bound in the 1960s were more conscious of their choices than their predecessors. They were less likely to find home and work as tightly confined by legal and cultural boundaries. Access to higher education improved. Not coincidentally, it was from this age cohort that our upwardly mobile Southern Appalachian school leaders came. Changes were on the horizon, but the stigma of women's work remained and continues to this day. Negative experiences with regard to salaries, autonomy, and status persist.

The Danger of Homogeneity

If deciding among alternatives is anxiety inducing, then it makes sense that the only flavor of ice cream is vanilla. When Henry Ford began producing cars, he famously quipped that his customers could buy them in any color they wanted, as long as it was black (quoted in Allen 1969, 98). In spite of a desire to choose among flavors or colors, Americans prefer, feel more comfortable with, a narrow rather than an infinite range of options. Sameness promotes a certain kind of efficiency. Mass production depends on identical, interchangeable parts. In spite of rhetoric to the contrary and a certain set of physical laws, it is not opposites that we find attractive, but similarities. Predictability brings with it a reassuring sense of security.

Perhaps that is one reason that homogeneity is so appealing. We have a long and occasionally checkered history of enforcing a degree of sameness on public school students. Required Bible readings in nineteenth- and twentieth-century schools came from the King James version, notwithstanding the objections of Catholic parents, who did not want their children using that text. Disagreement about which Bible to read was one of the reasons for the popularity of parochial schools. Being Christian was insufficient to those Protestants who sought to eliminate the possibility of a parochial alternative. Real Americans were Protestant, weren't they?

Public schools have long been an acculturating institution, teaching not only the ABCs or reading and writing, but also how to be an American. If immigrants lacked the appropriate cultural credentials to be considered part of the grand American whole, then schools would supply them. One of the most misguided efforts at Americanization was designing boarding schools for Native Americans on Richard Pratt's Carlisle model. Pratt told a group of supporters that his goal was to immerse "Indians in our civilization and when we get them under" to hold "them there until they are thoroughly soaked" (quoted in Reyhner and Eder 1989, 79–80). Toward that end, he and his teachers collected their students from western tribes and transported them to Pennsylvania, far removed from their parents. Cutting their hair, replacing their native dress with military uniforms for the boys and proper western-style dresses for the girls, and disciplining any of them who dared to speak anything other than English, Pratt's followers ensured that their charges at least gave the appearance of being "civilized."

In an 1889 bulletin on education Thomas Morgan, Commissioner of Indian Affairs, wrote that "children should be taken at as early an age as possible, before camp life has made an indelible stamp upon them" (quoted in Spring 1994, 23). Geographic displacement was an important part of Pratt's training protocol. To take the Indian out of an Indian required an environment without cultural artifacts to which a student might cling.

Educators found ways to Americanize diverse populations without having to resort to the costly expedient of distant boarding schools or to unseemly compulsion. Joel Spring describes several alternatives in *Deculturalization and the Struggle for Equality* (1994). They include: (1) "segregation and isolation," (2) "forced change of language," (3) "imposition of dominant culture through the curriculum," (4) "imposition of dominant culture through textbooks," (5) "denial of expression of dominated group's culture," and (6) "use of teachers from dominating group" (39). Separate children into groups, in English-only settings, teaching a set curriculum using approved texts in classrooms in which almost all teachers are white females, and assimilation is almost certainly an attainable goal.

We have moved beyond Americanization by blunt instrument to more sophisticated methods. Curriculum battles over what constitutes "true" American history and how much diversity needs to be included in textbooks are as much a thing of the present as of the past (Gitlin 1995; Miller 1998; Nash, Crabtree, and Dunn 1997; Ravitch 2001, 2003; Zimmerman 2002). Minority teachers are underrepresented in our public school classrooms. "English only" is in the ascendancy. At the core of acculturation is a desire to change one set of people so that they look, sound, think, and believe like another. To make people the same is too make them equal. Schools mint standardized Americans stamped with an official seal of approval (a diploma) at the culmination of the process.

In spite of lip service and nods to toleration and diversity, standardization is commonplace in the United States. America is eternally a nation is search of a best system. George Ritzer (1993) labels the process of applying a certain set of business principles to multiple sectors of American society "McDonaldization." Fast-food industries strive to attain maximum market advantage by attending four elements of production: efficiency, quantification, predictability, and control. Visible productivity is the measure of almost all things. We "McDonaldize" to rationalize our society. Ritzer argues McDonaldization is everywhere in our modern world, including our public schools.

In 1993 he pointed to the use of multiple choice, machine-scored tests, and custom publishing as examples of efficiency. Our preoccupation with numbers like IQs or SAT and GRE results is a sign of our affection for quantification. Although he did not specify an example for predictability, even in his 1996 revision of McDonaldization, one can certainly find it in the standards movement, in which all students will reach the same set of standards by a certain time. The textbook approval process ensures predictability in curricular scope and sequence nationally. An indicator of its success is the almost universal penchant for having a year of geometry between the traditional two years of algebra. The appropriate sequence for generic high school science is, in order, earth science, biology, chemistry, and then physics. Literature moves from the world stage (tenth grade generally), to the United States (eleventh grade), and finally to Great Britain (twelfth grade). There are some pesky nuances, of course. Each state insists on teaching its own state history. However, they usually do it in the same grades. Control efforts include formal and informal instruction in obedience to authority. There is, for example, the tyranny of the clock. Students, particularly in secondary school, must master concepts within a confined span of minutes, conveniently demarked in most schools by beginning and ending bells. Strict adherence to lesson plans means that students learn what someone has determined they must. Teachable moments are unacceptable digressions in a McDonaldized school.

Emphasis on educational productivity has not lessened since Ritzer wrote his book. Most educators could readily extend the complaints he offered about education. North Carolina in the 1980s pioneered teacher evaluation systems that assumed a remarkable homogeneity in teaching style. Legislators tied the system to earning a continuing license, thereby ensuring compliance. Want to stay employed? Master the six-step lesson plan. Worried about what, as opposed to how, teachers were teaching? By the late 1990s, Carolina linked bonus pay to test results. Administrators pressured teachers to focus their attention on the state's curriculum, taught in a format and pace that enhanced success on prescribed state exams. The art of bubbling answer sheets and mastering writing templates became, in many public schools, the curriculum. Educators narrowed the content to reflect what would likely appear on annual assessments. Students sometimes practice monthly for the annual tests.

McDonaldization is not confined to North Carolina or the South, although one could argue that its recent incarnation was ably assisted by a bevy of Southern "education governors," like South Carolina's Richard Riley, North Carolina's Jim Hunt, Tennessee's Lamar Alexander, and Texas's George W. Bush, who adopted remarkably similar paths to educational salvation. Americans are in the midst of a national school rationalization movement that began with *A Nation at Risk* (National Commission on Excellence in Education 1983) and whose end does not yet appear in sight. Using legislation, educational reformers standardize schools, schooling, and school men and women in an effort to boost educational productivity.

The cost of our efforts, according to Ritzer (1993, 1996), is likely to be great. Too many schools emphasize unquestioning obedience to authority, including the authority of a state-authorized curriculum often taught in set ways using endorsed materials to ensure reaching approved conclusions. Students master content by rote and demonstrate competency on "objective" tests. "Spontaneity and creativity tend not to be rewarded, and may even be discouraged" (115). McStudents might be as intellectually nutritious as most fast-food products are physically good for us.

Ritzer bases much of his analysis on the work of Max Weber. Bureaucracies, according to Weber (1968), evolved in the nineteenth and twentieth centuries as ways to bring order to (rationalize) the West's rapidly changing world, to give it shape, provide clear boundaries, and control it as much as possible. Yet as bureaucracies developed, they enclosed their workers in cages of rationality, thereby minimizing their uniqueness and their humanity. When bureaucracies operate mechanistically, according to rules that are beyond question, in a culture governed by "that's the way it is," judgment is unnecessary and even detrimental. Paradoxically, rational systems, as Weber and Ritzer observe, become irrational when they supersede human reason.

Weber was concerned primarily with what he labeled "formal rationality," a search for the one right system to attain a particular goal, a system elaborated by specific procedures and monitored by social structures. Bureaucrats, good organization men and women, do not search for a particular solution to a particular problem. The solution already exists in a technical manual. Formal rationality is Taylorism applied to all human endeavors. The good news about this approach to problem solving is that no one need ever reinvent the wheel. The bad news is that there is only one concept of wheel available, only one best way to go about making it, and only one best way to use it. Unfortunately, sometimes people need something without wheels.

Educational institutions fit Weber's definition of formal rationality. They have policy manuals and handbooks that spell out the rules. People who follow them gain rewards. Those who fail to abide by the approved process invite sanctions. Educational standardization appears, at first consideration, to have more positives than negatives. It is an efficient way to teach many students brought together in large schools. It yields a predictable and eminently quantifiable product and controls the behaviors of both educators and educatees. What is there to dislike about a common curriculum taught in common schools by appropriately credentialed teachers and judged by scores on common tests? To begin with, it limits choices, the essence of liberty.

Not all the cages in which modern organizations place workers are made of iron. Some are rubber and others velvet. The bars are sufficiently elastic to allow periodic escapes from sustained routines. Like Ferris Bueller, students can escape for a day. Teachers can suspend the curriculum for a special unit, as long as their students are ready for those tests. Or the bars are sufficiently pleasant that they do not appear onerous. Some teachers relish the competition of state tests, making education a game that they play through surrogates (their students). Administrators buffer teachers from the potential depersonalization of the system, serving up donuts and coffee. They offer feel-good bromides like shared decision making, as long as the decisions do not contradict or challenge the system proper. If Ford's cars were Weberian cages, they would be black when the cage was made of iron, Chevrolets if they were rubber, and any of six colors if they were velvet.

The few bureaucrats who rail against cages seem regularly to escape or are asked to leave. They go to colleges or editorial boards of newspapers and journals. Outsiders, they critique the system. Down with organized Little Leagues in manicured parks and up with disorderly pickup games in sandlots and backyards.

The problem inherent in education either by Americanization or McDonaldization is that it denies the particular and the individual, exchanging them for a set of interchangeable processes and people. A modern rational society wants people who play by the rules, color within the lines, and ask few difficult or troubling questions. It is that way because it is that way, period, end of discussion, because the authoritarian "I" say so. McDonald's does not need nor does it want a chef, someone who will be creative, use fresh local ingredients, and prepare seasonal menus. A McDonald's is a McDonald's is a McDonald's. It serves customers who want safe, predictable food, food that will look and taste the same in Oregon and Rhode Island, that will be ready on demand, can be consumed on site or on the go, and will cost as little money as possible. Homogeneity is good; differences are, if not bad, suspect or less desirable.

The greater the rationalization, the less human or distinctive need be the participants in a particular system. Write down all the rules and there is no need for judgment, a decidedly human behavior. Mechanize and segment the processes and machines do the work while a human services them with a well-placed shot of oil. Training replaces education. Workers need to know the system, but they do not necessarily need to know how to think. In North Carolina, students must write formal, state-scored essays at three points in their education, each one ostensibly of greater sophistication. They are taught, in the grades in which state essay tests occur, strict templates to follow. A certain type of composition has this general structure, with so many paragraphs, each of which does these specific things, in no less than and ideally no more than this number of sentences that contain these types of examples, supporting statements, and/or pieces of evidence. A remarkable essay, a creative one, that fails to model the template, is also less likely to receive a high score than an adequate one that hits all the right template notes.

When these students arrive at a class in which they are asked to write essays in their own voice, they do not have one. It was never really part of the template. Their initial products are uniformly predictable, strained, and distant. The essay, both read and written, can be a powerful instrument for change. (Remember Thomas Paine's "Common Sense" and the colonial insistence on freedom of the press?) It is not a potentially powerful tool in the minds and hands of young people for whom it has become a mechanical task fraught with the anxiety attendant a high-stakes accountability system. "Why do we gotta do it this way?" they ask. "Because that's the template the assessors use to grade it," the teachers reply. A measure of the rigidity of those templates is an observation made by a North Carolina grader of essay tests. "I know this sounds very bizarre, but you could put a number on these things without actually reading the paper" (quoted in Kohn 2000, 12).

There is a danger in all that sameness and in the objectification of human beings. Wes Jackson points out that "the agricultural human's pull historically has been toward monoculture of annuals. Nature's pull is toward a polyculture of perennials" (quoted in Berry 1990, 107). We strive to do one thing in quantity, to produce a cash crop for market. Yet nature, left on its own, tends toward diversity, as does the subsistence farmer who must provide whatever goes on the family table. Nature understands that if everything is the same, its extinction is far more likely than if there is variety. To Jackson (1998), our species is "Homo the Homogenizer, pursuer of an unnatural world." Wendell Berry (1987), farmer and social critic, notes that "one of the principles of an ecosystem is that diversity increases capacity" (63). Yet we have become trapped in "the monocultures of industrial civilization," a world that limits capacity and is inhospitable to its human inhabitants (151).

Conrad Geller (2001), a secondary school teacher of long standing, claims that local, as opposed to consolidated, public schools encourage innovation. They are not all the same. They might make short-term mistakes, but their close ties to particular communities have "given vigor to the whole enterprise." After all, centralization, a part of McDonaldization, "is not protection against folly." And, when folly happens on grand scales it is sometimes difficult to step back from the abyss. No Child Left Behind legislation jeopardizes Geller's schools. It reinforces grand-scale sameness.

When the World Economic Forum recently published a competitiveness index, the United States did well on all indices, but was distinctive in two. Unlike highly educated people elsewhere, educated Americans stay in the country. The United States profits mightily from being the destination of choice for educated people from elsewhere. On a national scale, the United States has a negative brain drain. Few of our smart folks leave and many of "theirs" come here. But the real distinguisher is our "national innovation capacity." Americans invent. In the past our schools have done well at encouraging habits that contribute to creativity. Students are relatively free to ask questions. Discussions are a common part of classroom experiences. In some other countries, public scrutiny of ideas is not a given; sometimes it is not even a part of the culture. Such societies might be more civil, but they are less likely to push at borders or to connect with something outside the proverbial box (Bracey 2002). We are unlikely to continue that tradition with an emphasis on sameness.

A Place for Place

There is a growing acknowledgement that school size is important not only for enhanced student achievement but also for meeting the emotional needs of young people. The school within a school movement is a recognition of the need to find ways to ameliorate the numbing effects of large institutions (Fine and Somerville 1998). The work of Deborah Meier (1995, 1996, 2000) in New York City and Boston testifies to the efficacy of maintaining a school size fit for humans rather than efficiency managers. Policies that create multiage groupings of students or programs in which one teacher follows a set of children for several years are attempts to replace bureaucratic, hierarchical organizations with patterns of association reflective of what one might have found and still can find in small schools.

Moreover, the literature on the advantages of smallness has proliferated, much of it sponsored by the ERIC Clearinghouse on Rural Education and Small Schools located in Charleston, West Virginia (Anderson 1998; Barker 1986; Clinchy 2000; Conway 1994; Cotton 1996; Howley 1989, 1994, 1996; Irmsher 1997; Lee and Smith 1995, 1997; and Raywid 1996, 1999). One can find moving accounts of the loss associated with the disappearance of small schools (DeYoung 1995) or of the connections between community sustainability and a local school (Peshkin 1978). There are books that address the ways in which rural communities and their local schools work together to construct meaning (Miller and Hahn 1997). And there are books that argue passionately for the connection between schooling, community, and identity (Theobald 1997). The role of African American schools to African American community, particularly in rural areas, has also been documented (Cecelski 1994; Smith 2000; Walker 1996).

The divisions of *Local Schools of Thought*, a 1996 publication by Webb, Shumway, and Shute, reflect the connection of place and community, of place and identity, of place and meaning. Among the chapters contained there are: "The Significance of Perspective," "The Search for Meaning," "Meaningful Student Outcomes," and "Thoughtful Teachers." They argue for schools that are more than training grounds for economic men and women. Schools should promote "thoughtfulness," which is far more than acquisition of knowledge and skills that fit one for the marketplace.

They, as well as other advocates of small schools (see, for example, Theobald 1992) frequently borrow the arguments of Wendell Berry to advance their own. "The child is not educated to return home and be of use to the place and community; he or she is educated to leave home and earn money in a provisional future that has nothing to do with place or community. . . . School systems innovate as compulsively and as eagerly as factories" (Berry 1990, 163). "A mind unreminded would be no mind at all" (Berry 1995, 95). "The right scale of work gives power to affection. . . . An adequate local culture, among other things, keeps work within the reach of love" (Berry 1993, 24). "Education in the true sense, of course, is an enablement to serve—both the living human community in its natural household or neighborhood and the precious cultural possessions that the living community inherits or should inherit. To educate is, literally, to 'bring up,' to bring young people to a responsible maturity, to help them to be good caretakers of what they have been given, to help them to be charitable toward fellow creatures" (Berry 1987, 52). "In a society in which nearly everybody is dominated by somebody else's mind or by a disembodied mind, it becomes difficult to learn the truth" (Berry 1997, 126). Berry argues for a global consciousness raising grounded in community-based, embodied education.

When a reporter asked him how he would improve education, Berry replied:

> I'd change the standard. I would make the standard that of community health rather than the career of the student. . . . [Now] we're teaching as if the purpose of knowledge is to help people have careers or to make them better employees, and that's a great and tragic mistake. . . . Adding to knowledge is not the first necessity. The first necessity is to teach the young . . . the knowledge that people have in their bones by which they do good work and live good lives" (quoted in Webb et al., v).

What romantic claptrap, Chester Finn and his educational standards allies would reply. "How do we possibly measure such things?" ask education governors as they expand their state's testing programs.

If the goal is better student achievement, there is evidence that small works. If the goal is parental participation, there is evidence that school connections with communities work. If the goal is that students feel more confident and possess greater senses of agency and efficacy, there is evidence that small learning communities work. If American policymakers are concerned with the types of citizens that schools are graduating, with their sense of affiliation to a local and global community, there is also some evidence that schools that teach embodied (locally centered) knowledge work.

To do those things we must center schooling not simply on affirmations of hopefulness that are race, gender, and class conscious. We must center schooling on thoughtfulness and critique, rather than facts to be paraded at some annual testing date. And we must be willing to acknowledge that the center changes with the topography, that place matters in both small and large ways. Young people need to know, before they move into adulthood, who they are in places where that matters.[9]

The Alchemy of Place Revisited

Categories of difference generally mean of some variation of race, class, and gender. That tripart designation is almost automatic, as though we have managed within those three divisions to capture the fault lines of our body politic.

That is, of course, folly. We are riven by other divides as well—for example, religion, ethnicity, sexual orientation, age, size, ability, degree of optimism, education, and agility. Nor have we described each other when we settle on a category or two because such descriptors intersect. We are not a matter of "or" so much as of "and." Individuals embody sets of characteristics that link them with some people and distance them from others. Attributes blur. Race, for instance, is no longer as clearly defined for many Americans as it once was. Someone might be born and raised a Methodist, only to convert to Judaism later in life. People differ and are alike, altering their proximity in minor and major ways throughout their shared lifetimes. At various times certain attributes become norms. They attain and sometimes retain a position of privilege. For example, doors open more easily in the United States if one is a Christian, white, physically able male from the upper or professional classes.

A missing marker in most discussions about identity is place. There is an unstated assumption that, because everyone is a North American, everyone is the same (except if that someone is a Canadian or Mexican.) The most anyone needs to know geographically about people is their country of origin, or maybe their state. Pizza Huts, Wal-Mart, and television have minimized all but the most inconsequential of differences.

There is still something about certain places that lingers, that shapes distinct cultures with unique value sets. Quentin, in William Faulkner's *Absalom, Absalom!*, claims that the South is inexplicable to outsiders. Eudora Welty told an interviewer that place was not only her source of inspiration, but "a definer and confiner" of her knowledge (Kuehl 1984, 87). Fred Chappell (1985) closes a novel set in Haywood County with a question addressed to his fictional self: "Well, Jess, are you one of us or not?" And his answer is implicit in the title of the book: *I Am One of You Forever*.

Some places are more indelible than others, places less disturbed by outsiders, homogeneous and stable, and of a size that renders their residents personalities rather than numbers. Like other aspects of identity, place consciousness, the stamp of geography, fluctuates. It dims over time, diminishing faster with time spent elsewhere. It changes with the introduction of new phenomena. It loses some of its power as transportation and communication innovations break down isolation. As Chappell's Joe Robert, father of Jess, observes in another novel (*Farewell, I'm Bound to Leave You*) "the time of your grandmother was a steady time that people could trust. But you can see for yourself that we are losing it" (1996, 5).

Losing it we are, but our own experiences in Southern Appalachia, living some distance removed from metropolitan mainstreams, as well as our experiences talking with educators from the region have convinced us that geography deserves attention. Today's generations of women may have lost some of "their hardiness and savor" (78), at least according to Jess's grandmother, but they, too, are bound to a place of memories and family. We found both them and their male colleagues savory enough.

The Errant Seductiveness of Simplicity

In 1970, on the occasion of his departure from Nixon's White House staff, Daniel Patrick Moynihan observed that Jacob Burckhardt, a Swiss historian, predicted that "ours would be the age of 'the great simplifiers' and that the essence of tyranny was the denial of complexity." "He was," Moynihan concluded, "right. This is the greatest temptation of the time. . . . What we need are great complexifiers" (quoted in "Competence and Complexity" 2003, 9). In an effort to simplify, Americans seek universal theories to explain human endeavors, to find absolute and straightforward solutions to vexing social problems. The current measure of educational effectiveness, performance on a patchwork quilt of standardized tests, is an example of a simple means of calculating something quite complex.

For what problem is it "the" (never "a" in the land of simplification) solution? To many reformers the problem is *everything* or, at least, a big dose of *anything*. In 1983 the United States was a nation at risk because of failed schools. If there are too many adolescents pregnant, too many young people abusing drugs, a faltering economy, an imbalance of trade, global instability, a rising prison population, more bullies, road rage, or lackadaisical factory workers, the problem is bad schooling. "Educationists," a common pejorative used by public school critics, have destroyed family values, questioned patriotism, and encouraged social deviancy. If those indicators cease to be troubling (say, the economy gets better or crime rates go down), the problem changes. The nation is not number one on international measures of academic achievement. It does not matter that debate is probably about apples and oranges comparisons. Americans love numbers, believe truth resides in rankings, and hate to lose, even if the contest is rigged or not worth their efforts.

The current solution, while not original (schools have been using some form of common tests since at least the nineteenth century to measure students), is relentlessly simple and simple-minded. Information is now defined as education. A demonstrable ability to remember, at least on paper, is its true sign. In an effort to make schools efficient and predictable, to control those who do it, we have turned to a common set of assessments. Forget individual differences. Forget local needs. Policymakers know a good school district by its collective and, increasingly, disaggregated test scores. They can recognize our best teachers and administrators by the numbers.

There is, as there often is in such an argument, some truth. Most people do want schools, the professional practitioners who work in them, and their district leaders to be accountable for the use they make of public dollars. They also want them to be accountable for the quality of the time that they spend with our nation's children. Tests measure things. Enumerating educational progress has a sense of scientific accuracy to it. Industrialists account for the productivity of a manufacturing enterprise by its bottom line; its quality is summarized by the size of its immediate profitability. High productivity translates into making a lot of something for as little cost as possible and doing it right now. It does not account for eventual environmental degradation or the social costs of a culture grounded on consumption. Tomorrow is not part of today's profit margin.

Widgets lend themselves to counting. Children and education do not translate quite so neatly into numbers. High performers in educational institutions might not generate the highest scores on standardized tests. They may be individuals who encourage students to consider options to which there are no bubbles that they can easily darken or templates to which they can write acceptable essays. Life lived well does not necessarily reduce to a topic sentence and three supporting ones, or a choice among a, b, c, or d. Educators whose students pursue something independently, at length, over time, and without someone checking over their shoulders to see that they have completed a set of steps in prescribed order and fashion may be the very ones best kept in our public schools.

What, you may ask, does any of that have to do with system administrators and insiderness? To access and retain a superintendency or another senior-level position, an individual must adopt behaviors that are relatively congruent with local expectations. If they think that schools should be about education and children in ways that fail to match expectations, they are either unlikely to get a job or, if they do, to retain it long after their first major clash with the community and its official representatives, the school board. Power to shape certain school outcome expectations, power for local communities to be local, has diminished over the past twenty years. Its decline is moving ever more rapidly toward extinction. Decisions are being made elsewhere about what constitutes schools and what young people need to know and be able to do. They are being made all too often by groups who neither know nor respect education. (They do tend to respect job readiness training.) These individuals are making decisions, because they have found a simple solution to challenging dilemmas. Unfortunately, they are creating settings in which ideological outsiders will not be welcomed. To become and remain a player in the new school game, a participant will have to meet new, potentially perilous, insider standards.

Critics, too, are sometimes guilty of simple solutions. Will changing the emperor's clothes (sex, race, place of birth) change the emperor's foolishness?

In another context, Bell and Chase (1995) observe that they are "wary of approaches that are too general, too decontextualized, and too unitary to reflect the realities of leadership practice in schools" (209). We have entered a new era of one-best system-ing and the current rules of the game have lowered the odds for changing it from within. Even well-intentioned and hardworking practitioners who care about children and learning will find it difficult to alter our present educational cage. Good ones will velvetize it; bad ones will make schools seem like the iron bars are all too real.

Conclusion

Based on our data we believe that the number of women and people of color in superintendencies and other senior-level positions will increase in Southern Appalachia. That trend is not only observable in other sections of the country but has proceeded there at a somewhat faster rate. We also think that the numbers are there to "tip" the profession, to gender it feminine. Whether that will happen remains to be seen, but the odds favor tipping rather than the establishment of an occupational equilibrium.[10]

If that is the case, then, based on historical precedents, we expect that following things to happen:

- the profession (district superintendent) will diminish in status;
- salaries will stagnate or decline relative to comparable positions (occupations that require roughly the same level of preparation and that entail the same level of responsibility);
- the role will become standardized and, potentially, deskilled, with an emphasis on technical performance at the expense of professional judgment (the job will be rationalized);
- autonomy will narrow and external supervision will increase (there will be more quantifiable accountability and less independence);
- the current mission of public schooling, with its emphasis on productivity and workers, will go unchallenged, although the leadership styles evident in schools and districts will become more collaborative; and
- the real power in education will migrate from individual school districts to places that remain in the control of those groups that now lead them. It will flow to Raleigh or Washington, D.C., where institutions continue to be white male-dominated and reflect the traditional, business-oriented values that have long characterized American public schools (Protestant, heterosexual, politically conservative, and economically, aggressively capitalistic).

The status quo will change in form and personnel, but not in substance. In other words, the glass ceiling to the superintendency might be broken but, in terms of fundamental alterations to the nature and goals of our nation's schools, little else will change.

That conclusion is not one that gives us any pleasure. It and the implications derived from it are consistent with long-standing cautions about authority and bureaucracy raised by scholars like Max Weber, novelists like George Orwell, and curmudgeons like Neil Postman and Wendell Berry. It leads neither to the schools we want for our nation's children (for any children) nor to the type of society in which we wish to live.

There is, of course, more than one possible ending to the scenario that we have constructed. The number game might turn in another direction and districts will remain in the hands of the people who now run them. If that is the case, it leaves both the current mission and organization of our public schools relatively untouched. Access for previously marginalized people will stall and recede.

Perhaps before the numbers tip, public schooling as we know it will be redefined by the charter school and/or voucher movements. That would make the notion of districts obsolete and, with it, the roles of district administrators. Given the impetus toward a national accountability model described by No Child Left Behind legislation, we assume that such schools would be subject to the curricula, standards, and achievement measures currently in place. Form and personnel might change, but substance would not. The desires and efforts of some educational reformers, including our current president, notwithstanding, vouchers and charter schools seem unlikely on a large scale in the near future.

Or, as the numbers tip, the negative consequences attendant previous occupational tippings will not occur. The profession will become blind to differences. The superintendency will remain as attractive and powerful a position as it was when the women were chased out initially. Meritocracy will prevail. Candidates will be judged not by who they are but by what they can do. The fact that anyone appropriately credentialed is eligible for candidacy does not automatically translate into diverse ways to run a school system. The nation appears to be relentlessly turning to an externally enforced, standardized school system at the very time that it is hiring less standardized-looking system leaders. The system is being rigged to ensure that former outsiders work toward narrowly defined insider goals, even as they work in less narrowly defined ways. They improve the condition of Max Weber's velvet cage, but it remains a cage.

In a rosier scenario, as more women, people of color, and majority race males in touch with their nurturing, collaborative side move into positions of power in school districts, they will rise above the less desirable effects of professional socialization and assimilation. They will find ways to reclaim local power. They will lead schools in different directions. The most optimistic finding in our study, to put it in language that Goffman would appreciate, is that people retain the freedom to rewrite their scripts, alter their settings, vary the props, and shuffle the cast. Accommodation experiences mean that people know how to exercise choice. As long as they remain conscious of their dissembling and retain critical distance, there remains the possibility that they (we) can step back from the precipice of unconscious assimilation.

Even if policymakers open wide access to the highest positions of leadership in school districts, that may have little effect on our ongoing ideological war for the hearts and souls of our nation's public school systems. Audre Lorde (1993) once wrote that we couldn't dismantle the master's house with the master's tools. If she is right, educators face the need to rally to another house—a different kind of school organization from the one currently in place. If they hope to retain public school districts, then we must find new ways to use those tools or refashion different ones out of the materials available. They must dismantle and rebuild from within the existing bureaucracies.

Can the current system be remade and become equitable? Along the lines suggested by people like Nel Noddings (1982, 2002, 2003) and Jane Roland Martin (1992, 2002), as schools that teach children rather than institutions that train future workers? To do that will require more than simple solutions. We cannot afford to wait for the one right person to arrive on the scene, clean up the town, slay the dragon, find the magic slippers, and return the Golden Fleece. Helping schools align with the ideas of a Noddings or a Martin requires acknowledging that the struggle is precisely that, a struggle, and that our means are politics writ larger than tussles over schools and schooling. In the United States, ivory tower critiques rarely fall far from the tower. Here there is no fear of poets and little of people who have the troublesome habit of asking questions that have complex answers. So the arenas will be legislatures and boardrooms. The winners this time should be children, local communities, and education, not politicians, businessmen, and educators.

·APPENDIX·

TABLES

TABLE 1. Selected Demographic Comparisons of the Male and Female Samples: Means

Category	Females	Males
Years in Education	28.2	27.4
Years in Teaching	12.25	6.64
Years in Administration	15.9	20.6
Length of Time in the County in Which They Work	36.3	17.04
Years Lived in North Carolina	46.29	32.5

TABLE 2. Central Office Survey Results: Item Frequencies (n=30)

	Vital	Very important	Important	Useful, but not crucial	Not particularly important
Being from the area	3 10%	2 7%	7 23%	15 50%	3 10%
Being familiar with the area	6 20%	8 27%	9 30%	6 20%	1 3%
Being from the South	3 10%	4 13%	6 20%	11 37%	6 20%
Being certified-educational administration	17 57%	8 27%	1 3%	2 7%	2 7%
Knowledge of curriculum and instruction	14 47%	7 23%	5 17%	2 7%	1 3%
Business management skills	13 43%	9 30%	6 20%	1 3%	1 3%
Facilities knowledge	6 20%	11 37%	11 37%	1 3%	1 3%
School/Community relations skills	14 47%	12 40%	3 10%	0 —	1 3%
Knowledge of educational research	4 13%	12 40%	11 37%	2 7%	1 3%
Teaching experience	11 37%	10 40%	4 13%	2 7%	3 10%
Principal experience	12 40%	7 23%	4 13%	4 13%	3 10%

Percents in the table above are rounded to the nearest whole number; thus the percents for some items may total slightly more or less than 100%.

TABLE 3. Central Office Mean Responses to Survey Items (n=30)

	Mean	Standard Deviation
Being from the area	3.43	1.10
Being familiar with the area	2.6	1.13
Being from the South	3.43	1.25
Being certified-educational administration	1.8	1.21
Knowledge of curriculum and instruction	1.87	1.17
Business management skills	1.93	1.05
Facilities knowledge	2.0	0.96
School/Community relations skills	1.73	0.91
Knowledge of educational research	2.47	0.94
Teaching experience	2.2	1.30
Principal experience	2.30	1.40

1= vital, one of the one or two most important things

2= very important, something not want to be without, but not the top 1 or 2

3= important

4= useful, but not crucial, at least initially

5= not particularly important

TABLE 4. School Board Survey Results: Item Frequencies (n=30)

	Vital	Very important	Important	Useful, but not crucial	Not particularly important
Being from the area	2 7%	9 30%	6 20%	9 30%	4 13%
Being familiar with the area	4 13%	8 27%	7 23%	8 27%	2 7%
Being from the South	1 3%	5 17%	10 33%	7 23%	7 23%
Being certified-educational administration	15 50%	9 30%	2 7%	4 13%	0 —
Knowledge of curriculum and instruction	13 43%	10 33%	3 10%	4 13%	0 —
Business management skills	12 40%	12 30%	6 20%	0 —	0 —
Facilities knowledge	3 10%	11 37%	13 43%	2 7%	0 —
School/Community relations skills	14 47%	12 40%	4 13%	0 —	0 —
Knowledge of educational research	1 3%	9 30%	14 47%	5 17%	1 3%
Teaching experience	6 20%	13 43%	9 30%	2 7%	0 —
Principal experience	7 23%	15 50%	6 20%	1 3%	1 3%

Percents in the table above are rounded to the nearest whole number; thus the percents for some items may total slightly more or less than 100%.

TABLE 5. School Board Mean Responses to Survey Items (n=30)

	Mean	Standard Deviation
Being from the area	3.13	1.20
Being familiar with the area	2.80	1.21
Being from the South	3.47	1.14
Being certified-educational administration	1.83	1.05
Knowledge of curriculum and instruction	1.93	1.04
Business management skills	1.80	0.76
Facilities knowledge	2.47	0.77
School/Community relations skills	1.67	0.71
Knowledge of educational research	2.87	0.86
Teaching experience	3.0	0.86
Principal experience	2.13	0.94

1= vital, one of the one or two most important things

2= very important, something not want to be without, but not the top 1 or 2

3= important

4= useful, but not crucial, at least initially

5= not particularly important

TABLE 6. Mean Responses Compared: School Board Members and Central Office Staff

	Central Office	School Board
Being from the area	3.43	3.13
Being familiar with the area	2.6	2.80
Being from the South	3.43	3.47
Being certified-educational administration	1.80	1.83
Knowledge of curriculum and instruction	1.87	1.90
Business management skills	1.93	1.80
Facilities knowledge	2.0	2.50
School/Community relations skills	1.73	1.67
Knowledge of educational research	2.47	2.87
Teaching experience	2.2	2.23
Principal experience	2.30	2.13

1= vital, one of the one or two most important things

2= very important, something not want to be without, but not the top 1 or 2

3= important

4= useful, but not crucial, at least initially

5= not particularly important

TABLE 7. Academic Performance in the Region: District Profiles Based on 2002–2003 Data

District	Stud. Pop.	No. Schools	EG* % Elem. Schools	% State	EG % Middle Schools	% State	EG% High Schools	% State
Asheville	3830	8	100	79	100	58	100	81
Buncombe	24180	41	100	79	86	58	86	81
Cherokee	3501	13	100	79	100	58	50	81
Clay	1221	3	100	79	100	58	100	81
Graham	1157	3	100	79	100	58	0	81
Haywood	7611	15	78	79	67	58	50	81
Henderson	11423	21	83	79	100	58	50	81
Jackson	3548	7	NA*	79	NA**	58	0	81
Macon	3949	19	50	79	0	58	100	81
Madison	2471	6	83	79	0	58	0	81
McDowell	6295	11	100	79	50	58	100	81
Mitchell	2336	8	100	79	50	58	0	81
Polk	2362	6	100	79	0	58	0	81
Swain	1661	5	50	79	0	58	100	81
Transylvan.	3780	9	75	79	100	58	100	81
Yancey	2459	9	100	79	100	58	100	81

* EG represents the percentage of schools making expected growth in performance on state testing. North Carolina students in grades 3–8 must complete annual ABC's End of Grade test in reading and mathematics. Students at the high school level in any of 10 courses—English I, Algebra I, Algebra II, Geometry, Biology, Chemistry, Physical Science, Physics, ELPS, and US History—must complete ABC's End of Course testing. As the data above reveal, most of the systems do well compared to the state percentages; in three of the systems, 100% of the students met expected growth.

** All Jackson County elementary schools are grades K-8. There is one K-12 school. Seventy-one percent of these schools made Expected Growth.

Of the sixteen districts in the study, only two have larger populations at 11,423 and 24,180, the first with 21 schools and the second with 41. All other districts are 7611 or under with the smallest population being 1157 in three schools. There is another district with only three schools. The average number of schools in these fourteen counties is 10.

Source: North Carolina Department of Public Instruction

NOTES

Chapter 1

1. For purposes of this chapter and the ones that follow, when Carolina appears without a North or South preceding it, it refers to North Carolina. We know there are two Carolinas on the map (Anna is from the southern one), so we mean no disrespect to either place by occasionally using a shorthand for the state in which we conducted the study.
2. A notable exception to that trend is the work done in Texas, particularly by activist, social justice-oriented faculty at its universities and by the Texas Council of Women School Executives (TCWSE). Through its *Women as School Executives* series (Brown and Irby 1993; Irby and Brown 1995; Funk, Pantake, and Reese 1998; Pantake, Schroth, and Funk 2000; and Korcheck and Reese 2002), the TCWSE ensures that the Lone Star State is a well-tended site of scholarly inquiry.
3. Ratings cited can be found in various editions of *Modern Maturity*, *Barron's Online*, *Outside*, *Rand McNally's Places Rated Almanac*, *Employment Review*, *Water Paddling*, *Bike Magazine*, *Kiplinger's Personal Finance Magazine*, *Men's Journal*, and *American Style* and are repeated in part of a number of Internet sites about Asheville.
4. The quotation is attributed to Isabella Mary Beeton, who included the advice in her 1861 *The Book of Household Management*. It is a measure of the power of the idea of order that it held sway even in the arena of domestic science. See Bartlett (1980), *Familiar Quotations*, 627:3.
5. As explained in greater detail in chapter 2, the counties in our study were Buncombe, Cherokee, Clay, Graham, Haywood, Henderson, Jackson, McDowell, Macon, Madison, Mitchell, Polk, Swain, Transylvania, and Yancey.
6. The literature on feminist perspectives is extensive. For an elaboration of the elements that we have enumerated here, see J. S. Chafetz (1988), *Feminist Sociology: An Overview of Contemporary Theories*.
7. We have found that much that has been written recently, particularly by sociologists and social psychologists, about gender and gender roles agrees with the theoretical constructs associated with proponents of sociology of knowledge. *The Handbook of the Sociology of Gender* (1999) provides a broad overview of the research in that area. Two additional literature reviews that proved particularly

helpful can be found in the fourth edition of *The Handbook of Social Psychology* (Gilbert, Fiske, and Lindzey 1998): Deaux and LaFrance's chapter entitled "Gender" and Baumeister's contribution "The Self." Note also Lorber and Farrell's (1991) *The Social Construction of Gender* and Schiebinger's (1993) *Nature's Body: Gender in the Making of Modern Science*. There is also a significant body of work on the social construction of race. Note, for example, Gates's (1997) *Racial Classification and History*, Smedley's (1999) *Race in North America: Origin and Evolution of a Worldview*, as well as Ferrante and Brown's (2000) *The Social Construction of Race and Ethnicity in the United States*.

8. We will not trace American historiography over the past century here, but we want to point to a few historians and their work that have influenced us. Appleby, Hunt, and Jacob (1994) have authored a very accessible book that does precisely that; see *Telling the Truth about History*. A more specialized account of fluctuating interpretations in the profession over time, specifically in the United States, is Novick's *That Noble Dream* (1992).
9. We assume that, were they writing today, they would include women in that formula.
10. The theoretical work of feminist researchers is large and growing. Note, for example, Stanley (1990), Nielsen (1990), and Harding (1998). For a more comprehensive look at standpoint theory, consult Allen (1996), Hartsock (1997), and Hallstein (1999). A large number of critiques of feminist research exists. Most of them defend a traditional approach to scholarship while simultaneously ridiculing its challengers. See, for instance, Gross and Levitt, *Higher Superstition: The Academic Left and Its Quarrels with Science* (1994).
11. So controversial was the book when it was published that it stimulated numerous refutations, conferences focused on the argument, and Lane's *The Debate over Slavery: Stanley Elkins and His Critics* (1971).

Chapter 2

1. A simple exercise illustrates the enduring sense of Southern uniqueness. On the Internet, plug into any search engine variations of "(region) studies" and tally the results. There are far more sites devoted to Southern Studies than Midwestern Studies or Pacific Northwest Studies or New England Studies or any of the many variations we tried. The only place that comes close is Appalachia, and some of those entries are related to the South.
2. See Boney (1971) for a more complete description of the stereotype. Bultman's (1996) book, marketed for a general audience, also provides a broad description of redneck America. Her treatment is sympathetic, draws on a variety of sources, and serves as an excellent starting point in sorting through the ways we construct identity for that subgroup.
3. That statistic is particularly noteworthy when one considers that the United States incarcerates its citizens at a far higher rate than most of the other nations on the planet. For example, it is three times as likely to place men and women in jail than sixty-three other countries reviewed by the Justice Policy Institute.

4. Johnny Paycheck, "Take This Job and Shove It"; McGuffey Lane, "Making a Living's Been Killing Me."
5. As scholars like Scott (1970) and Wolfe (1995) point out, the plantation mistress was responsible for organizing and managing a large household, including assuming primary responsibility for the domestic oversight of slaves, children, members of the extended family in residence, and other dependents. Note also diary entries of Southern women in O'Brien's (1993) *An Evening When Alone: Four Journals of Single Women in the South, 1827–67.*
6. The book traces a group of women attending a historically black college and another group that matriculated at the state's flagship institution. Both schools are in North Carolina.
7. Shakespeare's *Hamlet, The Taming of the Shrew,* and *The Merchant of Venice* respectively.
8. Glenda Gilmore's book *Gender and Jim Crow: Women and the Politics of White Supremacy in North Carolina, 1896–1920* (1996) is a explication of the various ways that gender and race intersected in challenging and preserving the hegemony of white men in the South. It illustrates how much more complex those intersections were than the overview here (white women exercising power to suppress race challenges; black women using feminist positions to confront racism; challenges from black women altering the style of white supremacy).
9. The literature on Southern slavery is extensive, contentious, and analytically rich. Note Blassingame (1979), Elkins (1963), Genovese (1969, 1972), Stampp (1956). For information about the general history of African Americans in North Carolina, see Anderson (1981), Crow, Escott, and Hatley (1992), Escott (1985), Franklin (1943), and Gavins (1989). The role of African Americans in North Carolina public education is documented in Brown (1964), Hanchett (1988), and Murray (1985). For additional information about race in Appalachia, see Margo (1990) and Inscoe (2001).
10. The center identified the essays by author name, grade, school, and state. We determined other information from evidence in the essays proper. Seventeen young writers were recognized by the center. The resulting sample included three males, twelve females, and two entries with ambiguous first names, but whom we believe are females. Fifteen of the writers are native Southerners; two are not. Thirteen are European Americans, one is African American, and one has a father from India and is part of an international, well-traveled family. Seven winners are in their senior year in high school. Eleven are juniors, one is a sophomore, and four are freshmen. We estimate that the age range for the sample is fourteen to eighteen years. The number and award designation of the categories appears to be contingent on the number of entries from a particular state as well as the quality of those entries. Essays ranged from one to slightly less than two pages in length and were single-spaced and typed. The topic was "What does it mean to be Southern?" and the format was apparently unrestricted beyond length and subject. In discussing the essays, we decided to omit specific student attributions when we quoted from them for two reasons: to be consistent with how we will treat our own data later and to retain a measure of confidentiality.
11. For more information on the difficulties of defining the region, see Raitz and Ulack (1984) and Williams (1996).

12. The United Way State of Caring index ranked states according to their level of state-assisted nurturing on a composite of factors measuring citizen well-being. Of the bottom ten states, seven were in the South and two were southwestern states that were populated by former Southerners in the nineteenth century (*The Warm North/The Chilly South* 2003). Yet Robert Levine (2003) found that the most altruistic people in the United States were in the Southeast, a finding he attributes to the endurance of a Southern way of life in the small towns of the region. An apparent contradiction, it actually serves to highlight the deep suspicion residents in the region have of centralized control (government) and the persistence of a sense of obligation to neighbors. Appalachians are especially representative of that contradiction.
13. Both researchers worked in Yancey County (Beaver also did field work in neighboring Watauga and Ashe Counties). Hicks's original study was conducted in the 1970s, but he returned to the county in the 1990s to see how his original findings held up. Beaver did her work in the 1980s.
14. A sense of the extreme paternalism that once pervaded the Carolina mountains can be gleaned from early accounts of its residents written for popular consumption elsewhere. See Dargan 1998/1925; Morley 1913; Kephart 1913; and Campbell 1921.
15. We decided to include a lengthy description of the area from which we took our sample and the people of the region because place plays a major role in the study proper and our findings. Unless otherwise indicated above, statistical information about the region was obtained from public access Internet sources via a portal maintained by the state of North Carolina at www.ncgov.com. Information cited above was obtained in May, June, and July of 2003.
16. The counties in our study were Buncombe, Cherokee, Clay, Graham, Haywood, Henderson, Jackson, McDowell, Macon, Madison, Mitchell, Polk, Swain, Transylvania, and Yancey.
17. "Thru-hikers" start either in Maine or Georgia and hike the entire trail in a single season.
18. In 1863 Confederate soldiers executed thirteen local citizens after torturing members of their families, including women, in an effort to secure the location of local irregulars loyal to the union. That incident precipitated a violent reaction. It is no accident that one community in Madison County is named Democrat (Williams 2002).
19. In addition to the people listed above, the list included Martin Luther King Jr., Billy Graham, Jimmy Carter, Lyndon Johnson, George Wallace, Woodrow Wilson, Sam Walton, Bill Clinton, Ted Turner, Huey Long, and Booker T. Washington. Three of the fourteen panel members (inclusive of Reed) were women.

Chapter 3

1. Education has never attained the recognition as a profession that all branches of science and most branches of social science hold. Lamentably, the notion that anyone can teach and that only those people who lack the requisite skills or drive to do otherwise end up in K–12 classrooms persists. Moreover, the literature on

whether the requisite skills for effective practice are more art than craft or more craft than science or can ever be a science at all continues to be debated. That debate notwithstanding, P–12 education followed patterns established by other disciplines with claims to professional status, setting up criteria for certifying individuals who attained a recognized level of competence. Similarly, it also established the requisite professional organizations, such as the American Educational Research Organization and, at least until it became a teacher advocacy group, the National Education Association, that placed their seal of approval on research methods and findings. They also assisted in creating preparation programs that served as vehicles for conveying professional truth claims. Students interested in the evolution of educational research can profitably begin their studies with Travers (1983) and Lagemann (2000). For information on the process of professionalization in general, see Haskell (2000).

2. Jones established a religious colony in Guyana, persuading and/or coercing hundreds of followers to commit mass suicide by ingesting poison-laced Kool-Aid in 1978. Charles Manson had a band of followers named the Manson Family who went on a ritualistic murder spree in California in 1969. David Koresh's Branch Davidians died in a confrontation with federal agents in Waco, Texas, in 1993.
3. Students in pursuit of more information would find no better starting place than Tyack and Hansot's *Managers of Virtue* and Tyack's *One Best System*. Beck and Murphy (1993) provide another way of looking at dominant ideas in administration by chronicling metaphorical themes by decade from the 1920s through the 1990s in *Understanding the Principalship*. For perspectives on the history of educational administration theory, see also Campbell, Fleming, Newell, and Bennion (1987); Fairholm (2000); English (1994); Foster (1986); Murphy (1992); Northouse (2001); and Rost (1993). For the development of supervision as a distinct specialty, see Glanz (1991). For brief histories of theory building and scholarship on educational administration and/or school leadership, see Leithwood and Duke (1999), Willower and Forsyth (1999), Griffiths (1988), and Culberson (1988).
4. Whether there exists a knowledge base in administration or leadership studies in general and in educational administration in particular is a topic of ongoing debate. The difficulty stems both from the nature of the subject and from disagreements about what constitutes trustworthy support for truth claims. Is, for example, qualitative research acceptable? Can a discipline build a knowledge base on anecdote? Must evidence meet certain prescribed tests for validity and reliability? Those debates are not germane here, except to acknowledge that they exist and thereby make more problematic the likelihood of agreement on how educational leaders should behave. Note Donmoyer, Imber, and Scheurich (1995) for an elaboration on recent work in this area.
5. The two functions were frequently separated. Business managers ran the fiscal side of school systems and superintendents were responsible for personnel and curriculum. Because power follows money, failing to control the budget was about more than adding up figures on a regular basis. Early boosters of the superintendency advocated merged functions almost from the introduction of professional preparation programs.
6. Glass (1986) believes that it was only in the 1920s that a literature sufficiently robust to constitute a fledgling knowledge base emerged. It is for that reason that Beck and Murphy begin their metaphor study with 1920. For a survey of the

development of educational administration programs, see Callahan, *Education and the Cult of Efficiency*, 1962, chapter 8: "A New Profession Takes Form," 179–220.

7. Not coincidentally, Cubberley was one of several higher education administration experts who profited professionally from such surveys, predecessors to accreditation processes that stressed on-site assessment by professionals keyed to specific standards of performance. See Tyack 1974, 137, 192–93, and Callahan 1962, 116–17.
8. The first books Rost found that specifically addressed leadership as opposed to management or administration were written in the 1930s. Books written before that date were few in number, even though he searched across disciplines and looked in both academic and trade journals. He acknowledges that other scholars have found and reviewed more citations than did he (Bass, for example, listed over 4,700 references when he reviewed the literature in 1981), but that his survey is representative. Rost omitted textbooks from consideration.
9. One group of educational historians has focused their critique of the common school movement on the role it played in maintaining the power of privileged classes. It provided instructions in following rules and obeying authority, while preparing prospective employees for their roles in a modern work setting. See Bowles and Gintis 1976; Katz 1975, 1987, 2001; Spring 1980; and Violas 1978.
10. The overview of general changes in school governance and the evolution of the superintendency in North Carolina is based on Smith (1888), Knight (1916), Noble (1930), Johnson (1937), Brown (1964), Lefler and Newsome (1973), Prather (1979), Powell (1989), Peek (1993), and Leloudis (1996).
11. In 2001 there were only seventeen special charter districts and none of them were in the state's largest towns. Only twelve counties had town districts, five of which had two. They ranged in size from Chapel Hill/Carrboro's 8,992 students (more than the county district's total) to Elkins's 1, 068. The state legislature continues to offer incentives for merger and penalties for continued separate existence. Legacies of special tax supplements, support from local industries, and/or demographic patterns perpetuate their status. Time is on the side of the counties and the state.
12. Town districts included Asheville (Buncombe), Murphy and Andrews (Cherokee), Canton (Haywood), Hendersonville (Henderson), Marion (McDowell), and Tryon (Polk).
13. Of our fifteen counties, today eight have only one high school. Two have one high school and one or two union or K–12 schools in a remote part of the county. The Asheville City Schools house only one high school. Of the remaining four counties, not counting alternative or union schools, only Henderson and Buncombe have more than two 9–12 schools.
14. The collective portrait, admittedly an incomplete picture, is based on comments from study informants and other education personnel elsewhere in the state, including individuals then working at the State Department of Public Instruction and at various professional organizations.
15. Information on Buncombe County superintendents comes from Allison (1944), the Asheville *Citizen* (1900–1991), Asheville *Citizen-Times* (1978–1991), Asheville *Democrat* (1889–1891), Asheville *Times* (1930–1991), Bird (1963), Miller

(1965), Roberson (1969), Tessier (1992), and Van Noppen and Van Noppen (1973).

16. Weaverville College, located in Buncombe County, can trace its origin back to the antebellum period. It shortened its name in 1912 to Weaver College, operating until 1934 when it merged with Brevard College in Transylvania County. Reagan's father was one of the institution's founders (Van Noppen and Van Noppen 1973, 154–55).
17. Reynolds was much like the superintendents described by Tyack (1976) and Tyack and Hansot (1982). See pp. 264–68 and pp. 168–80 respectively.
18. Information on Roberson's superintendency comes from Roberson (1969), Miller (1965), and the Asheville *Citizen-Times*, various issues, 1936–1969.

Chapter 4

1. This particular person did not appear in our original data collection, so she is not included in the descriptions of our sample.

Chapter 7

1. The North Carolina testing system uses a range of scores from one through four, with one and two being below standard. Meeting accountability criteria is based on the percentage of students who score three and above.
2. Since our interview with this participant, she has remarried.
3. Neither sex actually talked in terms of being an intellectual, but the actions that many of the men described indicated that they were conscious of the advantages of being perceived as a "regular Joe." Men had to downplay their academic preparation. Women, conversely, had to emphasize aspects of it.
4. Respondents rated items on a five-point scale, with a rating of three being "important." Ratings under three were considered useful or not particularly important.
5. Federal impact money is particularly important in counties in which the federal government owns large tracts of land. If land is exempt from taxation and ineligible for future, potentially taxable, development, that limits the potential of a county to supplement its local budget through county property taxes. In Western Carolina, the Forest Service and/or the Park Service is responsible for over half of all property in one county.

Chapter 8

1. That is not to say that we oppose new orders. When it comes to public schooling, we incline precipitously in that direction. But change-seekers are better prepared for initiating that process if they come to it with an understanding of the loci and bases of resistance.

Chapter 9

1. A good beginning place for information on occupational segregation is the 1976 spring supplement to the first volume of *Signs*, entitled "Women and the Workplace: The Implications of Occupational Segregation" (Blaxall and Reagan). See particularly Bernard ("Historical and Structural Barriers to Occupational Desegregation"), Lipman-Blumen ("Toward a Homosocial Theory of Sex Roles: An Explanation of the Sex Segregation of Social Institutions"), and Strober ("Toward Dimorphics: A Summary Statement to the Conference on Occupational Segregation").
2. For additional information on the nature of work and the history of labor in the United States, with particular attention to gender and race, see Baron (1991b), Byerly (1986), Greenwald (1990), Jones (1985, 1990, 1998), and Kessler-Harris (1982).
3. Among the factors that contributed to making that system the most likely to break the race ceiling were: the presence of the largest African American population in Western North Carolina; the disproportionately high percentage of African Americans in the system (many white students attend private schools); a rich history of segregation-era educational excellence in both private and public African American schools; the presence of a number of minority teachers and administrators; visibility of local black leaders (including the publisher of the only daily paper in the region as well as a member of the city council, who is also the vice-mayor); a diverse and, for the area, liberal electorate; and being an early insiderness expander (several previous geographic outsiders, and an immediate predecessor who was female.)
4. One consideration that might accelerate the inclusion of black women as insiders is that there are more African American females employed in the region's public schools and they have reached principalships in some systems.
5. Data on superintendents was culled from a review of the past fifty years of system directories (North Carolina Department of Public Instruction, 1952–2002).
6. Our participants, like those studied by Chase (1995) and Schmuck and Schubert (1995), saw gender discrimination as something that related specifically to them. It was not directed, necessarily, toward a group. The women who had a more global, as opposed to personal, perspective were the ones who had the most difficulty accommodating their behaviors to narrow definitions of insider.
7. "Remember, Ginger Rogers did everything Fred Astaire did, but she did it backwards in high heels." That observation comes from Faith Whittlesey and can be found on a feminist poster entitled "The Wisdom Quilt."
8. Obviously, majority race men can also act in the interest of social justice. However, they then become subject to being labeled outsiders, proponents of positions that are not "with us." They become privilege traitors. Even worse, they are unsexed as men and made to (choose to) sit with the women.

Chapter 10

1. Mertz has accumulated data from 1972 through 2002 on gender splits in the following categories: superintendent, deputy or associate superintendent, assistant

superintendent, high school principal, high school assistant principal, middle school principal, middle school assistant principal, elementary school principal, and elementary school assistant principal.

2. Gay and lesbian candidates, for example, are unlikely to find employment in superintendencies in many school districts in the South.
3. In the United States, when something is feminized, it becomes unattractive for whatever group is privileged, and acceptable for marginalized groups. African American men, for instance, might be relegated to feminized roles.
4. French feminists, like Hélène Cixous and Julia Kristeva, have argued that emphasizing differences is advantageous. It is people at the margins who have the power to disrupt society. (See Marks and de Courtivrons 1981.) Early American feminists also saw the potential power of assuming a difference orientation (Eisenstein and Jardine 1980). For examples of advocates of difference in leadership styles or explications of a feminine/feminist styles of leadership, see Eagly and Johnson (1990); Eagly, Karau, and Johnson (1992); Helgesen (1990); Regan (1990); Regan and Brooks (1995); Rosener (1990); Shakeshaft (1989); and Tibbetts (1980). Collins (1991b) has written about the perspective gained from being an "outsider within," suggesting that even inside, an outsider perspective will always influence behaviors.
5. Equally adamant in their arguments that differences are less important than similarities are critics of difference theory. Typical of that position are Collard (2001) and Reay and Ball (2000).
6. We believe that might be precisely the goal many of these educators prefer to work toward. Policymakers have skewed the school's mission toward specific social benefits and away from others. Paradoxically, they have taken choices away from local districts at the very time they claim to be freeing them to be more creative.
7. There were some exceptions. Many millinery shops, for instance, were owned and operated by single women or widows. Boarding houses were also the domain of women. For examples of choice, cultural constraints, and resistance, see Lebsock (1985) and Pease and Pease (1990).
8. Increased demand and inadequate supply are currently pushing nursing salaries up. Given likely baby boomer demand for services, there might develop external pressures that break the pattern of depressed wages for women's work. Crisis disrupts occupational segregation (Lippman-Blumen 1996).
9. Bill Moyers has a moving autobiographical commentary on that very point in his documentary *Marshall, Texas, Marshall, Texas*. He deftly weaves together two stories of one place—a story of his European-American town and of the African-American community that shared the same geography, but populated another place.
10. With regard to support for the timing of tipping, see England, Allison, Thompson, Mark, and Budig (2002). In a comprehensive review of college majors, they found that within five years of women increasing their presence in previously gendered male majors, men slowed their entry into those fields and found other, still traditional male majors. Their findings were consistent and statistically significant.

BIBLIOGRAPHY

Alexander, J. B., R. Groller, and J. Morris. 1990. *The warrior's edge: Front-line strategies for victory on the corporate battlefield*. New York: Avon Books.

Allen, B. 1996. Feminist standpoint theory: A black woman's (re)view of organizational socialization. *Communication Studies* 47 (winter): 257–71.

Allen, F. L. 1969. *The big change: America transforms itself, 1900–1950*. New York: Perennial Library.

Allison, J. 1944. The history of education in Buncombe County. *North Carolina Education* 10 (May): 443–46, 466–71.

Allison, D. 1992. *Bastard out of Carolina*. New York: Dutton.

Anderson, E. 1981. *Race and politics in North Carolina, 1872–1901: The Black Second*. Baton Rouge: Louisiana State University Press.

Anderson, V. 1998. Smaller is better. *Catalyst* 6 (May): 1–7.

Andrews, R., and M. Grogan. 2002. Defining preparation and professional development for the future. Paper commissioned for the first meeting of the National Commission for the Advancement of Educational Leadership Preparation.

Applebome, P. 1997. *Dixie rising: How the South is shaping American values, politics, and culture*. San Diego, CA: Harvest Book, Harcourt Brace.

Appleby, J. 2000. *Inheriting the Revolution: The first generation of Americans*. Cambridge, MA: Harvard University Press.

Appleby, J., L. Hunt, and M. Jacob. 1994. *Telling the truth about history*. New York: Norton.

Armas, G. C. 2002. South, Midwest led income gains: Census long forms show coasts lagging. *Post-Gazette.com*, June 5, 2002. http://www.postgazette.com/census/20020605censusap3.asp (accessed May 26, 2003).

Arthur, J. P. 1914. *Western North Carolina: A history from 1730 to 1913*. Johnson City, TN: Overmountain Press, 1996.

Asheville (NC) *Citizen*, 1900–1991.

Asheville (NC) *Citizen-Times*, 1978–1991.

Asheville (NC) *Democrat*, 1889–1891.

Asheville (NC) *Times*, 1930–1991.

Ayers, E. L. 1996. What we talk about when we talk about the South. In *All Over the Map: Rethinking American Regions*, ed. E. L. Ayers, P. N. Limerick, S. Nissenbaum, and P. S. Onuf, 62–82. Baltimore, MD: Johns Hopkins Press.

Barker, B. O. 1986. *The advantages of small schools*. Charleston, WV: ERIC Clearinghouse on Rural Education and Small Schools. (ED265988)

Baron, A. 1991a. Gender and labor history: Learning from the past, looking to the future. In *Work engendered: Toward a new history of American labor*, ed. A. Baron, 1–46. Ithaca, NY: Cornell University Press.

———. 1991b. *Work engendered: Toward a new history of American labor*. Ithaca, NY: Cornell University Press.

Bartlett, J. 1980. *Familiar quotations: A collection of passages, phrases, and proverbs traced to their sources in ancient and modern literature*. 15th ed. Ed. E. M. Beck. Boston: Little, Brown and Company.

Baumeister, R. F. 1998. The Self. In *The handbook of social psychology*. Vol. 1. Ed. D. T. Gilbert, S. T. Fiske, and G. Lindzey, 680–740. Boston: McGraw-Hill.

Beaver, P. D. 1986. *Rural community in the Appalachian south*. Prospect Heights, IL: Waveland Press.

Beck, L. G., and J. Murphy. 1993. *Understanding the principalship: Metaphorical themes, 1920s–1990s*. New York: Teachers College Press.

Belenky, M., B. Clinchy, N. Goldberger, and J. Tarfule. 1986. *Women's ways of knowing: The development of self, voice and mind*. New York: Basic Books.

Bell, C. S., and S. E. Chase. 1993. The underrepresentation of women in school leadership. In *The new politics of race and gender: The 1992 yearbook of the politics of education association*, ed. C. Marshall, 140–54. London: Falmer.

———. 1995. Gender in theory and practice of educational leadership. *Journal for a Just and Caring Education* 1 (10): 200–23.

Benson, S. P. 1986. *Counter culture: Saleswomen, managers, and customers in American department stores, 1890–1940*. Urbana: University of Illinois Press.

Berger, P. L., and T. Luckmann. 1967. *The social construction of reality: A treatise in the sociology of knowledge*. New York: Anchor Books.

Bernard, J. 1976. Historical and structural barriers to occupational desegregation. *Signs* 1 (3, spring supplement): 87–94.

Berry, W. 1987. *Home economics*. New York: North Point Press.

———. 1990. *What are people for?* New York: North Point Press.

———. 1993. *Sex, economy, freedom, and community*. New York: Pantheon Books.

———. 1995. *Another turn of the crank*. Washington, DC: Counterpoint.

———. 1997. *The hidden wound*. New York: North Point Press.

Best of the Blue Ridge Region: Our readers' views. *Blue Ridge Country* 16 (7/8): 38–43.

Billings, D. B., G. Norman, and K. Ledford, eds. 1999. *Back talk from Appalachia: Confronting stereotypes*. Lexington: University Press of Kentucky.

Bird, W. E. 1963. *The history of Western Carolina College: The progress of an idea*. Chapel Hill: University of North Carolina Press.

Biro, B. D. 2001. *Beyond success: The 15 secrets of effective leadership and life based on legendary Coach John Wooden's Pyramid of Success*. New York: Perigee.

Björk, L. G. 1999. Collaborative research on the superintendency. *AERA Research on the Superintendency SIG Bulletin* 2 (1): 1–4.

Blackwelder, J. K. 1991. Ladies, belles, working women, and civil rights. In *The South for new Southerners*, ed. P. D. Escott and D. R. Goldfield, 94–113. Chapel Hill: University of North Carolina Press.

Blackwell, D. L. 1998. The ability "to do much larger work:" Gender and reform in Appalachia, 1890–1935. PhD diss., University of Kentucky, Lexington.

Blanchard, K., and S. Johnson. 1983. *The one-minute manager: The quickest way to increase your own prosperity*. New York: Berkley Books.

Blassingame, J. W. 1979. *The slave community: Plantation life in the antebellum south*. Rev. ed. New York: Oxford University Press.

Blaxall, M., and B. D. Reagan, eds. 1976. Women and the workplace: The implications of occupational segregation. *Signs* 1 (3, part 2, spring supplement).

Blevins, T. 1995. Yesterday a total stranger called me white trash. *Southern Cultures* 1 (4, summer): 533–34.

Bloch, M. 1973. *The royal touch: Sacred monarchy and scrofula in England and France*. Trans. J. E. Anderson. London: Routledge and Kegan Paul.

Blount, J. M. 1998. *Destined to rule the schools: Women and the superintendency, 1873–1995*. Albany: State University of New York Press.

———. 1999. Turning out the ladies: Elected women superintendents and the push for the appointive system, 1900–1935. In *Sacred dreams: Women and the superintendency*, ed. C. C. Brunner, 9–28). Albany: State University of New York Press.

Blumberg. A., with P. Blumberg. 1985. *The school superintendent: Living with conflict*. New York: Teachers College Press.

Bolton, F. E., T. R. Cole, and J. H. Jessup. 1939. *The beginning superintendent*. New York: Macmillan.

Bolton, R. 1994. *Gal: A true life*. New York: Harcourt Brace.

Boney, F. N. 1971. The redneck. *Georgia Review* 25 (fall): 333–42.

Boudreau, C. 1994. Professional challenges and coping strategies of women superintendents from selected school districts in Illinois. *Dissertation Abstracts International* 55 (01A): 4631. (University Microfilm no. AAG9416934)

Bowles, S., and H. Gintis. 1976. *Schooling in capitalist America: Educational reform and the contradictions of economic life*. New York: Basic Books.

Bracey, G. 2002. Why scapegoat schools? *Liberal Opinion Week* (May 20): 26.

Braudel, F. 1972. *The Mediterranean and the Mediterranean world in the age of Phillip II*. Trans. Siân Reynolds. New York: Harper & Row.

Brown, G., and B. J. Irby, eds. 1993. *Women as school executives: A powerful paradigm*. Huntsville, TX: Sam Houston Press.

Brown, H. V. 1964. *E-qual-ity education in North Carolina among Negroes*. Raleigh, NC: Irving-Swain Press.

Brown, R. M. 1974. The last straw. In *Class and feminism*, ed. C. Bunch and N. Myron, 14–23. Baltimore, MD: Diana Press.

Browne, J. C. 1999. *The Sweet Potato Queens' book of love*. New York: Three Rivers Press.

——. 2001. *God save the Sweet Potato Queens*, New York: Three Rivers Press.

——. 2003. *The Sweet Potato Queens' big-ass cookbook and financial planner*. New York: Three Rivers Press.

Brubaker, D. L., and L. D. Coble. 1995. The derailed superintendent. *The Executive Educator* (October): 34–36.

——. 1997. *Staying on track: An educational leader's guide to preventing derailment and ensuring personal and organizational success*. Thousand Oaks, CA: Corwin Press.

Brubaker, D. L., and M. Shelton. 1995. The disposable superintendent. *The Executive Educator* (February): 16–19.

Brunner, C. C. 2000. Unsettled moments in settled discourse: Women superintendents' experiences of inequality. *Educational Administration Quarterly* 36 (1): 76–116.

Bultman, B. 1996. *Redneck heaven: Portrait of a vanishing culture*. New York: Bantam Books.

Burgess, S. 1995. Constructive forethought and the school administrator. Paper presented at a meeting of the UNCG Alumni Association, May 2. Greensboro, NC.

Burroughs, E. R. 1924. *The land that time forgot*. New York: Modern Library, 2002.

Byerly, V. 1986. *Hard times cotton mill girls: Personal histories of womanhood and poverty in the South*. Ithaca, NY: ILR Press.

Bynum, V. E. 1992. *Unruly women: The politics of social and sexual control in the Old South*. Chapel Hill: University of North Carolina Press.

Callahan, R. E. 1962. *Education and the cult of efficiency: A study of the social forces that have shaped the administration of the public schools*. Chicago: University of Chicago Press.

Campbell, J. 1949. *The hero with a thousand faces*. New York: MJF Books.

Campbell, J. C. 1921. *The Southern highlander and his homeland*. Lexington: University of Kentucky Press, 1969.

Campbell, R.F., T. Fleming, L. Jackson Newell, and J. W. Bennion. 1987. *A history of thought and practice in educational administration*. New York: Teachers College Press.

Carlton, D. L. 1995. How American is the American South? In *The South as an American problem*, ed. L. J. Griffin and D. H. Doyle, 33–56. Athens: University of Georgia Press.

——. 2001. Rethinking Southern history. *Southern Cultures* 7 (spring): 38–49.

Carnes, J. 1995. *Us and them: A history of intolerance in America*. Montgomery, AL: Southern Poverty Law Center.

Carter, D. 1999. A world turned upside down: Southern politics at the end of the twentieth century. In *The Southern state of mind*, ed. J. N. Gretlund, 49–63. Columbia: University of South Carolina Press.

Cash. W. J. 1941. *The mind of the South*. New York: Vintage Books, 1969.

Cashin, J. E., ed. 1996. *Our common affairs: Texts from women in the old South*. Baltimore, MD: Johns Hopkins University Press.

——. 1991. *A family venture: Men and women on the southern frontier*. New York: Oxford University Press.

Cecelski, D. 1994. *Along freedom road: Hyde County, North Carolina, and the fate of black schools in the South*. Chapel Hill: University of North Carolina Press.

Chadwick, D. 1999. *The 12 leadership principles of Dean Smith*. Kingston, NY: Total Sports Illustrated.

Chafetz, J. S. 1988. *Feminist sociology: An overview of contemporary theories*. Itasca, IL: Peacock.

———. 1999. *Handbook of the sociology of gender*. New York: Kluwer Academic/Plenum.

Chappell, F. 1985. *I am one of you forever*. Baton Rouge: Louisiana State University Press.

———. 1996. *Farewell, I'm bound to leave you*. New York: Picador.

Chase, S. E. 1995. *Ambiguous empowerment: The work narratives of women school superintendents*. Amherst: University of Massachusetts Press.

Clinchy, E., ed. 2000. *Creating new schools: How small schools are changing American education*. New York: Teachers College.

Clinton, H. 2003. *Living history*. New York: Simon & Schuster.

Cobb, J. 1990. The Sunbelt South: Industrialization in regional, national, and international perspective. In *Searching for the Sunbelt: Historical perspectives on a region*, ed. R. A. Mohl, 25–46. Knoxville: University of Tennessee Press.

Cobb, J. C. 1999. "We ain't white trash no more:" Southern whites and the reconstruction of Southern identity. In *The Southern state of mind*, ed. J. N. Gretlund, 135–46. Columbia: University of South Carolina Press.

Coclanis, P. A. 2000. Tracking the economic divergence of the North and the South. *Southern Cultures* 6 (4, winter): 82–103.

Cohen, A. 1985. *The symbolic construction of community*. London: Routledge.

Collard, J. L. 2001. Leadership and gender: An Australian perspective. *Educational Management and Administration* 2 (July): 343–55.

Collins, P. H. 1991a. *Black feminist thought: Knowledge, consciousness, and the politics of empowerment*. New York: Routledge.

———. 1991b. Learning from the outsider within: The sociological of black feminist thought. In *Beyond methodology: Feminist scholarship as lived research*, ed. M. Fonow and J. Cook, 35–59. Bloomington: Indiana University Press.

Competence and complexity. 2003. *Wilson Quarterly* 27 (3): 9.

Conger, J. A., and R. N. Kanungo, eds. 1988. *Charismatic leadership*. San Francisco: Jossey-Bass.

Conway, G. E. 1994. *Small scale and school culture: The experience of private schools*. Charleston, WV: ERIC Clearinghouse on Rural Education and Small Schools. (ED376996)

Cotton, K. 1996. *Affective and social benefits of small-scale schooling*. Charleston, WV: ERIC Clearinghouse on Rural Education and Small Schools. (ED401088)

Coumbe, P. 2001. What's happened to our school leaders? *New Jersey Department of Education*. http://www.njsba.org/members_only/publications/school_leader/July–August–2001 /what_happened_to_leaders.htm (accessed June 3, 2002).

Covey, S. R. 1989. *The 7 habits of highly effective people: Powerful lessons in personal change*. New York: Simon & Schuster.

———. 1992. *Principle-centered leadership*. New York: Simon & Schuster.

Crawford, F. B. 1992. A case study of women superintendents in Georgia: Explaining the common grounds. *Dissertations Abstracts International* 53 (12A): 4144. (University Microfilms no. AAG9312148)

Cremin, L. A. 1964. *The transformation of the school: Progressivism in American education, 1876–1957*. New York: Vintage Books

Crews, H. 1995. *A childhood: The biography of a place*. Athens: University of Georgia Press.

Crow, J. J., P. D. Escott, and F. J. Hatley. 1992. *A history of African Americans in North Carolina*. Raleigh: North Carolina Division of Archives and History.

Cubberley, E. 1922. *Public school administration: A statement of the fundamental principles underlying the organization and administration of public education*. Boston: Houghton-Mifflin.

———. 1924. Public school administration. In *Twenty-five years of American education*, ed. I. L. Kandal, 177–95. New York: Macmillan.

Culberson, J. A. 1988. A century's quest for a knowledge base. In *Handbook of research on educational administration*, ed. N. Boyan, 3–26. Englewood Cliffs, NJ: Prentice-Hall.

Cunningham, R. 1989. Appalachianism and Orientalism: Reflections on reading Edward Said. *Journal of the Appalachian Studies Association* 1:125–40.

Curti, M. 1974. *The social ideas of American educators*. Totowa, NJ: Littlefield, Adams.

Dargan, O. T. 1988. *From my highest hill*. Knoxville: University of Tennessee Press. Published in 1925 as *Highland annals*.

Deaux, K., and M. LaFrance. 1998. Gender. In *The handbook of social psychology*. Vol. 1. Ed. D. T. Gilbert, S. T. Fiske, and G. Lindzey, 788–827. Boston: McGraw-Hill.

Deep South Regional Humanities Center. 2003. The Deep South: What does it mean to be Southern? http://deepsouth.tulane.edu/deepsouth/besouthern.html (accessed June 5, 2003).

DeHart, J. S. 1997. Second wave feminism(s) and the South: The difference that differences make. In. *Women of the American South: A multicultural reader*, ed. C. A. Farhnam, 273–301. New York: New York University Press.

Department of Public Instruction. 2002. *Principal supply and demand study*. Raleigh: North Carolina State Department of Public Instruction.

DeYoung, A. J. 1995. *The life and death of a rural American high school: Farewell Little Kanawha*. New York: Garland.

Donmoyer, R., M. Imber, and J. J. Scheurich, eds. 1995. *The knowledge base in educational administration: Multiple perspectives*. Albany: State University of New York Press.

Douglas, A. 1977. *The feminization of American culture*. New York: Avon Books.

Drake, R. B. 2001. *A history of Appalachia*. Lexington: University Press of Kentucky.

Dublin, T. 1979. *Women at work: The transformation of work and community in Lowell, Massachusetts, 1826–1860*. New York: Columbia University Press.

———. 1994. *Transforming women's work: New England lives in the Industrial Revolution*. Ithaca, NY: Cornell University Press.

Dyer, K. M., and J. Carothers. 2000. *The intuitive principal: A guide to leadership*. Thousand Oaks, CA: Corwin Press.

Eagly, A. H., and B. T. Johnson. 1990. Gender and leadership style: A meta-analysis. *Psychological Bulletin* 108:233–56.

Eagly, A. H., S. J. Karau, and B. T. Johnson. 1992. Gender and leadership style among school principals: A meta-analysis. *Educational Administration Quarterly* 28 (1, February): 76–102.

Edson, S. 1995. Ten years later: Too little too late? In *Women leading in education*, ed. D. Dunlap and P. Schmuck, 36–48. Albany: State University of New York Press.

Educational Policies Commission. 1965. *The unique role of the superintendent of schools*. Washington, DC: National Education Association.

Edwards, L. 2000. *Scarlett doesn't live here anymore: Southern women in the Civil War era*. Champaign: University of Illinois Press.

Eggleston, E. 1892. *The Hoosier schoolmaster*. New York: Orange Judd.

Eisenstein, H., and A. Jardine, eds. 1980. *The future of difference*. Boston: Hall.

Eisler, B. 1977. *The Lowell offering*. New York: Lippincott.

Elkins, S. M. 1963. *Slavery: A problem in American institutional and intellectual life*. New York: Grosset and Dunlap.

Eller, R. 1981. *Miners, millhands, and mountaineers: The modernization of the Appalachian South, 1880–1930*. Knoxville: University of Tennessee Press.

England, P., P. Allison, J. Thompson, N. Mark, and M. Budig. 2002. Why are some academic fields tipping toward female? Paper presented at the Northwestern University Institute for Policy Research winter colloquium, January 7, Evanston, IL.

English, F. W. 1994. *Theory in educational administration*. New York: Harper Collins.

Escott, P. D. 1985. *Many excellent people: Power and privilege in North Carolina, 1850–1900*. Chapel Hill: University of North Carolina Press.

———. 1991. The special place of history. In *The South for new Southerners*, ed. P. D. Escott and D. R. Goldfield, 1–17. Chapel Hill: University of North Carolina Press.

Fairholm, G. W. 2000. *Perspectives on leadership: From the science of management to its spiritual heart*. Westport, CT: Praeger.

Fanon, F. 1971. *Black skin, white masks*. New York: Grove Press.

Farnham, C. A. 1994. *The education of the Southern belle: Higher education and student socialization in the antebellum South*. New York: New York University Press.

Faulkner, W. 1936. *Absalom, Absalom!* In *William Faulkner, Novels, 1936–1940*. New York: Library of America, 1990, 5–313.

Federal Glass Ceiling Commission. 1995a. *Good for business: Making full use of the nation's human capital*. Washington, DC: Government Printing Office.

———. 1995b. *A solid investment: Making full use of the nation's human capital*. Washington, DC: Government Printing Office.

Ferrante, J., and P. Brown, eds. 2000. *The social construction of race and ethnicity in the United States*. 2nd ed. Upper Saddle River, NJ: Prentice Hall.

Fine, M., and J. Somerville, eds. 1998. *Small schools, big imaginations: A creative look at urban public schools*. Chicago: Cross City Campaign for Urban School Reform.

Fischer, D. H. 1991. *Albion's seed: Four British folkways in America*. New York: Oxford University Press.

Florida Department of Education. 2003. Gender representation among professionals in Florida's public schools. *Florida Department of Education*. Series 2004–02F. http://www.fldoe.org (accessed October 30, 2003).

Flowers, L. 1992. *Throwed away: Failures of progress in Eastern North Carolina*. Knoxville: University of Tennessee Press.

Ford, D. 2003. *The GRITS (girls raised in the south) guide to life*. New York: Dutton.

Forsyth, P., and T. Smith. 2001. Patterns of principal retention: What the Missouri case tells us. *Michigan State University*. http://edtech.connect.msu.edu/Searchaera2002/viewproposaltext.asap?propID=3113 (accessed October 30, 2003).

Foster, W. 1986. *Paradigms and promises: New approaches to educational administration*. Buffalo, NY: Prometheus Books.

Fox, J. 2000. *Five sisters: The Langhornes of Virginia*. New York: Simon & Schuster.

Fox-Genovese, E. 1993. The anxiety of history: The Southern confrontation with modernity. *Southern Cultures* (inaugural issue): 65–82.

Franklin, J. 1964. *The militant South*. New York: Beacon Press.

Franklin, J. H. 1943. *The free Negro in North Carolina, 1790–1860*. Chapel Hill: University of North Carolina Press.

Fredrickson, G. M. 1965. *The inner Civil War: Northern intellectuals and the crisis of union*. New York: Harper & Row.

French, S. 1995. What is social memory? *Southern Cultures* 2 (1, fall): 9–18.

Friedan, B. 1971. *The feminine mystique*. New York: Dell.

Funk, C., A. Pankake, and M. Reese, eds. 1998. *Women as school executives: Realizing the vision*. Commerce: Texas A&M University-Commerce Press.

Gaddis, J. L. 2002. *The landscape of history: How historians map the past*. New York: Oxford University Press.

Gates, E. N. 1997. *Racial classification and history*. New York: Garland.

Gavins, R. 1989. The meaning of freedom: Black North Carolina in the Nadir, 1880–1900. In *Race, class, and politics in Southern history: Essays in honor of Robert F. Durden*, ed. J. J. Crow, P. D. Escott, and C. L. Flynn Jr., 192–93. Baton Rouge: Louisiana State University Press.

Geertz, C. 1973. *Interpretation of cultures: Selected Essays.* New York: Basic Books.

———. 1983. *Local knowledge: Further essays in interpretive anthropology*. New York: Basic Books.

Geller, C. 2001. Failing public schools? Who says? *The Irascible Professor*. http: //irascibleprofessor.com/comments-3-23-01.htm (accessed June 2, 2003).

Genovese, E. D. 1969. *The world the slaveholders made: Two essays in interpretation*. New York: Vintage Books.

———. 1972. *Roll, Jordan, roll: The world the slaves made*. New York: Pantheon Books.

———. 1994. *The Southern tradition: The achievement and limitations of an American conservatism*. Cambridge, MA: Harvard University Press.

———. 2002. The dulcet tones of Christian disputation in the Democrat up-country. *Southern Cultures* 8 (4, winter): 56–68.

Gilbert, D. T., S. T. Fiske, and G. Lindzey, eds. 1998. *The handbook of social psychology*. Vols. 1–2. Boston: McGraw-Hill.

Gilligan, C. 1982. *In a different voice: Psychological theory and women's development*. Cambridge, MA: Harvard University Press.

Gilmore, G. E. 1996. *Gender and Jim Crow: Women and the politics of white supremacy in North Carolina, 1896–1920*. Chapel Hill: University of North Carolina Press.

Gitlin, T. 1995. *The twilight of common dreams: Why America is wracked by culture wars*. New York: Henry Holt.

Giuliani, R. W. 2002. *Leadership*. New York: Hyperion.

Gladwell, M. 2000. *The tipping point: How little things can make a big difference*. Boston: Little, Brown.

Glanz, J. 1991. *Bureaucracy and professionalism: The evolution of public school supervision*. Rutherford, NJ: Fairleigh Dickinson University Press.

Glaser, B. G., and A. L. Strauss. 1967. *The discovery of grounded theory: Strategies for qualitative research*. New York: Aldine de Gruyter.

Glass, T. E., ed. 1986. *An analysis of texts on school administration, 1820–1985: The reciprocal relationship between the literature and the profession*. Danville, IL: Interstate.

———. 1992. *The 1992 study of the American school superintendency*. Arlington, VA: American Association of School Administrators.

———. 2000. Where are all the women superintendents? *The School Administrator*. June. http://www.aasa.org/publications/sa/2000_06/glass.htm (accessed May 26, 2003).

Glass, T. E., L. Bjork, and C. C. Brunner. 2000. *The study of the American school superintendency*. Arlington, VA: American Association of School Administrators.

Goffman, E. 1959. *The presentation of self in everyday life*. New York: Doubleday.

Gordon, J. W. 1970. *My country school diary*. New York: Dell. Originally published in 1946 under the author's maiden name, Julia Weber.

Graff, O. B., and C. M. Street. 1956. *Improving competence in educational administration*. New York: Harper and Brothers.

Grantham, D. W. 1994. *The South in modern America: A region at odds*. New York: HarperCollins.

Gray, R. 1999. Recorded and unrecorded histories: Recent Southern writing. In *The Southern state of mind*, ed. J. N. Gretlund, 67–79. Columbia: University of South Carolina Press.

Greene, M. F. 1992. *Praying for sheetrock*. New York: Viking/Ebury.

Greenfield, T. 1991. Re-forming and re-valuing educational administration: Whence and when cometh the Phoenix? *Educational Management and Administration* 19 (4): 200–17.

Greenfield, T., and P. Ribbins, eds. 1993. *Greenfield on educational administration: Towards a humane science*. London: Routledge.

Greenwald, M. W. 1990. *Women, war, and work: The impact of World War I on women workers in the United States*. Ithaca, NY: Cornell University Press.

Gretlund, J. N., ed. 1999. *The Southern state of mind*. Columbia: University of South Carolina Press

Gribskov, M. 1980. Feminization and the woman school administrator. In *Women and educational leadership*, ed. S. K. Biklen and M. B. Brannigan, 77–91. Lexington, MA: D.C. Heath.

Griffin, L. J. 1995. Why was the South a problem to America? In *The South as an American problem*, ed. L. J. Griffin and D. H. Doyle, 10–32. Athens: University of Georgia Press.

Griffiths, D. 1959. *Administrative theory*. New York: Appleton-Century-Crofts.

———. 1988. Administrative theory. In *Handbook of research on educational administration*, ed. N. Boyan, 27–51. Englewood Cliffs, NJ: Prentice-Hall.

Gross, P. R., and N. Levitt. 1994. *Higher superstition: The academic left and its quarrels with science*. Baltimore, MD: Johns Hopkins University Press.

Guralnik, B., ed. 1970. *Webster's new world dictionary of the American language*. 2nd College ed. Englewood Cliffs, NJ: Prentice-Hall.

Haber, S. 1964. *Efficiency and uplift: Scientific management in the Progressive Era, 1880–1920*. Chicago: University of Chicago Press.

Hagman, H. L. 1951. *The administration of American public schools*. New York: McGraw-Hill.

Hall, J. D. 1998. Open secrets: Memory, imagination, and the refashioning of Southern identity. *American Quarterly* 50 (1): 109–24.

Hallstein, L. O. 1999. A postmodern caring: Feminist standpoint theories, revisioned, caring, and communication ethics. *Western Journal of Communication* 63 (winter): 32–56.

Hammer, C., and C. Rohr. 1994. *Public and private school principals: Are there too few women?* Washington, DC: National Center for Education Statistics. NCES Issue Brief 94192.

Hammond, L. 2000. Building bridges by building differences: The career life history of Winifred Wrisley. EdD diss. Western Carolina University, Cullowhee, NC.

Hanchett, T. W. 1988. The Rosenwald Schools and black education in North Carolina. *North Carolina Historical Review* 65 (October): 387–444.

Haraway, D. 1991. *Simians, cyborgs, and women: The reinvention of nature*. New York: Routledge.

Harding, S., ed. 1987. *Feminism and methodology*. Bloomington: Indiana University Press.

———. 1993. Rethinking standpoint epistemology: What is "strong objectivity?" In *Feminist epistemologies*, ed. L. Alcoff and E. Potter, 49–82. New York: Routledge.

———. 1998. *Is science multicultural? Postcolonialisms, feminisms, and epistemologies*. Bloomington: Indiana University Press.

Harmel, K. 1999. UF researcher studies changes in the elementary school principalship. *University of Florida*. February 11, 1999. http://www.napa.ufl.edu/99news/principa.htm (accessed October 30, 2003).

Harney, W. W. 1873. A strange land and peculiar people. *Lippincott's Magazine* 12 (October): 429–38.

Harrington, M. 1992. *The other America: Poverty in the United States*. New York: Macmillan.

Harris, T. 1996. Porch-sitting as a creative Southern tradition. *Southern Cultures* 2 (3/4): 441–60.

Hartsock, N. 1983. *Money, sex, and power: Towards a feminist historical materialism*. New York: Longman.

——, ed. 1987. The feminist standpoint: Developing the ground for a specifically feminist historical materialism. In *Feminism and methodology*, ed. S. Harding, 157–80. Bloomington: Indiana University Press.

——. 1997. Standpoint theories for the next century. *Women and Politics* 19:93–101.

Harvey, P. 1995. "Sweet home Alabama:" Southern culture and the American search for community. *Southern Cultures* 1 (3, spring): 321–34.

Harwell, R. B. 1964. The stream of self-consciousness. In *The idea of the South: Pursuit of a central theme*, ed. F. E. Vandive, 17–25. Chicago: University of Chicago Press.

Haskell, T. L. 2000. *The emergence of professional social science: The American Social Science Association and the nineteenth-century crisis of authority*. Baltimore, MD: Johns Hopkins University Press.

Heider, J. 1986. *The tao of leadership: Lao Tzu's Tao Te Ching adapted for a new age*. New York: Bantam Books.

Heilbrun, C. G. 1988. *Writing a woman's life*. New York: Norton.

Helgesen, S. 1990. *The female advantage: Women's ways of leadership*. New York: Doubleday Currency.

Heyrman, C. L. 1997. *Southern cross: The beginnings of the Bible Belt*. New York: Knopf.

Hicks, G. L. 1976. *Appalachian valley*. Prospect Hills, IL: Waveland Press.

Hodgkinson, C. 1991. *Educational leadership: The moral art*. Albany: State University Press of New York.

Hofstadter, R. 1966. *Anti-intellectualism in American life*. New York: Vintage Books.

Holland, D. C., and M. A. Eisenhart. 1990. *Educated in romance: Women, achievement, and college culture*. Chicago: University of Chicago Press.

Hood, S. 1996. *Ohio superintendent benchmark data and the derailment issue: An essay*. Greensboro: University of North Carolina Greensboro, Humanistic Education Project.

Howley, C. B. 1989. *What is the effect of small-scale schooling on student achievement*. Charleston, WV: ERIC Clearinghouse on Rural Education and Small Schools. (ED308062)

——. 1994. *The academic effectiveness of small-scale schooling (An update)*. Charleston, WV: ERIC Clearinghouse on Rural Education and Small Schools. (ED372897)

——. 1996. *Ongoing dilemmas of school size: A short story*. Charleston, WV: ERIC Clearinghouse on Rural Education and Small Schools. (ED401089)

Huber, P. 1995. A short history of *redneck:* The fashioning of a Southern white masculine identity. *Southern Cultures* 1 (2, winter): 145–66.

Hughes, L. 1995. Harlem [2]. In *The collected poems of Langston Hughes*, ed. A. Rampersad and R. David, 426. New York: Vintage Classics.

Inscoe, J. C., ed. 2001. *Appalachians and race: The mountain South from slavery to segregation*. Lexington: University Press of Kentucky.

Institute for Women's Policy Research. 2002. *The status of women in the states: Overview*. Washington, DC: Institute for Women's Policy Research.

Irby, B. J., and G. Brown, eds. 1995. *Women as school executives: Voices and visions.* Huntsville, TX: Sam Houston Press.

Irmsher, K. 1997. *School size.* Charleston, WV: ERIC Clearinghouse on Rural Education and Small Schools. (ED414615)

Irving, W. 1819–20. The legend of Sleepy Hollow. In *History, tales and sketches: The sketch book of Geoffrey Crayon, Gent,* 1058–88. New York: Library of America, 1983.

Jackson, W. 1998. Ignorance-based world view: Fund-raising letter. *Land Institute*. December 1998. http://www.landinstitute.org/vnews/display.v/ART/1998/12/01/3aa7fec59 on July 3, 2003.

Janiewski, D. 1991. Southern honor, Southern dishonor: Managerial ideology and the construction of gender, race, and class relations in southern industry. In *Work engendered: Toward a new history of American labor,* ed. A. Baron, 76–91. Ithaca, NY: Cornell University Press.

Jefferson, T. 1813. Letter to John Adams, October 28. In *Thomas Jefferson: Writings.* New York: Library Classics of the United States, 1984, 1304–10.

Johnson, G. G. 1937. *Ante-bellum North Carolina*. Chapel Hill: University of North Carolina Press.

Johnson, S. 1998. *Who moved my cheese? An amazing way to deal with change in your work and in your life.* New York: G. P. Putnam's Sons.

Jones, A. G. 1996. The work of gender in the Southern Renaissance. In *Southern writers and their words,* ed. C. Morris and S. G. Reinhart, 41–56. College Station: Texas A&M University Press.

Jones, E. H., and X. P. Montenegro. 1982. *Recent trends in the representation of women and minorities in school administration and problems in documentation.* Arlington, VA: American Association of School Administrators.

Jones, J. 1985. *Labor of love, labor of sorrow: Black women, work, and the family from slavery to the present.* New York: Basic Books.

———. 1990. *A social history of the laboring classes: From colonial times to the present.* Malden, MA: Blackwell.

———. 1998. *American work: Four centuries of black and white labor*. New York: Norton.

Jones, L. 1994. *Appalachian values*. Ashland, KY: Jesse Stuart Foundation.

———. 1999. *Faith and meaning in the Southern uplands*. Chicago: University of Illinois Press.

Jordan, W. D. 1973. *White over black: American attitudes toward the Negro, 1550–1812.* Baltimore, MD: Penguin.

Joy, L. 1998. Why are women underrepresented in public school administration? An empirical test of promotion discrimination. *Economics of Education Review* 17 (2): 193–204.

Juster, N. 1979. *So sweet to labor: Rural women in America, 1865–1895*. New York: Viking Press.

Justice Policy Institute. 2003. Doing time south of the Mason-Dixon Line. *Sojourners Magazine* 32 (4, July–August): 13.

Karr, M. 1995. *The liar's club: A memoir*. New York: Viking.

———. 2000. *Cherry: A memoir*. New York: Viking.

Katz, M. B. 1975. *Class, bureaucracy, and schools: The illusion of educational change in America*. New York: Praeger Publishers.

———. 1987. *Reconstructing American education*. Cambridge, MA: Harvard University Press.

———. 2001. *The irony of early school reform: Educational innovation in mid-nineteenth century Massachusetts*. New York: Teachers College.

Kaye, J. L. 1992. *The wisdom of Baltasar Gracián: A practical manual for good and perilous times*. New York: Pocket Books.

Keller, E. F. 1983. *A feeling for the organism: The life and work of Barbara McClintock*. New York: Freeman.

Kemp, A. A. 1990. *A women's wage: Historical meanings and social consequences*. Lexington: University Press of Kentucky.

———. 1994. *Women's work: Degraded and devalued*. Englewood Cliffs, NJ: Prentice Hall.

Kephart, H. 1913. *Our Southern highlanders*. Knoxville: University of Tennessee Press, 1992.

Kessler-Harris, A. 1982. *Out to work: A history of wage-earning women in the United States*. New York: Oxford University Press.

Kilbride, D. 2000. The cosmopolitan South: Privileged Southerners, Philadelphia, and the fashionable tour in the antebellum era. *Journal of Urban History* 26 (5, July): 563–590.

King, F. 1993. *Southern ladies and gentlemen*. New York: St. Martin's Press.

King, M. C. 1993. Black women's breakthrough into clerical work: An occupational tipping point. *Journal of Economic Issues* 28 (4, December): 1097–125.

Knight, E. W. 1916. *Public school education in North Carolina*. Boston: Houghton-Mifflin.

Knight, E. W., and C. L. Hall, eds. 1951. *Readings in American educational history*. New York: Appleton-Crofts.

Kohn, A. 2000. *The case against standardized testing: Raising the scores, ruining the schools*. Portsmouth, NH: Heinemann.

Korchech, S. A., and M. Reese, eds. 2002. *Women as school executives: Research and reflections on educational leadership*. Austin: Texas Council of Women School Executives.

Krzyzewski, M., and D. T. Phillips. 2000. *Leading with heart: Coach K's successful strategies of basketball, business, and life*. New York: Warner Books.

Kuehl, L. 1984. *Conversations with Eudora Welty*. Vol. 47 of The Art of Fiction, ed. P. W. Prenshaw, 74–91. Jackson: University Press of Mississippi.

Kuhn, T. 1973. *The structure of scientific revolutions*. Chicago: University of Chicago Press.

Kyriakoudes, L., and P. Coclanis. 1997. The "Tennessee Test of Manhood": Professional wrestling and Southern cultural stereotypes. *Southern Cultures* 3 (fall): 8–27.

Lagemann, E. C. 2000. *The elusive science: The troubling history of education research*. Chicago: University of Chicago Press.

Lambert, L., D. Walker, D. P. Zimmerman, J. E. Cooper, M. D. Lambert, M. E. Gardner, P. J. Ford Slack. 1995. *The constructivist leader*. New York: Teachers College Press.

Lane, A. J., ed. 1971. *The debate over slavery: Stanley Elkins and his critics*. Urbana: University of Illinois Press.

Larimore, W. 2002. *Bryson City tales: Stories of a doctor's first year practicing in the Smoky Mountains*. Grand Rapids, MI: Zondervan.

Lea, R. A. 1989. Career paths and perceived success levels of women superintendents of public schools in the state of Texas. *Dissertation Abstracts International* 50 (06A). (University Microfilms no. AAG8921236)

Leach, E. 1976. *Culture and communication: The logic by which symbols are connected.* Cambridge: Cambridge University Press.

Lebsock, S. 1985. *The free women of Petersburg: Status and culture in a southern town, 1784–1860*. New York: Norton.

Lee, V. E., and J. B. Smith. 1995. Effects of high school restructuring and size on early gains in achievement and engagement. *Sociology of Education* 68 (4): 241–70.

———. 1997. High school size: Which works best and for whom? *Educational Evaluation and Policy Analysis* 19 (3): 205–27.

Lefler, H. T., and A. R. Newsome. 1973. *The history of a southern state: North Carolina*. 3rd ed. Chapel Hill: University of North Carolina Press.

Leithwood, K., and D. L. Duke. 1999. A century's quest to understand school leadership. In *Handbook of research on educational administration*, ed. J. Murphy and K. S. Lewis, 45–72. San Francisco: Jossey-Bass.

Leloudis, J. L. 1996. *Schooling in the new South: Pedagogy, self, and society in North Carolina, 1880–1920*. Chapel Hill: University of North Carolina Press.

Leslie, J. B., and E. V. Velsor. 1996. *A look at derailment today: North American and Europe*. Greensboro, NC: Center for Creative Leadership.

Levine, R. V. 2003. The kindness of strangers. *American Scientist* 91 (3): 226–33.

Lewis, S. 1922. *Babbitt*. New York: Harcourt Brace Jovanovich, 1961.

Lippman-Blumen, J. 1976. Toward a homosocial theory of sex roles: An explanation of the sex segregation of social institutions. *Signs* 1 (3, spring supplement): 15–31.

Logan, J. 1998. School leadership of the 90s and beyond: A window of opportunity for women educators. *Advancing Women in Leadership* 1 (3): 2–10.

Lombardo, M., and C. McCasuley. 1988. *The dynamics of management derailment*. Greensboro, NC: Center for Creative Leadership.

Lorber, J., and S. A. Farrell. 1991. *The social construction of gender*. Newbury Park, CA: Sage Publications.

Lorde, A. 1993. *Zami, Sister Outsider, Undersong*. New York: Quality Paperback Book Club.

Lovejoy, A. J. 1936. *The great chain of being*. Cambridge, MA: Harvard University Press.

Machiavelli, N. 1515. *The Prince*. 2nd ed. Trans. Robert M. Adams. New York: Norton, 1992.

Magers, J. E. 1987. Education. In *The history of Jackson County*, ed. M. R. Williams, 281–318. Sylva, NC: Jackson County Historical Association.

Malone, B. C. 1993. *Singing cowboys and musical mountaineers: Southern culture and the roots of country music*. Athens: University of Georgia Press.

Mann, H. 1951. Tenth Annual Report to the Massachusetts State Board of Education, 1846. In *Readings in American educational history*, ed. E. W. Knight and C. L. Hall, 163–65. New York: Appleton-Century-Crofts.

Mannheim, K. 1936. *Ideology and utopia*. Trans. L. Wirth and E. Shils. New York: Harvest Books.

Marchalonis, S. 1989. *The worlds of Lucy Larcom, 1824–1893*. Athens: University of Georgia Press.

Margo, R. A. 1990. *Race and slavery in the South, 1880–1950: An economic history*. Chicago: University of Chicago Press.

Marks, E., and I. de Courtivrons, eds. 1981. *The new French feminists*. New York: Schocken.

Martin, J. R. 1992. *The schoolhouse: Rethinking schools for changing families*. Cambridge, MA: Harvard University Press.

———. 2002. *Cultural miseducation: In search of a democratic solution*. New York: Teachers College Press.

McCall, M. W., and M. M. Lombardo. 1983. *Off track: Why and how successful executives get derailed*. Greensboro, NC: Center for Creative Leadership.

McCauley, D. V. 1995. *Appalachian mountain religion: A history*. Urbana: University of Illinois Press.

McCreight, C. 1999. *Female superintendents: Barriers and the struggle for equity*. Charleston, WV: ERIC Clearinghouse on Rural Education and Small Schools. (ED432041)

Meier, D. 1995. Small schools, big results. *The American School Board Journal* 182 (7, July): 37–40.

———. 1996. The benefits of smallness. *Educational Leadership* 54 (1, September): 12–15.

———, ed. 2000. *Will standards save public education?* Boston, MA: Beacon Press.

Mencken, H. L. 1920. The Sahara of the Bozart. In *Prejudices: Second Series*, 136–54. New York: Knopf.

Mertz, N. 2003. The promise of Title IX: Longitudinal study of women in administration, 1972–2002. Paper presented at the 29th annual fall conference on Research on Women in Education, Knoxville, TN.

———. 1991. Females in school administration: Making sense of the numbers. *Planning and Changing* 22 (1): 34–45.

Miller, B. A., and K. J. Hahn. 1997. *Finding their own place: Youth in three small rural communities take part in instructive school-to-work experiences*. Charleston, WV: ERIC Clearinghouse on Rural Education and Small Schools.

Miller, J. J. 1998. *The unmaking of Americans: How multiculturalism has undermined the assimilation ethic*. New York: Free Press.

Miller, L. 2002. Superintendent official: Hedrick sworn in. *Cherokee Scout*, July 3, 1.

Miller, L. P. 1965. *Education in Buncombe County, 1793–1965*. Asheville, NC: Miller Printing.

Mitchell, M. 1936. *Gone with the wind*. New York: Avon, 1976. Originally published by Macmillan.

Moehlman, A. B. 1951. *School administration*. 2nd Ed. Cambridge, MA: Riverside.

Morgan, L. 2002. *Mountain born, mountain molded*. Boone, NC: Parkway Publishers.

Morgan, L., and B. LeGette. 1958. *Gift from the hills: Miss Lucy Morgan's story of her unique Penland School*. Indianapolis, IN: Bobbs-Merrill.

Morie, E. D., and B. B. Wilson. 1996. Women superintendents: New role models in leadership for change. Paper presented at the annual conference of the Association for Supervision and Curriculum Development, New Orleans, LA.

Morley, M. W. 1913. *The Carolina mountains*. Alexander, NC: Land of the Sky Books, 2002.

Morrison, A. M., R. P. White, E. Van Velsor, and the Center for Creative Leadership. 1987. *Breaking the glass ceiling: Can women reach the top of America's largest corporations?* Reading, MA: Addison-Wesley.

Moynihan, D. P. 1965. *The Negro family: The case for National Action*. Washington, DC: Office of Policy Planning and Research, Department of Labor.

Munroe, F. 1912. *New demands in education*. New York: n.p.

Murphy, J. 1992. *The landscape of leadership preparation: Reframing the education of school administrators*. Newbury Park, CA: Corwin Press.

Murray, B. n.d. Tracking religious membership in the United States. *Foundation for American Communications*. http://www.facsnet.org/issues/faith/sanchagrin.php (accessed June 23, 2003). Article based on *Religious Congregations and Membership in the United States: 2000*, published by the Glenmary Research Center in Cincinnati, Ohio.

Murray, P. E. 1985. *History of the North Carolina Teachers Association*. Washington, DC: National Education Association.

Nafisi, A. 2003. *Reading Lolita in Tehran: A memoir in books*. New York: Random House.

Nash, G. B., C. Crabtree, and R. E. Dunn. 1997. *History on trial: Culture wars and the teaching of the past*. New York: Knopf.

National Center for Education Statistics. 2000a. *School and staffing survey*. Washington, DC: United States Department of Education, Office of Educational Research and Improvement.

———. 2000b. *Dropout rates in the United States: 2000*. Washington, DC: United States Department of Education, Office of Educational Research and Improvement.

National Commission on Excellence in Education. 1913. *A nation at risk: The imperative for educational reform*. Washington, DC: National Commission on Excellence in Education.

Newby, I. A. 1989. *Plain folk in the new South: Social change and cultural persistence, 1880–1915*. Baton Rouge: Louisiana State University Press.

Nielsen, J. M., ed. 1990. *Feminist research methods: Exemplary readings in the social sciences*. Boulder, CO: Westview Press.

Nisbett, R., and D. Cohen. 1996. *Culture of honor: The psychology of violence in the south*. Boulder, CO: Westview Press.

Noble, M. C. S. 1930. *A history of the public schools of North Carolina*. Chapel Hill: University of North Carolina Press.

Noddings, N. 1982. *The challenge to care in schools: An alternative approach to education*. New York: Teachers College Press.

———. 2002. *Educating moral people: A caring alternative to character education*. New York: Teachers College Press.

———. 2003. *Happiness and education*. New York: Cambridge University Press.

North Carolina Department of Public Instruction. 1952–2002. *North Carolina education directory*. Raleigh: State Department of Public Instruction.

Northouse, P. G. 2001. *Leadership: Theory and practice*. 2nd Ed. Thousand Oaks, CA: Sage.

Norton, M. S., L. D. Webb, L. L. Dlugosh, and W. Sybouts. 1996. *The school superintendency: New responsibilities, new leadership*. Boston: Allyn and Bacon.

Novick, P. 1992. *That noble dream: The "objectivity question" and the American historical profession*. New York: Cambridge University Press.

O'Brien, M., ed. 1993. *An evening when alone: Four journals of single women in the South, 1827–67*. Charlottesville: University Press of Virginia.

Oakley, E., and D. Krug. 1991. *Enlightened leadership: Getting to the heart of change*. New York: Simon & Schuster.

Obermeyer, L. E. 1996. Profiles of women superintendents and women aspiring to the superintendency in California and barriers encountered during their careers. *Dissertation Abstracts International* 57 (04A). (University Microfilm no. AAG9622243)

Odem Institute for Research in Social Science. 2000. *Southern Focus Poll*. Chapel Hill: University of North Carolina Center for the Study of the American South.

———. n.d. Southern Focus Poll stories: Lazy workers in the South? *Odem Institute*. http://www2.irss.unc.edu/irss/insidethetute/irss_news_article.asp?id=185 (accessed June 7, 2003).

Owsley, F. L. 1936. The old south and the new. *American Review* 6 (February): 475–85.

Paddock, S. 1981. Male and female paths in school administration. In *Educational policy and management: Sex differentials*, ed. P. Schmuck, W. Charters, and R. Carlson, 187–98. New York: Academic Press.

Painter, J. B. 1996. *The season of Dorland-Bell: History of an Appalachian mission school*. Boone, NC: Appalachian Consortium Press.

Pankake, A., G. Schroth, and C. Funk, eds. 2000. *Women as school executives: The complete picture*. Commerce: Texas A&M University-Commerce Press.

Pavan, B., et al. 1995. Eight years later: Has the superintendency changed for women? Paper presented at the annual meeting of the American Educational Research Association. San Francisco, California. (ED384962)

Pease, J. H., and W. H. Pease. 1990. *Ladies, women, and wenches: Choice and constraint in antebellum Charleston and Boston*. Chapel Hill: University of North Carolina Press.

Peek, W. 1993. *History of education in North Carolina*. Raleigh: North Carolina Department of Public Instruction.

Perin, C. 1988. *Belonging in America: Reading between the lines*. Madison: University of Wisconsin Press.

Peshkin, A. 1978. *Growing up American: Schooling and the survival of community*. Chicago: University of Chicago Press.

Peters, T. 1987. *Thriving on chaos: Handbook for a management revolution*. New York: Harper & Row.

Phillips, U. B. 1928. The central theme of Southern history. *American Historical Review* 34 (October): 30–43.

Polanyi, K. 1944. *The great transformation: The political and economic origins of our time*. Boston: Beacon Press, 1971.

Pope, A. 1733–34. An essay on man. In *The Harvard Classics: Vol. 40. English Poetry*. 55th ed. Ed. C. W. Eliot, 406–40. New York: Collier & Son, 1963.

Potter, D. M. 1961. The enigma of the South. *Yale Review* 51 (October): 142–51.

——. 1964. On understanding the South: A review article. *Journal of Southern History* 30 (November): 451–62.

——. 1972. *The South and the concurrent majority*. Baton Rouge: Louisiana State University Press.

Pounder, D. 2000. Book review. *Educational Administration Quarterly* 36 (1): 143–48.

Powell, L. W. 1966. *Who are these mountain people? An intimate historical account of Southern Appalachia*. New York: Exposition Press.

Powell, W. S. 1989. *North Carolina through four centuries*. Chapel Hill: University of North Carolina Press.

Prather, H. L. 1979. *Resurgent politics and educational progressivism in the new south: North Carolina, 1890–1913*. Rutherford, NJ: Fairleigh Dickinson University Press.

Proctor, B. D., and J. Dalaker. 2002. *Poverty in the United States, 2001*. Washington, DC: U.S. Census Bureau.

Pugh, D. S., D. J. Hickson, and C. R. Hinings. 1964. *Writers on organizations*. London: Hutchinson.

Raitz, K. B., and R. Ulack. 1984. *Appalachia: A regional geography: Land, people and development*. Boulder, CO: Westview Press.

Ravitch, D. 2001. *Left back: A century of battles over school reform*. New York: Simon & Schuster.

——. 2003. *The language police: How pressure groups restrict what students learn*. New York: Knopf.

Ray, J. 1999. *Ecology of a cracker childhood*. Minneapolis, MN: Milkweed.

Raywid, M. A. 1996. *Downsizing schools in big cities*. Charleston, WV: ERIC Clearinghouse on Rural Education and Small Schools. (ED393958)

——. 1999. *Current literature on small schools*. Charleston, WV: ERIC Clearinghouse on Rural Education and Small Schools. (ED425049)

Reay, D., and S. Ball. 2000. Essentials of female management: Women's ways of working the educational market place. *Education Management and Administration* 2 (April): 145–59.

Reed, B. 2000. The Brevard Rosenwald School. EdD diss., Western Carolina University, Cullowhee, NC.

Reed, J. S. 1986. *The enduring South: Structural persistence in mass society*. Rev. ed. Chapel Hill: University of North Carolina Press.

——. 1990. *Whistling Dixie: Dispatches from the South*. San Diego: Harvest Book, Harcourt Brace.

——. 1993. *My tears spoiled my aim and other reflections on Southern culture*. San Diego: Harvest Book, Harcourt Brace.

——. 1994. Images of Southern women. *Southern Cultures* 1 (1, fall): 125–27.

——. 1995. Southern manners. *Southern Cultures* 1 (2, winter): 275–77.

——. 1996. Happy New Year! *Southern Cultures* 2 (3/4): 421–23.

——. 1997. South polls: A double-wide what? *Southern Cultures* 3 (winter): 112–114.

——. 2001. South polls: The twenty most influential Southerners of the twentieth century. *Southern Cultures* 7 (spring): 96–100.

Regan, H. 1990. Not for women alone: School administration as a feminist activity. *Teachers College Record* 91 (4): 565–77.

Regan, H. B., and G. H. Brooks. 1995. *Out of women's experience: Creating relational leadership*. Thousand Oaks, CA: Corwin Press.

Reyhner, J., and J. Eder. 1989. *A history of Indian education*. Billings: Eastern Montana College.

Rice, J. M. 1914. *Scientific management in education*. New York: Arno Press, 1969.

Rich, R. 1999. *What Southern women know (that every woman should): Timeless secrets to get everything you want in love, life, and work*. New York: Perigee.

Riehl, C., and M. Byrd. 1997. Gender differences among new recruits to school administration: Cautionary footnotes to an optimistic tale. *Educational Evaluation and Policy Analysis* 19 (1): 45–64.

Ritzer, G. 1993. *The McDonaldization of society: An investigation into the changing character of contemporary social life*. Thousand Oaks, CA: Pine Forge Press.

——. 1996. *The McDonaldization of society*. Rev. ed. Thousand Oaks, CA: Pine Forge Press.

Roberson, Z. H. 1969. *Public school education in Buncombe County, 1935–1969*. Asheville, NC: Miller Printing.

Rose, H. 1983. Hand, brain and heart: A feminist epistemology for the natural sciences. *Signs* 9:73–90.

——. 1986. Beyond masculinist realities: A feminist epistemology for the sciences. In *Feminist approaches to science*, ed. R. Bleier, 57–76. New York: Pergamon Press.

Rosener, J. B. 1990. Ways women lead. *Harvard Business Review* 68 (3): 119–25.

Rost, J. C. 1993. *Leadership for the twenty-first century*. Westport, CT: Praeger.

Sartre, J. P. 1968. *Anti-Semite and Jew*. Trans. G. J. Becker, Trans. New York: Schocken.

Schiebinger, L. 1993. *Nature's body: Gender in the making of modern science*. Boston: Beacon Press.

Schmuck, P. 1999. Introduction. In *Sacred dreams: Women and the superintendency*, ed. C. Cryss Brunner, 1–6. Albany: State University of New York Press.

Schmuck, P., and J. Schubert. 1995. Women principals' views on sex equity: Exploring issues of integration and information. In *Women leading in education*, ed. D. M. Dunlap and P. A. Schmuck, 274–87. Albany: State University of New York Press.

Schuster, D. J., and T. H. Foote. 1990. Differences abound between male and female superintendents. *School Administrator* 47 (2): 14–16, 18–19.

Schwartz, M. 2001. *A Southern belle primer or why Princess Margaret will never be a Kappa Kappa Gamma*. New York: Broadway Books.

Scott, A. F. 1970. *The Southern lady: From pedestal to politics, 1830–1930*. Charlottesville: University Press of Virginia, 1995.

Searles, P. D. 1995. *A college for Appalachia: Alice Lloyd on Caney Creek*. Lexington: University Press of Kentucky.

Sewell, W. 1848. Wm. Sewell to Horace Mann, July 21, 1848. In *Readings in American educational history*, ed. E. W. Knight and C. L. Hall, 166–67. New York: Appleton-Century-Crofts, 1951.

Shackelford, L., and B. Weinberg, eds. 1977. *Our Appalachia*. New York: Hill & Wang.

Shakeshaft, C. 1987. *Women in educational administration*. Newbury Park, CA: Sage.

——. 1989. The gender gap in research in educational administration. *Educational Administration Quarterly* 25 (4): 324–37.

Shakespeare, W. 1601–03. *Troilus and Cressida*. In *The Yale Shakespeare*. 3rd ed. Vol. 37. Ed. J. J. Campbell. New Haven: Yale University Press, 1965.

Shapiro, H. D. 1978. *Appalachia on our mind: The Southern mountains and mountaineers in the American consciousness, 1870–1920*. Chapel Hill: University of North Carolina Press.

Sheldon, T. D., and L. W. Munnich Jr. 1999. *Administrative autumn: A study of Minnesota's aging educational leaders and the difficulty in finding their replacements*. Minneapolis, MN: Hubert H. Humphrey Institute of Public Affairs.

Sheppard, M. E. 1935. *Cabin in the laurel*. Chapel Hill: University of North Carolina Press, 1991.

Shuptrine, H., and J. Dickey. 1974. *Jericho: The South beheld*. Birmingham, AL: Oxmoor House.

Slater, R. 1998. *Jack Welch and the G.E. Way: Management insights and leadership secrets of the legendary CEO*. New York: McGraw Hill.

Slater, R. O. 1994. Symbolic educational leadership and democracy in America. *Educational Administration Quarterly* 30 (1): 97–101.

Sloop, M. T. M., with L. Blythe. 1953. *Miracle in the hills: The lively personal story of a woman doctor's forty-year crusade in the mountains of North Carolina*. New York: McGraw-Hill.

Smedley, A. 1999. *Race in North America: Origin and evolution of a worldview*. Boulder, CO: Westview Press.

Smith, C. L. 1888. *The history of education in North Carolina*. Washington, DC: Government Printing Office.

Smith, D. 1987. *The everyday world as problematic: A feminist sociology*. Boston, MA: Northwestern University Press.

——. 1992. Sociology from women's experience: A reaffirmation. *Sociological Theory* 10:88–98.

Smith, P. 1996. "A history of their own": Nine African American school administrators. Paper presented at the annual meeting of the American Educational Research Association, New York.

———. 1997. And then there was one: Clay County Schools, 1926–1996: An introductory study in community. Paper presented at the annual meeting of the History of Education Society. Philadelphia, PA.

———. 2000. And then there were none: The African American school experience in Southern Appalachia. Paper presented at the annual meeting of the American Educational Research Association. New Orleans, LA.

Smith, S. A., and J. N. Rogers. 1995. Saturday night in country music: The gospel according to juke. *Southern Cultures* 1 (2, winter): 229–44.

Smith-Rosenberg, C. 1985. *Disorderly conduct: Visions of gender in Victorian America.* New York: Oxford University Press.

Spaulding, F. 1913. The application of the principles of scientific management. *Journal of the Proceedings and Addresses of the Fifty-First Annual Meeting of the National Education Association*, 259–79. Ann Arbor, MI: National Education Association.

Spring, J. 1980. *Educating the worker-citizen: The social, economic, and political foundations of education*. New York: Longman.

———. 1994. *Deculturalization and the struggle for equality: A brief history of the education of dominated cultures in the United States*. New York: McGraw-Hill.

Stampp, K. M. 1956. *The peculiar institution: Slavery in the antebellum South*. New York: Vintage Books.

Stanley, L., ed. 1990. *Feminist praxis: Research, theory, and epistemology in feminist sociology*. New York: Routledge.

Steadman, M. 1987. *Angel child*. Atlanta, GA: Peachtree Publishers.

Steiger, T., and B. F. Reskin. 1990. Baking and baking off: Deskilling and the changing sex makeup of bakers. In *Job queues, gender queues: Explaining women's inroads into male occupations*, ed. B. F. Reskin and P. A. Roos, 257–74. Philadelphia, PA: Temple University Press.

Stoddart, J., ed. 1997. *The quare women's journals: Mary Stone and Katherine Pettit's summers in the Kentucky Mountains and the founding of the Hindman Settlement School*. Ashland, KY: Jesse Stuart Foundation.

Stouder, J. G. 1998. A profile of female Indiana school superintendents. *Dissertation Abstracts International* 59 (03A), 0686. (University Microfilm no. AAG9825896)

Strauss, A. L. 1987. *Qualitative analysis for social scientists*. New York: Cambridge University Press.

Strober, M. 1976. Toward dimorphics: A summary statement to the conference on occupational segregation. *Signs* 1 (3, spring supplement): 293–302.

———. 1984. Toward a general theory of occupational sex segregation. In *Sex segregation in the workplace: Trends, explanations, remedies*, ed. B. F. Reskin, 144–56. Washington, DC: National Academy Press.

Strom, S. H. 1992. *Beyond the typewriter: Gender, class, and the origins of modern American office work, 1900–1930*. Urbana: University of Illinois Press.

Stuart, J. 1949. *The thread that runs so true: A mountain school-teacher tells his story*. New York: Charles Scribner's Sons, 1958.

Summitt, P. H., and S. Jenkins. 1998. *Reaching for the summit: The definite dozen system for succeeding at whatever you do*. New York: Broadway Books.

Tallerico, M., and J. N. Burnstyn. 1996. Retaining women in the superintendency: The location matters. *Education Administration Quarterly* 32 (December): 642–64.

Taylor, F. W. 1911. *The principles of scientific management*. New York: Norton, 1967.

Taylor, W. R. 1961. *Cavalier and Yankee: The old South and American national character*. New York: Harper Torchbooks.

Tessier, M. S. 1992. *The state of Buncombe*. Virginia Beach, VA: Donning.

Theobald, P. 1992. *Rural philosophy for education: Wendell Berry's tradition*. Charleston, WV: ERIC Clearinghouse on Rural Education and Small Schools. (ED345930)

——. 1997. *Teaching the commons: Place, pride, and the renewal of community*. Boulder, CO: Westview Press.

Tibbetts, S. 1980. The woman principal: Superior to the male. *Journal of the NAWDAC* [National Association of Women Deans, Administrators, and Counselors] 43 (4): 15–18.

Tichi, C. 1994. *The high lonesome: The American culture of country music*. Chapel Hill: University of North Carolina Press.

Tillyard, E. M. W. n.d. *The Elizabethan world picture*. New York: Vintage Books.

Tindall, G. B. 1964. Mythology: A new frontier in southern history. In *The idea of the South: Pursuit of a central theme*, ed. F. E. Vandiver, 1–15. Chicago: University of Chicago Press.

Towery, M. 1998. *Powerchicks: How women will dominate America*. Atlanta, GA: Longstreet.

Travers, R. M. W. 1983. *How research has changed American schools: A history from 1840 to the present*. Kalamazoo, MI: Mythos Press.

Twelve Southerners. 1977. *I'll take my stand: The South and the agrarian tradition*. Baton Rouge: Louisiana State University Press.

Tyack, D. 1974. *The one best system: A history of American urban education*. Cambridge, MA: Harvard University Press.

——. 1976. Pilgrim's progress: Toward a social history of the school superintendency, 1860–1960. *History of Education Quarterly* 16 (fall): 257–300.

Tyack, D., and E. Hansot. 1982. *Managers of virtue: Public school leadership in America, 1820–1980*. New York: Basic Books.

Tzu, S. 1971. *The art of war*. Trans. S. B. Griffith, Trans. New York: Oxford University Press.

U.S. Census Bureau. 2002. State and county quick facts. *U.S. Census Bureau*. http://quickfacts.census.gov/qfd/states/37000.html (accessed July 9, 2003).

Van Noppen, I. W., and J. J. Van Noppen. 1973. *Western North Carolina since the Civil War*. Boone, NC: Appalachian Consortium Press.

Vandiver, F. E. 1964. The Southerner as extremist. In *The idea of the South: Pursuit of a central theme*, ed. F. E. Vandiver, 43–55. Chicago: University of Chicago Press.

Violas, P. C. 1978. *The training of the urban working class: A history of twentieth-century American education*. Chicago: Rand McNally College.

Walker, V. S. 1996. *Their highest potential: An African American school community in the segregated South*. Chapel Hill: University of North Carolina Press.

Walton, S., and J. Huey. 1992. *Sam Walton: Made in America—My Story*. New York: Doubleday.

Warm North/The Chilly South (The). 2003. *Utne Reader* (March–April): 20.

Warren, M. R. 1912. Medieval methods for modern children. *Saturday Evening Post* (March 12): 11–13, 34–35.

Webb, C. D., L. K. Shumway, and R. W. Shute. 1996. *Local schools of thought*. Charleston, WV: ERIC Clearinghouse on Rural Education and Small Schools.

Weber, M. 1968. *Economy and society*. Ed. G. Roth and C. Wittich. Trans. E. Fischoff and others. Totowa, NJ: Bedminster Press.

Weiner, L. Y. 1985. *From working girl to working mother: The female labor force in the United States, 1820–1980*. Chapel Hill: University of North Carolina Press.

Welch, J., and J. A. Byrne. 2001. *Jack: Straight from the gut*. New York: Warner.

Whisnant, D. E. 1983. *All that is native and fine: The politics of culture in an American region*. Chapel Hill: University of North Carolina Press.

Wiebe, R. H. 1967. *The search for order, 1877–1920*. New York: Hill & Wang.

Williams, J. A. 1996. Counting yesterday's people: Using aggregate data to address the problem of Appalachia's boundaries. *Journal of Appalachian Studies* 2 (spring): 3–27.

———. 2002. *Appalachia: A history*. Chapel Hill: University of North Carolina Press.

Williams, M. 1979. *The Jeanes story: A chapter in the history of American education, 1908–1968*. Atlanta, GA: Southern Education Foundation.

Williamson, J. W. 1995. *Hillybillyland: What the movies did to the mountains and what the mountains did to the movies*. Chapel Hill: University of North Carolina Press.

Willower, D. J., and P. B. Forsyth. 1999. A brief history of scholarship on educational administration. In *Handbook of research on educational administration*, ed. J. Murphy and K. S. Lewis, 1–23. San Francisco: Jossey-Bass.

Wilson, C. R., and W. Ferris, eds. 1990. *Encyclopedia of Southern culture*. Chapel Hill: University of North Carolina Press.

Wimpelberg, R. K. 1988. Instructional leadership and ignorance: Guidelines for the new studies of district administrators. *Education and Urban Society* 20 (3): 302–10.

Wolfe, M. R. 1995. *Daughters of Canaan: A saga of Southern women*. Lexington: University Press of Kentucky.

Wolverton, M. 1999. The school superintendency: Male bastion or equal opportunity? *Advancing Women in Leadership* (spring). www.advancingwomen.com/ awl/ spring99/Wolverton/wolver.html (accessed October 30, 2003).

Wooden, J., and S. Jamison. 2003. *Wooden*. New York: McGraw Hill.

Wooden, J., and J. Torbin. 1988. *They call me coach*. New York: McGraw Hill.

Woodward, C. V. 1960. *The burden of Southern history*. Baton Rouge: Louisiana State University Press.

Wuthnow, R. 1988. *The restructuring of American religion*. Princeton, NJ: Princeton University Press.

Wyatt-Brown, B. 2001. *The shaping of Southern culture: Honor, grace, and war, 1760s–1890s*. Chapel Hill: University of North Carolina Press.

X, M., with the assistance of A. Haley. 1965. *The autobiography of Malcolm X*. New York: Grove Press.

Yeakey, C.C., G. S. Johnston, and J. A. Adkison. 1986. In pursuit of equity: A review of research on minorities and women in educational administration. *Educational Administration Quarterly* 22 (3, summer): 110–49.

Yoder, E. M. 1964. A Dixieland reverie. *Saturday Review* (May 30): 40.

Yuan, G. 1991. *Lure the tiger out of the mountains: The 36 strategies of ancient China*. New York: Simon & Schuster.

Zimmerman, J. 2002. *Whose America? Culture wars in the public schools*. Cambridge, MA: Harvard University Press.

Zinn, H. 1964. *The Southern mystique*. New York: Knopf.

INDEX

Studies in the Postmodern Theory of Education

General Editors
Joe L. Kincheloe & Shirley R. Steinberg

Counterpoints publishes the most compelling and imaginative books being written in education today. Grounded on the theoretical advances in criticalism, feminism, and postmodernism in the last two decades of the twentieth century, Counterpoints engages the meaning of these innovations in various forms of educational expression. Committed to the proposition that theoretical literature should be accessible to a variety of audiences, the series insists that its authors avoid esoteric and jargonistic languages that transform educational scholarship into an elite discourse for the initiated. Scholarly work matters only to the degree it affects consciousness and practice at multiple sites. Counterpoints' editorial policy is based on these principles and the ability of scholars to break new ground, to open new conversations, to go where educators have never gone before.

For additional information about this series or for the submission of manuscripts, please contact:

Joe L. Kincheloe & Shirley R. Steinberg
c/o Peter Lang Publishing, Inc.
275 Seventh Avenue, 28th floor
New York, New York 10001

To order other books in this series, please contact our Customer Service Department:

(800) 770-LANG (within the U.S.)
(212) 647-7706 (outside the U.S.)
(212) 647-7707 FAX

Or browse online by series:

www.peterlangusa.com